KOREAN 2
FROM ZERO!

Lilah Dugan

George Trombley
Reed Bullen
Jiyoon Kim
Myunghee Ham

special thanks to our
consulting authors
Jinhyun Park
Shi Eun An

Korean From Zero! Book 2
Proven Methods to Learn Korean with integrated Workbook

PREFACE

To learn Korean is to learn Korea. Without knowing Korean you can only scratch the surface of the Korean experience. **Korean From Zero!** was written by people just like you who studied the language from scratch and understand the struggles you face when trying to study Korean. Each book is crafted page by page and lesson by lesson to have relevant (and sometimes fun) Korean conversations and sentence structure patterns that enhance your ability to speak Korean faster and understand the small nuances of everyday Korean speech.

DEDICATION

This book is dedicated and made for those of you who truly want to learn Korean:

Korean culture lovers, Korean language learners, Korean drama watchers,
Korean beginners, KPOP music fans, people of Korean heritage connecting to their history, and anyone planning travel to Korea!

This began as a project for myself (George). This is the book I wanted when I started learning Korean, but it's also for anyone like me who loves Korea and the Korean language and wants to have a closer connection to Korea itself.

All of us on the *Korean From Zero!* team wish you success on your road to Korean fluency.

DISTRIBUTION

Distributed in the UK & Europe by:
Bay Foreign Language Books Ltd.
Unit 4, Kingsmead, Park Farm, Folkestone,
Kent. CT19 5EU, Great Britain
sales@baylanguagebooks.co.uk

Distributed in the USA & Canada by:
From Zero LLC.
10624 S. Eastern Ave. #A769
Henderson, NV 89052, USA
sales@fromzero.com

COPYRIGHT

Thanks for the nice comments! We love feedback!

I have already learned so much. I am excited for book 2 and 3!
Lauren C. – facebook

I'm not starting from zero but I had a ton of "now I get it moments" thanks to Korean From Zero!
Karen D. – twitter

I just finished reading Vol. 1 of this series and it was awesome! Basically under two months, I was able to get a deep understanding of the language. Some books would rely on heavy technically arranged jargon! I don't mean to say those books are awful, but they're really not handy for total beginners like me.
Andrei C. – via email

Excellent teaching. I understand so much better now. Having a native speaker present also gives me confidence that it is correct.
Permacore – youtube

I have tried other language books and software and nothing has had the affect on me that Korean From Zero has.
Josh F. – email

I tried many Korean books and found yours to be the best by far! Thanks again for such a great learning tool!
Christopher C. – email

I am from Morocco, I began to learn Korean 7 months ago and because of your book I can read, write and understand the Korean language.
I really enjoyed.
Zineb B. – email

I'm so glad I've found you, you're really helping me out and I appreciate it ❤
Kamsahamnida ❤ Hwaiting!!
Bella C. – facebook

I am a Russian guy, who admires your study book. It is really perfect, I understand everything fast and easily! My Korean becomes better day by day due to you!
Mikhail S. – email

안녕하세요!! I really looove this book! It teaches really clear and I understand easily, you guys did an amazing great job!
An L. – email

feedback@fromzero.com

Korean From Zero! 2

Introduction

Welcome to Korean From Zero! book 2

This is the second book in the *Korean From Zero!* series. We assume that you have already completed the first book in the series for beginners. We will build on the concepts taught in the first book and will also often refer to sections from the first book. It is by no means required that you have the first book in your possession. The first lesson of this book will provide a quick summary of key topics covered in book 1.

About the authors

This book would not be possible without the collaboration of each of the authors. Each author brings a different level of Korean language understranding that help make *Korean From Zero!* the highly rated book series that it is. I, George, have written a synopsis of what each of the authors of the *Korean From Zero!* series brings to the books.

George Trombley (written by self)

I lived in Japan for 9 years and co-authored eight Japanese language text books. Since the age of 17 I have worked as a Japanese interpreter and have created over 600 instructional videos in Japanese on YesJapan.com. The similarities in the Japanese and Korean languages gave me a great advantage when I began learning Korean. Teaching language for the last 15 years and then learning Korean from scratch from age 39 gave me a unique perspective when crafting each page of *Korean From Zero!*. Viewers of my videos are aware of my lack of love for most books that are heavy on grammar terms and overly complicated example sentences. Furthermore, just because something has been taught one way for years, doesn't mean it can't be improved.

I created the *Korean From Zero!* series to be the book that I personally wish I had when I started learning Korean. If a grammar point brings up a question, then that question should be answered. You should NOT require a teacher to learn from this book. It's written for the independent student.

Reed Bullen

Reed learned Korean initially for his missionary work in South Korea. During his stay in Korea he lived in Daejeon and met hundreds of Koreans, volunteered for farm work, and worked with local Korean orphanages. After his mission he continued studying Korean. I first met Reed at a Korean language learning meetup in Las Vegas. We become friends and Reed spent many of those meetings patiently explaining to me the way Korean grammar worked. He had to have patience as I am relentless in my questions. One of Reeds best qualities, is that despite his knowledge of Korean, he isn't afraid to challenge what he knows. These books would absolutely not be possible with his tireless efforts.

Myunghee Ham
Myunghee is a Korean teacher at Seoul Korean Academy. She is also fluent in Japanese and has taught foriegners for over 8 years. Myunghee was added to the *Korean From Zero!* series after her amazing work on the 3rd revision of book 1. Myunghee has an amazing talent for breaking down a grammar point to it's base points and not over explaining. After I personally attended her classes in Korea, I knew she would be perfect for book 2 and beyond.

Jiyoon Kim (Katie Kim)
Jiyoon grew up in Seoul and graduated from UNLV with a degree in hospitality management. I often communicated with Jiyoon during my intitial Korean studies. Jiyoon was able to clear up my early confusion in some of the more difficult Korean grammar concepts. She was a natural choice to join the *Korean From Zero!* team and has been instrumental in designing the sentences and debating the grammar that make up this book. Jiyoon brings a special perspective that the other authors don't share since she learned English as a second language and isn't classically trained in teaching Korean. Jiyoon is currently also studying Chinese.

Jinhyun Park (Orville Johnson)
Orville was born in Korea and his first language is Korean. He shares a unique trait among the authors as being the only half Korean in the group of authors. He was raised in Korea and moved to America before speaking any English. Orville is also currently studying Japanese. For the last 4 years he has taught Korean at the largest Korean meetup in Las Vegas. His passion for teaching Korean shows in his weekly self created lessons at the meetup where hundreds of students have learned Korean over the years. Orville has shown a special type of rare dedication to teaching Korean as he spends hours developing lessons that he voluntarily teaches at the University of Las Vegas Korean meetup.

Summary of Authors
As you can see we are not a group of linguists or high level academics writing this series. We are a mix of teachers and language lovers who, more than anything, love teaching and learning languages. We hope our love of Korean will help you on your journey to Korean fluency.

You can help with a book review!

Reviews help! Please visit any of the major book seller websites and post a review of *Korean From Zero!* We are fanatical about making the best books for students who don't have access to a Korean teacher. Your book reviews help make new books possible!

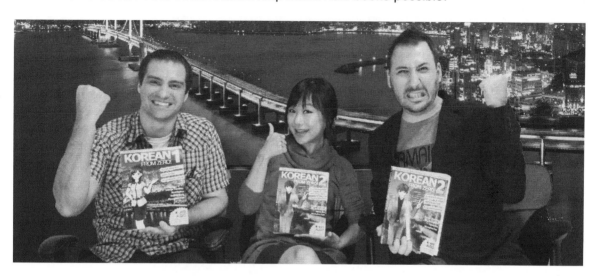

You can help with feedback!

If you love, hate, or are confused about any concept in this book please email as at feedback@fromzero.com with your feedback so we can improve future versions.

VISIT **KoreanFromZero.com**!

Support for your Korean Learning!
- PDF copy of *Korean From Zero!* book 1
- Mobile and Browser Audio Anytime Streaming
- FULL AUDIO sound pack for PC and WINDOWS
- Online Matching Course for book 1 and 2

Thank you and enjoy your Korean journey,

The entire KFZ! team

 How this book works:
Welcome!

 Getting Started

Play the sounds on mobile and in the browser!

To listen to the audio files on your mobile device or in any browser visit:

koreanfromzero.com/sounds2

Download the sound pack!

Visit **koreanfromzero.com** and download the100% Free Audio Files.

STEP 1:   Download the zipped audio file to your WINDOWS or MAC computer.
The direct link to the audio is **koreanfromzero.com/audio2**

STEP 2:   Unzip (uncompress) the zipped file.

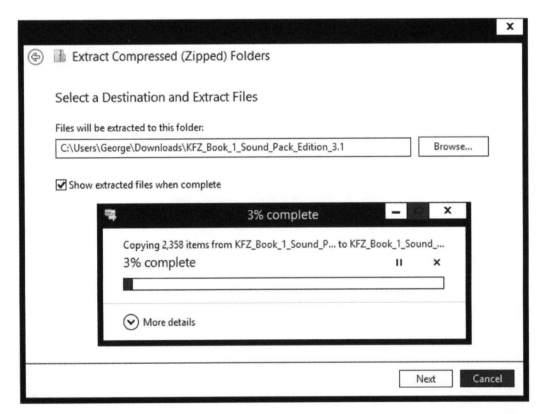

STEP 3:   Each lesson will have its own folder.

lesson_(A)	lesson_(B)	lesson_(C)
lesson_(E)	lesson_(G)	lesson_01
lesson_03	lesson_04	lesson_05
lesson_07	lesson_08	lesson_09
lesson_11	lesson_12	lesson_13
lesson_15	lesson_16	lesson_17

STEP 4:   Open any lesson to view the sections of that lesson.

Action_Verb_Usage_Examples	Additional_Vocabulary	Conversation_E-K
Descriptive_Verb_Usage_Examples	Grammar_Examples	New_Action_Verbs
New_Words	Question_and_Answer	

STEP 5:   In each section folder, you will find the sounds for that section in the order that they appear in the book.

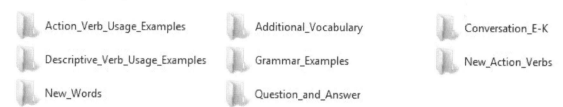

0001-What-...	1	What color do you like? 무슨 색깔을 좋아해요?
0002-What-f...	2	What foods do you dislike? 무슨 음식을 싫어해요?
0003-What-...	3	What kind of animals do you like? 어떤 동물을 좋아해요?
0004-What-t...	4	What type of things did you buy? 어떤 것을 샀어요?
0005-Which...	5	Which restaurant did you go to? 어느 식당에 갔어요?
0006-Which...	6	Which one is cheap? 어느 것이 싸요?
0007-There-...	7	There are a lot of red cars in front of my college. 제 대학교 ...
0008-I-boug...	8	I bought a black computer this Saturday. 이번주 토요일에 ...
0009-There-...	9	There are a lot of white things in hospitals. 병원에 하얀 것...
0010-Today-...	10	Today isn't so cold. 오늘은 별로 춥지 않아요.
0011-I-dont-...	11	I don't like apples that much. 나는 사과를 별로 좋아하지 않...
0012-I-dont-...	12	I don't go to America that much. 미국에는 별로 안 가요.
0013-I-dont-...	13	I don't watch basketball matches much. 농구시합을 별로 ...
0014-I-didnt...	14	I didn't get so many presents at the party. 파티에서 선물을 ...
0015-More-...	15	More water please. 물 더 주세요.
0016-I-boug...	16	I bought more fruits. 과일 더 샀어요.
0017-More-f...	17	More friends came. 친구들이 더 왔어요.

1

The Basics - Lesson 1:
20 Important Phrases

Learning grammar is more important than set phrases. However some phrases don't easily make sense to beginning and intermediate students so memorization is the best option.

1 Food Related Phrases

1. 잘 먹겠습니다.
I will eat well.
This is said before eating.

2. 잘 먹었습니다.
I ate well.
Said after eating.

3. 맛있게 드세요.
Eat deliciously.
This is said to other people to wish them a delicious meal.

4. 건배!
Cheers!
This means "dry glass". The idea is to drink until the glass is dry.

1 Acknowledgment Phrases

5. 알겠습니다. / 알아요.
I have understood. / Got it.
When someone gives you information, you respond with this phrase.

6. 당연하죠! / 당연하지요!
Of course! (without a doubt)
This is a strong way of saying "of course!" and shows strong agreement.

7. 대단해요!
That's great!
Said after someone has told you some great news.

8. 수고하셨습니다. / 수고하세요.
Great job.
This phrase acknowledges a person's hard work. It's said after a day of work or when a task or project ends.

1 | Apologetic Phrases

9. 미안해요.
I'm sorry.
This is a casual way to say "sorry".

10. 죄송합니다.
I'm sorry. / I apologize.
Compared to 미안해요, this phrase is heavier in meaning. Use it when you have caused or will cause more than a minor inconvenience to the person.

1 | Request Phrases

11. 부탁 드립니다. / 부탁 드려요.
I humbly request.
This is how it sounds, a very humble way to request something.

12. 잠시만 기다리십시오. / 잠시만 기다리세요.
Please wait a moment.
You might hear this a bank. If you push the walk button at a crosswalk you will also hear this very polite phrase.

13. 잠깐만요. / 잠시만요.
Just a moment.
Both of these phrases are normal level politeness.

1 | Greeting Phrases

14. 좋은 하루 되세요.
Have a good day.

15. 좋은 밤 되세요.
Have a good evening.

16. 안녕히 주무세요. / 잘 자요.
Sleep well. (polite) / Sleep well. (with friends)

17. 돼지 꿈 꾸세요.
Dream of pigs.
It's considered good luck to dream of pigs, as pigs bring wealth. You will sometimes see pigs in the entrance way of business to promote profit.

1 │ Phrases of Congratulation

18. 축하합니다.
Congratulations.

19. 생일 축하합니다.
Happy birthday.
This phrase literally means, "Congratulations on your day of birth".

20. 새해 복 많이 받으세요.
Happy New Year.
The direct translation of this phrase is "Receive many blessings in the New Year".

2 The Basics - Lesson 2: Must Know Polite Forms

It's easy to think that you can just always be polite or always use a certain level of politeness. When I first visited Korea, my goal was to only talk to people younger than me. This way I wouldn't have to learn the higher level forms. This, of course, doesn't work since OTHER people will say the polite forms to you, so you MUST learn them.

2 | Grammar and Usage 문법과 사용법

● 2-1. Why even learn anything polite or formal?

One of the most challenging parts of learning Korean is to determine which form to use among the many forms available. Many Korean learning materials err on the side of caution and focus on the higher level forms of politeness.

Unfortunately this leaves you unprepared to live in Korea, or talk naturally with your Korean friends. The majority of people reading this book are NOT learning Korean for business, and for this reason this series focuses on more everyday speaking styles.

However... even if you aren't learning for business, or will never be in a formal situation, you WILL need to learn higher forms because you will constantly hear them. Absolutely everytime you are in a coffee shop in Seoul, Busan, or even Daegu, you will be spoken to with respect at the register. Speaking with people for the first time will also always be polite Korean.

It will take experience to know the best TIMES, PLACES, and OCCASIONS ("TPO") for each of the forms. This chapter's main purpose is to remind you of what we briefly introduced in book 1 and to help you gain a better understanding of Korean speech levels.

● 2-2. Formal VS Polite VS Casual Korean

It's easy to mistakenly assume that "formal" Korean is the same as "respectful" Korean. But each style is used in different situations. Don't go crazy learning the following words, instead just remember the concepts they represent.

존댓말 Polite Speech

This is "polite speech" and you will use it the most. 요 form, used heavily in this series, is one of the most important forms. It's polite and friendly at the same time. It can really be considered "normal" Korean.

To make 요 form, you add 요 after any BASIC form (아/어/여) verb or adjective. To make questions you simply add a question mark and make it sound like a question with an upward tone.

Examples (요 form)

1. 여섯 시에 도착할 거예요.
   I will arrive at 6:00.

2. 아침에 학교에 가요.
   I go to school in the morning.

3. 책을 많이 읽어요?
   Do you read many books?

4. 이것은 제 책이에요.
   This is my book.

5. 고양이가 있어요.
   There is a cat. / I have a cat.

6. 한국 여자들은 예뻐요.
   Korean woman are pretty.

7. 사람들이 많아요.
   There are a lot of people.

8. 버스를 타고 싶어요.
   I want to take the bus.

9. 술을 마시지 않아요.
   I don't drink alcohol.

10. 매운 음식을 먹어 봤어요.
    I tried some spicy food.

Another form that is on the same level of politeness as the 요 form is the (으)ㅂ니다 form. This form FEELS more polite because it's used in more FORMAL situations.

If the verb / adjective STEM has a 받침, then you add 습니다, and without a 받침 you attach ㅂ to the bottom of the STEM followed by 니다.

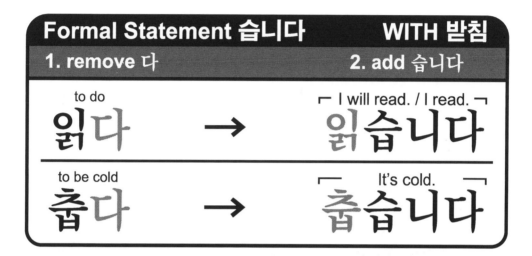

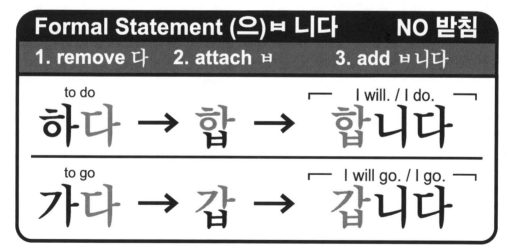

It's used when speaking to groups of people and has a more **distant** feeling to it. It's used in newspapers and news reports etc.

If you are in the Korean military, I have been told, that you will even be punched or hit if you answer in 요 form. This is because of the friendly nature of the 요 form.

The question form and statement form are different.

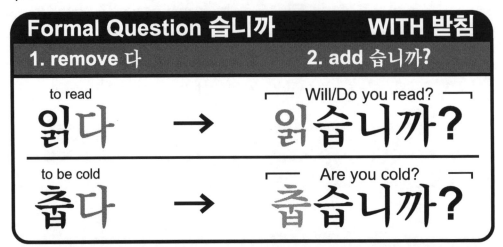

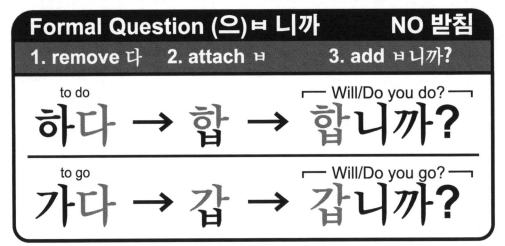

Let's look at the same sentences from page 20 in their formal forms.

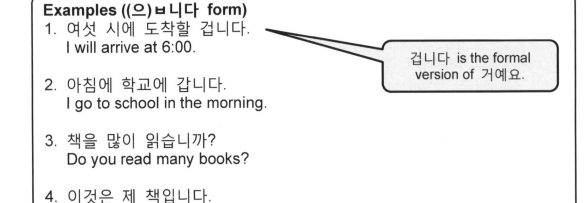

Examples ((으)ㅂ니다 form)
1. 여섯 시에 도착할 겁니다.
   I will arrive at 6:00.

   겁니다 is the formal version of 거예요.

2. 아침에 학교에 갑니다.
   I go to school in the morning.

3. 책을 많이 읽습니까?
   Do you read many books?

4. 이것은 제 책입니다.
   This is my book.

5. 고양이가 있습니다.
   There is a cat. / I have a cat.

6. 한국 여자들이 예쁩니다.
   Korean woman are pretty.

7. 사람들이 많습니다.
   There are a lot of people.

8. 버스를 타고 싶습니다.
   I want to take the bus.

9. 술을 마시지 않습니다.
   I don't drink alcohol.

10. 매운 음식을 먹어 봤습니다.
    I tried some spicy food.

반말 Casual Speech

반말 is "casual speech" in Korea. It's used with friends and people who are below you in status. It should never be used to talk to people above you in status as it will be considered rude.

In most cases just removing 요 from the 요 form makes 반말.
Look at the examples of the same set of sentences in their 반말 form.

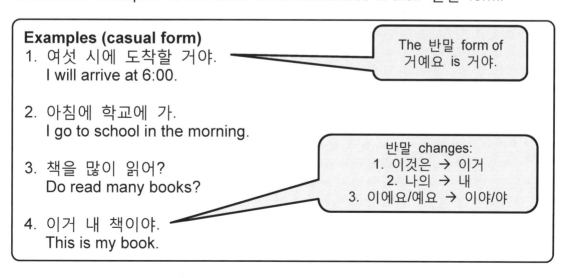

Examples (casual form)
1. 여섯 시에 도착할 거야.
   I will arrive at 6:00.

   The 반말 form of
   거예요 is 거야.

2. 아침에 학교에 가.
   I go to school in the morning.

3. 책을 많이 읽어?
   Do read many books?

   반말 changes:
   1. 이것은 → 이거
   2. 나의 → 내
   3. 이에요/예요 → 이야/야

4. 이거 내 책이야.
   This is my book.

5. 고양이가 있어.
   There is a cat. / I have a cat.

6. 한국 여자들이 예뻐.
   Korean woman are pretty.

7. 사람들이 많아.
   There are a lot of people.

8. 버스를 타고 싶어.
   I want to take the bus.

9. 술을 마시지 않아.
   I don't drink alcohol.

10. 매운 음식을 먹어 봤어.
    I tried some spicy food.

3 Conjugation Basics

The Basics – Lesson 3:

Nothing is more important than a strong understanding of the fundamentals. We understand the desire to move fast when learning a language, but if you build on top of a shaky foundation, you won't have a strong base to learn higher level topics. The following were covered in *Korean From Zero!* book 1.

3 | Grammar Review 문법 복습

● 3-1. The BASIC form conjugation rules for regulars

Depending on the context of the conversation, BASIC form can be future tense, present tense, or a command. This form is used in many Korean sentence patterns. It's just as important as the verb stem. The BASIC form of all Korean regular verbs and adjectives can be created using the rules below:

"BASIC" Form Rules   FOR REGULARS

Remove 다. Choose from A, then if there is a 받침 (final consonant) do B, if not do C.

case #	A Last vowel or character?	B HAS 받침	C NO 받침 — Modify last vowel ONLY!
1	하		change 하 to 해
2	ㅏ ㅗ	add 아	combine ㅏ with vowel
3	ㅣ	add 어	change ㅣ to ㅕ
4	ㅓ ㅐ ㅔ ㅜ	add 어	combine ㅓ with vowel
5	ㅡ	add 어	If prior character has ㅏ or ㅗ (change ㅡ to ㅏ) OR change ㅡ to ㅓ
6	ㅟ ㅚ and others		add 어

Using the rules chart and some verbs you might not know, make sure you can make the BASIC form. Always remove the 다 from the verb before conjugating into the BASIC form.

인쇄하다 (to print)	보여 주다 (to show)	닫다 (to close)
A) Last Hangul: 하 NO 받침	A) Last Vowel: ㅜ NO 받침	A) Last Vowel: ㅏ HAS 받침
B) change to 해	C) overlay ㅓ	C) add 아
BASIC Form: **인쇄해**	BASIC Form: **보여 줘**	BASIC Form: **닫아**
Case used: 1	Case used: 4	Case used: 2

● 3-2. The BASIC form conjugation rules for irregulars

The BASIC form for all irregular Korean verbs and adjectives can be made using the chart rules below. We haven't learned all irregulars yet so keep this chart handy for when new irregulars are introduced.

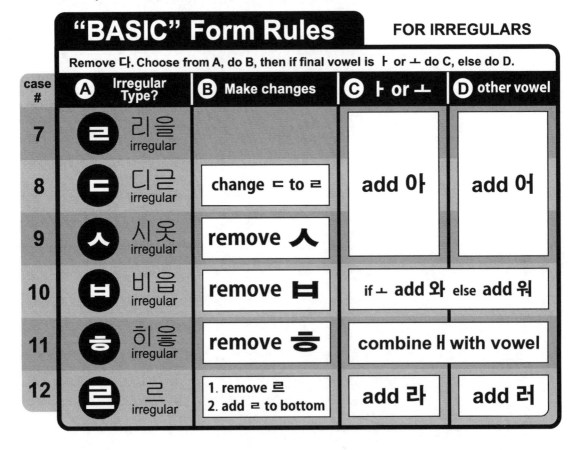

"BASIC" Form Rules   FOR IRREGULARS

Remove 다. Choose from A, do B, then if final vowel is ㅏ or ㅗ do C, else do D.

case #	A Irregular Type?	B Make changes	C ㅏ or ㅗ	D other vowel
7	ㄹ 리을 irregular			
8	ㄷ 디귿 irregular	change ㄷ to ㄹ	add 아	add 어
9	ㅅ 시옷 irregular	remove ㅅ		
10	ㅂ 비읍 irregular	remove ㅂ	if ㅗ add 와 else add 워	
11	ㅎ 히읗 irregular	remove ㅎ	combine ㅐ with vowel	
12	르 르 irregular	1. remove 르 2. add ㄹ to bottom	add 라	add 러

Using the rules chart and some verbs you might not know, make sure you can make the BASIC form. Always remove the 다 from the verb before conjugating into the BASIC form.

(ㄹ irregular) **놀다 (to play)**	**(ㄷ irregular)** **걷다 (to walk)**	**(ㅂ irregular)** **곱다 (to be pretty)**
A) Type: ㄹ	A) Type: ㄷ	A) Type: ㅂ
B) ---	B) change ㄷ to ㄹ	B) remove ㅂ
C) Last Vowel: ㅗ Add 아	D) Last Vowel: ㅓ Add 어	D) Last Vowel: ㅗ Add 어
BASIC Form: **놀아**	BASIC Form: **걸어**	BASIC Form: **고와**
Case used: 7	Case used: 8	Case used: 10

● **3-3. Verb tenses and patterns review**

You should know how to make and use all of the verb patterns taught in book 1 of this series. It's okay if you are missing or forgot a few, but we assume you won't be totally lost using them.

Verb patterns taught in book 1

1. 매일 해요.	I do it everyday.
2. 내일 해요.	I will do it tomorrow.
3. 할 거예요.	I will do it.
4. 했어요.	I did it.
5. 하지 않아요.	I won't do it. / I don't do it.
6. 하지 않았어요.	I didn't do it.
7. 하지 않을 거예요.	I won't do it.
8. 해 주세요.	Please do it.
9. 해!	Do it!
10. 해봐!	Try to do it!
11. 할까요?	Shall we do it?
12. 합시다. / 하자.	Let's do it.
13. 하고 있어요.	I am doing it.
14. 하고 있었어요.	I was doing it.
15. 하고 있지 않아요.	I am not doing it.
16. 하고 있지 않았어요.	I wasn't doing it.
17. 하고 싶어요.	I want to do it.
18. 하고 싶었어요.	I wanted to do it.
19. 하고 싶지 않아요.	I don't want to do it.
20. 하고 싶지 않았어요.	I didn't want to do it.

● 3-4. Directly modifying with adjectives

In book 1 you learned how to directly modify with adjectives. This allows you to say things like "pretty woman" etc. The simple rule is to attach ㄴ (if there is no 받침) or add 은/는 (if there is a 받침) to the adjective STEM.

Examples

1.	예쁜 여자	a pretty woman
2.	큰 고양이	a large cat
3.	작은 개	a small dog
4.	긴 머리	long hair
5.	짧은 치마	short skirt
6.	재미있는 영화	an interesting movie
7.	맛있는 음식	delicious food

3 | Test Yourself Activities 연습 문제

● A3-1. BASIC conjugation practice

Use the conjugation rules on page 25 to convert the following verbs and adjectives to their BASIC form (아/어/여).

NOTE: To make it more challenging some verbs haven't been taught yet.

1. 가다 (go)

_____

2. 하다 (do)

_____

3. 지키다 (protect)

_____

4. 앉다 (sit)

_____

5. 쓰다 (write)

_____

6. 먹다 (eat)

_____

7. 더럽다 (dirty) (ㅂ irregular)

_____

8. 보다 (see)

_____

9. 모르다 (not know) (르 irregular)

_____

10. 보내다 (send)

_____

3 | Self Test Answers 연습 문제 정답

● A3-1. BASIC conjugation practice

1. 가
2. 해
3. 지켜
4. 앉아
5. 써

6. 먹어
7. 더러워
8. 봐
9. 몰라
10. 보내

4 The Basics – Lesson 4: Particle Power

● **4-1. Particles and markers review**

Particles, also called markers, come after a word to define its role in the sentence. They come after a word to mark that word in a way that affects how it's used in the sentence. Prior to using this book you should understand how to use these markers:

Markers types taught in book 1

1. **은/는 topic marker**
   이것은 사과예요.
   This is an apple.

   사과는 과일입니다.
   Apples are fruit.

2. **이/가 subject marker**
   짠 음식이 맛있어요.
   Salty food tastes good.

   저는 차가 없어요.
   I don't have a car.

3. **을/를 object marker**
   치즈 피자를 정말 좋아해요.
   I really like cheese pizza.

   이 책을 별로 안 좋아해요.
   I don't like this book that much.

4. **도 inclusion marker (also, too)**
   맛있는 것도 있어요.
   There are also delicious things.

   가족도 같이 갈 거예요.
   My family is also going.

5. **에 location / time marker (in, on, at)**
   어디에 갔어요?
   Where did you go?

   제 집 옆에 가게가 있어요.
   There is a store next to my house.

6. **부터 start time marker (from)**
   일은 아침부터 시작해요.
   Work starts in the morning.

   몇 월부터 한국에 있어요?
   From what month are you in Korea?

7. **에서 from location**
   미국에서 왔어요.
   I am from America.

   오늘 일본에서 출발해요.
   I depart from Japan today.

8. **에서 event location**
   편의점에서 샀어요.
   I bought it at a convenience store.

   집에서 잘 거예요.
   I will sleep at my house.

9. **(으)로 method marker**
   택시로 갈 거예요.
   I will go by taxi.

   이메일로 보냈어요.
   I sent it by email.

   눈으로 봤어요.
   I saw it with my eyes.

10. **에게 / 한테 to person marker**
    친구한테 돈을 줬어요.
    I gave money to a friend.

남자친구한테 떡을 줄 거예요.
I will give rice cakes to my boyfriend.

제 아버지에게 선물을 줬어요.
I gave a present to my father.

선생님에게 사과를 줬어요.
I gave an apple to my teacher.

11. 에게서 / 한테서 from person marker
선생님한테서 연필을 받았어요.
I got pencils from the teacher.

12. 에 대해(서) about marker
저는 차에 대해(서) 몰라요.
I don't know about cars.

> The 서 is commonly dropped. The meaning doesn't change with or without it.

할머니에 대해(서) 알고 싶어요.
I want to know about grandmother.

13. 하고 and / with marker
친구하고 먹었어요.
I ate with a friend.

저는 어제 책하고 펜을 샀어요.
Yesterday I bought a book and a pen.

14. 랑/이랑 and / with marker
수요일이랑 목요일이 좋아요.
Wednesday and Thursday are good.

박가영 씨랑 여행을 할 거예요.
I am going to take a trip with Gayoung Park.

15. 와/과 and / with marker
김치와 김밥을 좋아해요.
I like kimchi and gimbab.

귤과 바나나가 달아요.
Tangerines and bananas are sweet.

● **4-2. Particle Instincts**
Particles / markers can be confusing to new students. There are a few "instincts" you can learn to make better choices about which particle to use.

Instinct 1 – When to use 이/가

When you are describing something using adjectives, or talking about the state of something, then the 이/가 subject marker is used. In other words, the thing you are describing is marked with 이/가.

1. 버섯이 맛있다.   Mushrooms are delicious.
2. 케이크가 달다.   Cake is sweet.
3. 귤이 쓰다.   Tangerines are bitter.
4. 차가 비싸다.   Car is expensive.

Instinct 2 – When to use 을/를

When someone does an action to something, then that "something" is marked with 을/를. In other words, when something "receives" the action it's marked with 을/를.

1. 차를 사다.   Buy a car.
2. 김밥을 먹다.   Eat gimbap.
3. 주스를 마시다.   Drink juice.
4. 영어를 하다.   Speak English.
5. 엄마를 사랑하다.   Love my mother.

Instinct 3 – When to use 은/는

When introducing a new topic it's best to use 은/는. It's also used when you are putting stress on the subject, for example when comparing. You should avoid using 은/는 twice in a sentence, if you feel you need it twice it's safe to think the second time should be 이/가.

1. 저는 미국 사람입니다.   I am American.
2. 한국어는 어렵다.   Korean is hard. (compared to others)
3. 선생님은 똑똑하다.   Teacher is smart.
4. 지금은 뭐 할 거예요?   What will you do now? (opposed to other times)

● 4-3. Particle Shuffle

Look at how the meaning of sentences containing the same words can change just by switching the particles.

Sentences correctly using particles will have a ✓.
Sentences using the wrong particles will have an ✗.

1. 저 친구 식당 먹었어요. ✗
    Best Translation:
    I friend restaurant ate.

    > Without particles we don't know the function of each of the words.

2. 저는 친구하고 식당에서 먹었어요. ✓
    I ate with a friend at the restaurant.

3. 저는 친구를 식당에서 먹었어요. ✗
    Best Translation:
    I ate a friend at the restaurant.

    > Using 을/를 in the wrong spot can make you a cannibal.

4. 저는 친구에서 식당을 먹었어요. ✗
    Best Translation:
    At a friend I ate the restaurant.

5. 저하고 친구를 식당은 먹었어요. ✗
    Best Translation:
    With me the restaurant ate a friend.

    > Wow! What a scary restaurant! All because you used 은/는 instead of 에서!

6. 저는 친구랑 식당에서 불고기를 먹었어요. ✓
    I ate bulgogi with a friend at the restaurant.

The following demonstrates what happens when you mix up 에서 and 에

7. 저는 친구랑 식당<u>에</u> 갔어요. ✓
    I went <u>to</u> a restaurant with a friend.

8. 저는 친구랑 식당<u>에서</u> 갔어요. ✗
    Best Translation:
    I went <u>at</u> a restaurant with a friend.

    > 에서 marks and "event location" and not a "destination".

4 | Test Yourself Activities 연습 문제

● A4-1. Fill in the blanks

Fill in the best matching particles in the sentences below. It's possible to have NO particle also.

1. 저<u>는</u> 한국어_____ 공부해요.
   I study Korean.

2. 제_____ 친구<u>가</u> 영국 사람이에요.
   My friend is English.

3. 아이폰<u>도</u> 비싸요.
   iPhones are also expensive.

4. 몇 시_____ 공항_____ 출발할 거예요?
   What time are you departing to the airport?

5. 선생님_____ 차는 어디_____ 있어요?
   Where is teacher's car?

6. 이 시계는 어디<u>에</u> 샀어요?
   Where did you buy this clock?

7. 친구_____ 선물을 주었어요.
   I gave a gift to my friend.

8. 누구_____ 갔어요?
   Who did you go with?

9. 할머니_____ 돈_____ 받았어요.
   I received money from my grandmother.

10. 저는 미국_____ 왔어요.
    I came from America.

11. 할아버지는 컴퓨터_____ 몰라요.
    Grandfather doesn't know about computers.

12. 이 책<u>이</u> 재미있어요.
    This book is interesting.

4 │ Self Test Answers 연습 문제 정답

● A4-1. Fill in the blanks

1. 저<u>는</u> 한국어<u>를</u> 공부해요.
   I study Korean.

2. 제(none) 친구(<u>는</u> / <u>가</u>) 영국 사람이에요.
   My friend is English.

3. 아이폰<u>도</u> 비싸요.
   iPhones are also expensive.

4. 몇 시<u>에</u> 공항<u>에</u> 갈 거예요?
   What time are you departing to the airport?

5. 선생님<u>의</u> 차는 어디<u>에</u> 있어요?
   Where is teacher's car?

6. 이 시계는 어디(<u>에서</u> or <u>서</u>) 샀어요?
   Where did you buy this clock?

7. 친구(<u>에게</u> or <u>한테</u>) 선물을 주었어요.
   I gave a gift to my friend.

8. 누구(<u>하고</u> or <u>랑</u> or <u>와</u>) 갔어요?
   Who did you go with?

9. 할머니(<u>한테서</u> or <u>에게서</u>) 돈을 받았어요.
   I received money from my grandmother.

10. 저는 미국<u>에서</u> 왔어요.
    I came from America.

11. 할아버지는 컴퓨터<u>에</u> <u>대해(서)</u> 몰라요.
    Grandfather doesn't know about computers.

12. 이 책(<u>이</u> or <u>은</u>) 재미있어요.
    This book is interesting.

5 Lesson 5: Action Frequency

The "New Vocabulary" section will include any new adjectives and verbs grouped together. Verbs and adjectives have slightly different conjugation rules.

The "Grammar and Usage" section will further explain each verb and adjective.

5 | New Vocabulary 새로운 단어

New Nouns etc.

항상	always
자주	often
가끔	sometimes
전혀	never, not at all, totally, ever
운동	physical activity, exercise
싱가폴	Singapore
도시	city
기분	feelings, mood
접시	plate, dish
카페	café
아이폰	iPhone

New Adjectives

따뜻하다	to be warm
깨끗하다	to be clean
더럽다	to be dirty
넓다	to be spacious, roomy, wide

New Verbs

끝나다	to end
기다리다	to wait
돌아가다	to return, to go back
돌아오다	to return, to come back

| 5 | Grammar and Usage 문법과 사용법 |

When a new verb and adjective is introduced in the "Grammar and Usage" section it will have a breakdown of information as follows.

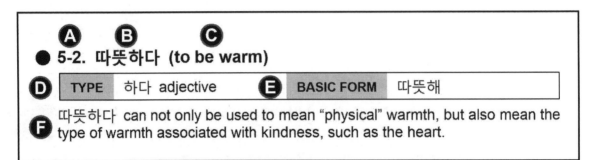

New Verb and Adjective Key

A Usage Reference Number

B Korean Verb or Adjective

C English Meaning

D Verb or Adjective Type

E Conjugated BASIC Form

F Other related information / Particle usage

● **5-1. Changing the "frequency" verb**
These are adverbs and ALWAYS come before any verb or verb phrase to change the frequency of the phrase.

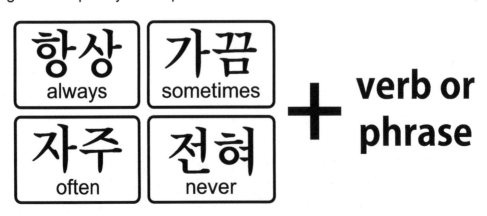

Example sentences
1. 저는 <u>항상</u> 10 시에 자요.   I <u>always</u> sleep at 10 o'clock.
2. 저는 <u>가끔</u> 10 시에 자요.   I <u>sometimes</u> sleep at 10 o'clock.
3. 저는 <u>자주</u> 10 시에 자요.   I <u>often</u> sleep at 10 o'clock.

4. 저는 <u>항상</u> 한식을 먹어요.   I <u>always</u> eat Korean food.
5. 저는 <u>가끔</u> 한식을 먹어요.   I <u>sometimes</u> eat Korean food.
6. 저는 <u>자주</u> 한식을 먹어요.   I <u>often</u> eat Korean food.

In English we say "I never go" or "I never eat" using a pattern of "NEVER + positive conjugation". However, in Korean 전혀 (never) must ALWAYS be used with a negative conjugation such as 안~, ~지 않다, 못~, ~지 못하다.

Example sentences
7. 저는 10 시에 <u>전혀</u> 안 자요.   I <u>never</u> sleep at 10 o'clock.
8. 저는 10 시에 <u>전혀</u> 자지 않아요.   I <u>never</u> sleep at 10 o'clock.
9. 저는 10 시에 <u>전혀</u> 못 자요.   I can't <u>ever</u> sleep at 10 o'clock.
10. 저는 10 시에 <u>전혀</u> 자지 못해요.   I can't <u>ever</u> sleep at 10 o'clock.

11. 저는 한식을 <u>전혀</u> 안 먹어요.   I <u>never</u> eat Korean food.
12. 저는 한식을 <u>전혀</u> 먹지 않아요.   I <u>never</u> eat Korean food.
13. 저는 한식을 <u>전혀</u> 못 먹어요.   I can't <u>ever</u> eat Korean food.
14. 저는 한식을 <u>전혀</u> 먹지 못해요.   I can't <u>ever</u> eat Korean food.

If a verb is naturally negative, as opposed to conjugated into a negative form, like 없다 (to not exist), or 모르다 (to not know) it can be used with 전혀.

Example sentences
15. 이 가게는 싼 것이 <u>전혀</u> 없어요.
    This store doesn't have any cheap things <u>at all</u>.

16. 중국어에 대해 <u>전혀</u> 몰라요.
    I don't know <u>anything</u> about Chinese language.

——— Special Information 특별 정보 ———

"Frequency words" sometimes have alternative versions. 항상 (always) can also be 늘 or 언제나. 가끔 (sometimes) can also be 가끔씩.

전혀 and 절대 both mean the same thing but 절대 is stronger in emotion and shows your intent. 전혀 is more "factual" such as "I never go", whereas 절대 is more definite such as "I will never go!".

● 5-2. 따뜻하다 (to be warm)

TYPE	하다 adjective	BASIC FORM	따뜻해

따뜻하다 can be used to mean physical warmth, and also with emotional warmth such as in a "warm heart".

Example sentences

1. 캘리포니아 날씨가 따뜻해요.
   California's weather is warm.

2. 날씨가 따뜻해요. 그래서 공원에 가고 싶어요.
   The weather is warm. So I want to go to the park.

3. 따뜻한 우유를 한 잔 줄까요?
   Shall I give you a glass of warm milk?

Example conversation

1. A: 어떤 남자하고 결혼하고 싶어요?
   B: 마음이 따뜻한 남자하고 결혼하고 싶어요.

   A: What type of man do you want to marry?
   B: I want to marry a warm hearted man.

● 5-3. 깨끗하다 (to be clean)

TYPE	하다 adjective	BASIC FORM	깨끗해

깨끗하다 is used to refer to the cleanliness of a room, car, or other objects. If a person is 깨끗하다 they have a good image or personality.

깨끗하다 doesn't mean "to clean". It just describes the state of being clean.

Example sentences

1. 제 방이 깨끗하지 않아요.
   My room isn't clean.

2. 제주도의 바다는 정말 깨끗해요.
   Jeju Island's beaches are very clean.

> 제주도 is a popular resort island in the southern part of South Korea.

3. 싱가폴은 깨끗한 도시예요.
   Singapore is a clean city.

● 5-4. 더럽다 (to be dirty)

TYPE	ㅂ irregular adjective	BASIC FORM	더러워

더럽다 is the opposite of being clean.

Example sentences
1. 이 접시가 더러워요.
   This plate is dirty.

> Remember that ㅂ irregulars conjugate to BASIC form by removing ㅂ then adding 워.

2. 더러운 물을 마시지 마세요.
   Don't drink dirty water.

> ㅂ irregulars become direct modifiers by removing ㅂ then adding 운 (not 은!)

3. 제 딸의 방은 가끔 더러워요.
   My daughter's room is sometimes dirty.

● 5-5. 끝나다 (to end)

TYPE	regular verb	BASIC FORM	끝나

끝나다 is a "passive" verb. It can not be used to say "I ended…" It's only used when the thing ending happens naturally or without direct interaction from the speaker.

Example sentences
1. 수업이 2 시에 끝납니다.
   Class ends in 2 hours.

2. 오늘은 회사일이 늦게 끝났어요.
   Work today ended late today.

> 회사일 is another way to say "work".

> This is 반말 (casual) since the 요 is missing.

3. 시험이 끝났어. 그래서 기분이 너무 좋아.
   My test is over. So I'm in a very good mood.

Special Information 특별 정보

In English we can modify verbs to be *active* (I did it) or *passive* (It was done). Korean also has several ways to make verbs *active* or *passive*.

However, in some cases there are completely independent verbs to express *active* and *passive*. For example, 끝나다 (to be ended) is *passive* while 끝내다 (to end) is *active*. More on this later!

● 5-6. 기다리다 (to wait)

TYPE	regular verb	BASIC FORM	기다려

The item / person being waited for is marked with the object marker 을/를.

Example sentences
1. 남자친구가 회사 앞에서 저를 기다리고 있어요.
   My boyfriend is waiting for me in front of the company.

2. 내일 7 시에 카페에서 기다릴 거예요.
   I'll wait for you at 7 o'clock at the cafe.

> Since this is 반말 (casual speech) you can assume friends are talking.

3. 버스를 30 분 기다렸어. 하지만 아직 안 왔어.
   I waited 30 minutes for the bus. However, it hasn't come yet.

● 5-7. 돌아가다 (to go back), 돌아오다 (to come back)

TYPE	regular verb	BASIC FORM	돌아가

TYPE	regular verb	BASIC FORM	돌아와

Both of these verbs are only used to *return* to a place where you once were.
If the person speaking is NOT at the location 돌아가다 (to go back) is used.
If the speaker IS at the location 돌아오다 (to come back) is used.

Example sentences
1. 언제 한국에 돌아와요?
   When are you coming back to Korea?

> We know that the speaker is IN Korea because 돌아오다 is used.

2. 내년에 미국에 돌아갈 거예요.
   I will go back to America next year.

3. 남편이 아직 집에 돌아오지 않았어요. 그래서 못 자요.
   My husband hasn't come home yet. So I can't sleep.

4. 언제 한국에 돌아가요?
   When are you going back to Korea?

> We know that the speaker is NOT in Korea because 돌아가다 is used.

5. 가족들이 미국에 돌아갔어요. 그래서 슬퍼요.
   My family went back to America. So I am sad.

● **5-8. The power of 하다 (to do) verbs**

하다 verbs are made by combining an activity with 하다 to make a verb.
This is really handy if you want to make a verb on the fly.

For example, in this lesson we learned the word 운동 (exercise). By adding
하다 you now have the verb 운동하다 (to exercise). Officially the verb would
also include the object marker 을/를 as in 운동을 하다 (to do exercise).
However it's VERY often dropped.

Here are some examples of 하다 verbs made with words you already know.

운동 (exercise)	→	운동하다	to exercise
질문 (question)	→	질문하다	to question
숙제 (homework)	→	숙제하다	to do homework
여행 (travel)	→	여행하다	to travel
미팅 (meeting)	→	미팅하다	to have a meeting
전화 (phone)	→	전화하다	to phone / call
일 (work)	→	일하다	to work
대답 (answer)	→	대답하다	to answer
샤워 (shower)	→	샤워하다	to shower

● **5-9. Reverse engineering 하다 (to do) verbs**

You can often reverse engineer a 하다 verb to gain a noun. For example
공부하다 (to study) without the 하다 is just 공부 (studies) and 연습하다 (to
practice) because 연습 (practice). NOTE: This typically won't work with
adjectives.

Here are some nouns "extracted" from 하다 verbs that you already know.

사랑하다 (to love)	→	사랑	love
공부하다 (to study)	→	공부	studies
연습하다 (to practice)	→	연습	practice
도착하다 (to arrive)	→	도착	arrival
출발하다 (to depart)	→	출발	departure
노래하다 (to sing)	→	노래	song
수영하다 (to swim)	→	수영	swimming

● **5-10. 넓다 (to be spacious, roomy, wide)**

TYPE	regular adjective	BASIC FORM	넓어

Example sentences
1. 우리 집은 진짜 넓어요.
   Our house is really spacious.

2. 이 길은 넓지 않아요.
   This street isn't wide.

Special Information 특별 정보

여행을 가다
In this lesson 여행을 하다 (to take a trip) is introduced. It's also common to say 여행을 가다 (to go on a trip). The usage of 을 with 가다 is unique in this usage. The destination of the trip is still marked with 에.

Example sentences
1. 우리 가족은 매년 중국에 여행을 가요.
   My family goes on a trip to China every year.

2. 영국에 여행을 가고 싶어요.
   I want to go on a trip to England.

5 | Q&A 질문과 대답

1. **언제 회사일이 끝나요?**
   오늘은 늦게 회사일이 끝나요.
   저는 항상 6 시에 끝나요.
   새벽까지 끝나지 않을 거예요.

   When will your work end?
   Today work will end late.
   Normally I end at 6 o'clock.
   It won't end until dawn.

2. **여자친구의 방은 깨끗해요?**
   아니요. 진짜 더러워요.
   네. 항상 깨끗해요.

   Is your girlfriend's room clean?
   No, it's really dirty.
   Yes, it's always clean.

3. **지금 뭐해요?**
   여자친구를 기다려요.
   집에 돌아가고 있어요.

   What are you doing now?
   I am waiting for my girlfriend.
   I am returning home.

4. **요즘 날씨가 어때요?**
   자주 비가 와요.
   오후에는 항상 따뜻해요.
   요즘 날씨가 너무 좋아요. 하지만 가끔 비가 와요.

   How is the weather these days?
   It often rains.
   In the afternoon it's always warm.
   Recently the weather is really good. However, sometimes it rains.

5. **올해 여행을 갔어요?**
   아니요. 시간이 없었어요.
   네. 가족이랑 싱가폴로 여행을 갔었어요.

   Did you go on a trip this year?
   No. I don't have time.
   Yes. I took a trip to Singapore with my family.

5 | Test Yourself Activities 연습 문제

● **A5-1. Sentence Jumble**
Using ONLY the words provided, create Korean sentences that match the English translation. <u>You can freely add ANY required particle or pronoun</u> in your sentences as needed. Also conjugate and reuse items as needed.

1. 도시, 더럽다, 이, 그, 저, 깨끗하다, 접시, 방, 차

   _____
   These dishes are dirty.

   _____
   Is your room clean?

   _____
   My car is not dirty.

2. 수업, 항상, 기다리다, 끝나다, 전혀, 자주, 공항, 남자친구, 일찍

   _____
   I am waiting for my boyfriend at the airport.

   _____
   The class often ends early.

   _____
   My boyfriend never waits for me.

3. 기분, 서울, 돌아가다, 돌아오다, 화요일, 월요일, 늦게, 좋다, 그래서

   _____
   I will go back to the Seoul on Tuesday.

   _____
   You came back early. So I feel good. (use 반말)

   _____
   Are you coming back again on Monday?

● **A5-2. Fill in the blanks**
Fill in the missing word based on the English sentence.

1. 저는 _____ 일찍 일어나요.
   I always wake up early.

2. 제 차는 정말 _____요.
   My car is really dirty.

3. 한국어 수업은 2 시에 _____요.
   Korean class will end at 2 o'clock.

4. 저는 한식을 전혀 _____요.
   I never eat Korean food.

5. 저는 _____ 날씨를 좋아해요.
   I like warm weather.

● **A5-3. Best Sentence**
Choose the BEST Korean translation for the English sentence.

1. I am going back to Korea in March.
   ○ 저는 삼월에 한국에 돌아올 거예요.
   ○ 저는 사월에 한국에 돌아갈 거예요.
   ○ 저는 삼월에 한국에 돌아갈 거예요.

2. I often eat gimbap at school.
   ○ 학교에서 김밥을 자주 먹어요.
   ○ 학교에 김밥을 가끔 먹어요.
   ○ 학교에서 김밥을 가끔 먹어요.

3. I never want to go to China.
   ○ 저는 중국에 가고 전혀 싶지 않아요.
   ○ 저는 중국에 전혀 가고 싶지 않아요.
   ○ 저는 중국에 항상 가고 싶지 않아요.

5 | Self Test Answers 연습 문제 정답

● **A5-1. Sentence Jumble**
1. 이 접시는 더러워요.
   네 방은 깨끗해? / 당신의 방은 깨끗해요?
   제 차는 더럽지 않아요.

2. 저는 공항에서 남자친구를 기다리고 있어요.
   수업이 자주 일찍 끝나요.
   제 남자친구는 전혀 저를 (안 기다려요. or 기다리지 않아요.)

3. 화요일에 서울에 돌아갈 거예요.
   너가 일찍 돌아왔어. 그래서 기분이 좋아.
   월요일에 돌아올 거예요?

● **A5-2. Fill in the blanks**
1. 저는 <u>항상</u> 일찍 일어나요.
2. 제 차는 정말 <u>더러워</u>요.
3. 한국어 수업은 2시에 (끝나 or 끝날 거예)요.
4. 저는 한식을 전혀 (안 먹어 or 먹지 않아)요.
5. 저는 <u>따뜻한</u> 날씨를 좋아해요.

● **A5-3. Best Sentence**
1. I am going back to Korea in March.
   ○ 저는 삼월에 한국에 돌아올 거예요.
   ○ 저는 사월에 한국에 돌아갈 거예요.
   ✓ 저는 삼월에 한국에 돌아갈 거예요.

2. I often eat gimbap at school.
   ✓ 학교에서 김밥을 자주 먹어요.
   ○ 학교에 김밥을 가끔 먹어요.
   ○ 학교에서 김밥을 가끔 먹어요.

3. I never want to go to China.
   ○ 저는 중국에 가고 전혀 싶지 않아요.
   ✓ 저는 중국에 전혀 가고 싶지 않아요.
   ○ 저는 중국에 항상 가고 싶지 않아요.

5 | **Vocabulary Builder** 단어 구축

During your studies you will soon realize that grammar points aren't so easily forgotten. But you need more than grammar to speak effectively – you need a lot of vocabulary too!

Continuing the tradition of book 1 we will introduce groups of words that are important for everyday Korean speaking. You don't have to try to memorize them all at once. Just familiarize yourself with each group since they might or might not show up in subsequent lessons.

■ **Group A: Body** 몸

목	neck, throat
무릎	knee
어깨	shoulder
등	back
허리	waist, lower back
팔꿈치	elbow
발뒤꿈치	heel
손목	wrist
손톱	finger nails
발톱	toe nails
입술	lips
엉덩이	buttocks (money maker)

목구멍 is the official word for "throat" but many Koreans just use 목

Should this be in the final edition? Consider removing? Nah...

■ Vocabulary Sentences

The following sentences might contain words and concepts not yet taught. Focus on the new vocabulary more than the grammar.

1. 목이 아파요.
   My throat hurts.

2. 책상에 무릎을 부딪쳤어요.
   I bumped my knee on the desk.

3. 아버지의 어깨가 넓어요.
   My father's shoulder's are wide.

4. 친구는 등에 문신이 있어요.
   My friend has a tattoo on their back.

5. 무거운 것을 들어서 허리가 아팠어요.
   Because I lifted a heavy thing I hurt my lower back.

6. 제 팔꿈치가 골절됐어요.
   I fractured my elbow.

7. 발뒤꿈치가 신발에 맞지 않아요.
   My heel doesn't fit in the shoe.

8. 손목에는 손목시계를 차요.
   I am wearing a wrist watch on my wrist.

9. 여자친구의 손톱은 너무 길어요.
   My girlfriend's fingernails are too long.

10. 내 발톱을 칠했어.
    I painted my toenails.

11. 너의 입술에 뽀뽀하고 싶어.
    I want to kiss your lips.

12. 청바지를 입었을 때 엉덩이가 섹시해요.
    When I wear jeans my butt is sexy.

6

Lesson 6:
Cause and Effect

6 | New Vocabulary 새로운 단어

New Nouns etc.

요즘	these days, recently
액정	screen (LCD)
규칙	rule
자켓	jacket
한국말	Korean language (similar to 한국어)
인형	a doll
문자	letters, text (message)

New Adjectives

졸리다	to be sleepy
피곤하다	to be tired, to be tiring
힘들다	to be exhausted, rough

New Verbs

깨다	to break, to shatter
깨지다	to become broken / shattered
만들다	to make

6 | Grammar and Usage 문법과 사용법

● **6-1. VERB / ADJECTIVE + 서 (because verb / adjective~)**
This form acts as a connector between two sentences. The first sentence is the REASON and the second sentence is the RESULT.

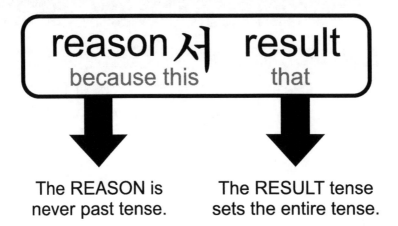

The REASON is never past tense.

The RESULT tense sets the entire tense.

Examples
1. 돈이 없어서...   Because I have no money...
2. 사람들이 많아서...   Because there are many people...
3. 아침을 먹어서...   Because I ate breakfast...
4. 날씨가 추워서...   Because the weather is cold...
5. 벌써 선물을 사서...   Because I already bought a present...

It's really important to understand, that <u>the final verb (result)</u> determines the tense of the entire statement. Let's look and see how the final verb changes the entire translation. The first verb (reason) can ONLY be BASIC form.

Example
1. 돈이 없어서 못 가요.
   Because I <u>have</u> no money I <u>can't</u> go.

2. 돈이 없어서 못 갔어요.
   Because I <u>had</u> no money I <u>couldn't</u> go.

3. 돈이 없어서 가고 싶지 않아요.
   Because I <u>have</u> no money I <u>don't want to</u> go.

Another rule is that the RESULT can never be a command or suggestion.

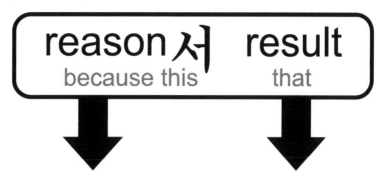

The RESULT can never be a command or suggestion.

Keeping the rules in mind let's look at some sentences.

Example sentences

1. 돈이 없어서 여행을 할 수 없어요.
   Because I don't have money, I can't go on a trip.

2. 사람들이 많아서 이 식당은 시끄러워요.
   Because there are many people, this restaurant is loud.

3. 아침을 너무 많이 먹어서 지금 배고프지 않아요.
   Because I ate too much breakfast, I'm not hungry now.

4. 날씨가 추워서 자켓이 필요해요.
   Because the weather is cold, I need a jacket.

5. 매일 한국말을 공부해서 한국말을 잘해요.
   I'm good at Korean, since I study Korean everyday.

   > In English "cause-result" order can change.
   > In Korean "cause" comes first.

6. 선물을 벌써 사서 케이크를 사고 싶지 않아요.
   Because I already bought a present, I don't want to buy the cake.

7. 요즘 바빠서 점심을 잘 먹지 못했어요.
   Recently I've been busy, so I haven't been able to eat lunch well.

8. 수영을 못해서 수영장에 가고 싶지 않아요.
   I can't swim so I don't want to go to the pool.

● **6-2. NOUN + 서 (because noun~)**

The Korean "be verbs" 이다 (is, am, are) and 아니다 (isn't, am not, aren't) are changed to "because" using the following pattern.

이다	
because it's a (noun)	
no 받침	**noun라서**
with 받침	**noun이라서**

이니다	
because it's NOT a (noun)	
no 받침	**noun가 아니라서**
with 받침	**noun이 아니라서**

Example sentences

1. 저는 학생이라서 숙제가 많아요.
   Because I'm a student, I have a lot of homework.

2. 우리는 친구라서 키스를 못 해요.
   Because we are friends we can't kiss.

3. 여름이라서 날씨가 더워요.
   Because it's summer it's hot.

4. 21 살이 아니라서 술을 못 마셔요.
   Because I am not 21 I can't drink alcohol.

5. 여기는 큰 도시가 아니라서 지하철이 없어요.
   Because this place isn't a big city, there isn't a subway.

● 6-3. Doing something for someone ~BASIC + 주다

When someone does something for you or you for them, the benefit of the action is "given". In English often "for" or "to" are added to the sentence when ~주다 is used. Add 주다 (to give) after the BASIC form of any verb.

$$\boxed{\begin{array}{c} \textbf{BASIC + 주다} \\ \text{to do verb for someone} \end{array}}$$

Here are just a few examples of new verbs that can be made.

하다 (to do)	해 주다	to do for someone
사다 (to buy)	사 주다	to buy for someone
쓰다 (to write)	써 주다	to write for someone

Important Point #1

주다 is used for "giving" to someone, and also for when someone "gives" to you. That means that the BASIC + 주다 pattern can be used to say "I did it for them" or "They did it for me".

A friend didn't have money…	**You didn't have money…**
빵을 사 줬어요.	빵을 사 줬어요.
I bought bread for them.	They bought bread for me.

Important Point #2

Adding ~주다 to a sentence creates the feeling that "a favor was done". Look at how the nuance changes in the following similar sentences.

1. 친구가 저를 기다렸어요.
   My friend waited.

2. 친구가 저를 기다려 <u>줬어요</u>.
   My friend waited <u>for me</u>.

3. 저는 선물을 샀어요.
   I bought a gift.

4. 저는 선물을 사 <u>줬어요</u>.
   I bought a gift <u>for them</u>.

Important Point #3
The BASIC form of 주다 is 줘. It's also commonly spread out to be 주어.
That means that the past tense for 주다 can be 줬어 and 주었어.

You can apply all the conjugation patterns you know to the new "combo"
verbs. Let's practice first just using 해 주다 (to do for someone).

Example sentences
1. 친구가 해 주었어요.
   My friend **did it** for me.

2. 친구가 해 줬어요.
   My friend **did it** for me.

3. 친구가 해 줄 거예요.
   My friend **will do it** for me.

4. 친구가 해 주지 않았어요.
   My friend **didn't do it** for me.

The person that is receiving the benefit of the action is marked with 에게 or
한테. Now let's mix in some other verbs into the examples.

Example sentences
1. 친구가 저에게 편지를 써 줬어요.
   My friend wrote a letter to me.

2. 여자 친구가 저에게 선물을 사 주었어요.
   My girlfriend bought a present for me.

3. 선생님이 학생들에게 한국어를 가르쳐 줬어요.
   The teacher taught Korean to the students.

4. 우리 아버지는 다섯 시까지 우리를 기다려 주었어요.
   Our Father waited for us until 5 o'clock.

5. 여동생이 항상 제 생일에 전화를해 주어요.
   My younger sister always calls me on my birthday.

6. 저는 친구에게 재미있는 책을 사 줬어요.
   I bought an interesting book for my friend.

● 6-4. 졸리다 (to be sleepy)

TYPE	regular adjective	BASIC FORM	졸려

졸리다 simply means you are "sleepy" regardless of how much sleep you got or how exhausted a task made you feel.

> **Example sentences**
> 1. 밥을 많이 먹어서 졸려요.
>   I ate too much so now I'm sleepy.
>
> 2. 커피를 많이 마셔서 졸리지 않아요.
>   I drank lots of coffee so now I'm not sleepy.
>
> 3. 너무 졸려서 공부를 할 수 없어요.
>   I can't study because I'm so sleepy.

● 6-5. 힘들다 (to be strenuous, hard, in a rough situation)

TYPE	regular adjective	BASIC FORM	힘들어

The base of 힘들다 comes from 힘 which means "power". The nuance is that you have used all your power. 힘들다 describes both PHYSICAL exhaustion or strain, and MENTAL strain.

> **Example sentences**
> 1. 아침부터 밤까지 일만 해서 너무 힘들어요.
>   From morning to night all I did was work, so I'm drained.
>
> 2. 힘들어서 운동을 할 수 없어요.
>   I exhausted so I can't exercise.
>
> 3. 요즘 안 바빠서 힘들지 않아요.
>   These days I'm not busy, so I'm not exhausted.
>
> 4. 숙제가 어려워서 힘들어요.
>   I'm exhausted since my homework is so hard.
>
> **Example conversation**
> A: 그 일 제가 해 줄까요?
> B: 아니요, 별로 힘들지 않아요.
>
> A: Shall I do this work for you?
> B: No, it's not that strenuous.

● 6-6. 피곤하다 (to be tired, exhausted)

TYPE	하다 adjective	BASIC FORM	피곤해

피곤하다 means "to be tired" in the classic sense that you didn't get enough sleep. 피곤하다 is used to describe the PHYSICAL state of your body.

Example sentences
1. 피곤해요?
   Are you tired?

2. 오늘 일이 너무 많아서 피곤해요.
   Since I had so much work today, I am exhausted.

3. 어제 피곤해서 숙제를 못 했어요.
   Since I was tired yesterday, I couldn't do my homework.

Special Information 특별 정보

피곤하다 and 힘들다 are used at different times even though sometimes the English definition overlaps. 피곤하다 is used expressly for being "tired" due to lack of sleep or going a long time without sleep. 힘들다 is used after a difficult physical or mental task. You don't need to be "tired" to use 힘들다. If you are simply tired, then using 피곤하다 is best. If you are "tired" or "exhausted" due to a difficult task, then 힘들다 is best.

● 6-7. 깨다 (to break, to shatter)

TYPE	regular verb	BASIC FORM	깨

Since this is an action verb, the shattered item is marked with marker 을/를.

Example sentences
1. 동생이 컵을 깼어요.
   My younger brother broke a cup.

2. 아이폰의 액정을 깼어요.
   I broke my iPhone's screen.

3. 할머니의 안경을 깼어요.
   I broke my grandmother's glasses.

> 의 usage is explained in the next Special Information section.

┌─────── **Special Information 특별 정보** ───────┐

In the prior section we used 아이폰의 액정 to say "iPhone's screen". In Korean 의 is used to show possession and also to make a noun into a direct modifier. However, 의 is commonly dropped from items that are considered a single unit or often said together. For example, we could have used just 아이폰 액정 to say "iPhone screen" and dropped the 의 since an iPhone screen is a commonly known item.

└──┘

● **6-8. 깨지다 (to be broken, to be shattered)**

TYPE	regular adjective	BASIC FORM	깨져

Whereas 깨다 is an action verb that is used to say "who" broke something. 깨지다 is used to show the "state" of an item. The item that is broke is marked with subject marker 이/가.

┌──┐

Example sentences
1. 계란이 깨졌어요.
   The egg is broken.

2. 아이폰 액정이 깨졌어요.
   The iPhone screen is broken.

└──┘

> 깨졌어요 literally means "to have gotten broke", but in English it's more natural to say "it's broke".

┌──┐

Example conversation
1. 학생: 선생님, 창문이 깨졌어요.
   선생님: 누가 창문을 깼어요?
   학생: 준호가 창문을 깼어요.

   Student: Teacher, the window (got) broke.
   Teacher: Who broke the window?
   Student: Junho broke the window.

NOTE: In the conversation above you should pay attention to how 깨다 and 깨지다 are interchanged to show the "state" of the window, and "who" broke the window.

└──┘

┌─────── **Special Information 특별 정보** ───────┐

깨다 and 깨지다 are not used to say "broke" with machines. These verbs are more commonly used for items that shatter such as glass and eggs. Later you will learn other verbs that mean "broke" for machines.

└──┘

● **6-9. 만들다 (to make)**

TYPE	ㄹ irregular verb	BASIC FORM	만들어

The item being made is marked with 을/를.

Example sentences
1. 학교에서 인형을 만들었어요.
   We made a doll at school.

2. 엄마는 아침에 빵을 만들어 줄 거예요.
   Mother will make bread for us in the morning.

3. 친구에게 귀여운 것을 만들어 주고 싶어요.
   I want to make a cute thing for my friend.

Special Information 특별 정보

ㄹ irregular verbs have special rules when conjugating into certain forms. So far, every form we have learned for ㄹ irregulars follow the standard "regular" rules. In the next lesson we will see a special case for them.

6 | Q&A 질문과 대답

1. **파티에 안 갔어요?**
   네. 너무 피곤해서 안 갔어요.
   아니요. 남자친구와 함께 갔어요.
   네. 숙제가 많아서 안갔어요.

   > In Korean you either agree or disagree with the statement. You can't use a double negative like English often does.

   You didn't go to the party.
   Yes. I didn't go because I was too tired.
   No. I went together with my boyfriend.
   Yes. I didn't go because I had a lot of homework.

2. **너 지금 졸려?**
   아니. 전혀 졸리지 않아.
   응. 커피를 안 마셔서 너무 졸려.

   Are you sleepy now?
   No. I'm not sleepy at all.
   Yes. I am very sleepy because I didn't drink coffee.

3. **오늘 기분이 어때요?**
   시험이 끝나서 기분이 좋아요.
   몸이 아파서 기분이 안 좋아요.

   How do you feel today?
   I feel good because the test is over.
   I don't feel good because my body hurts.

4. **어제 생일파티를 했어요?**
   네. 친구가 해 주었어요.
   아니요. 친구가 해 주지 않았어요.
   아니요. 하지만 부모님이 선물을 사 줬어요.

   Did you do a birthday party yesterday?
   Yes. My friend did it for me.
   No. My friends didn't do it for me.
   No. However, my parents bought a gift for me.

5. **저녁에 같이 공부하고 싶어요?**
   아니요. 요즘 저녁에 운동을 해요.
   네. 카페에서 이따가 만납시다.

   Do you want to study together in the evening?
   No. Recently I exercise in the evening.
   Yes. Let's meet later at the café.

6 | Test Yourself Activities 연습 문제

● A6-1. Sentence Jumble
Using ONLY the words provided, create Korean sentences that match the English translation. <u>You can freely add ANY required particle or pronoun</u> in your sentences as needed. Also conjugate and reuse items as needed.

1. 바쁘다, 돈, 시간, 없다, 아주, 너무, 일, 여행을 하다

   _____

   Because I have no money, I can't travel.

   _____

   Because I am too busy, I can't travel.

   _____

   I can't travel because I don't have time.

2. 친구, 만들다, 케이크, 사다, 차, 생일, 부모님, 엄마, 이다, 주다

   _____

   Because it's my birthday my parents bought me a car.

   _____

   My mother made me a cake on my birthday.

   _____

   I gave my friend a cake.

3. 많다, 일, 자다, 힘들다, 피곤하다, 졸리다, 바쁘다, 요즘, 별로, 이번 주

   _____

   Because I am so busy, I haven't slept that much.

   _____

   Because I haven't slept so much this week, I am tired.

   _____

   I had a lot of work this week, so I am exhausted.

● **A6-2. Fill in the blanks**
Fill in the missing word based on the English sentence.

1. 저는 친구_____ 재미있는 책을 사 주었어요.
   I bought an interesting book for my friend.

2. 제 컴퓨터의 액정이 _____요.
   My computer screen is broken.

3. 숙제가 어려워서 _____요.
   I'm exhausted since my homework is so hard.

4. 학생이 학교의 규칙을 많이 _____요.
   The student broke many of the school rules.

5. 우리 딸에게 인형을 _____요.
   I made a doll for my daughter.

● **A6-3. Best Sentence**
Choose the BEST Korean translation for the English sentence.

1. I need a jacket because it's so cold.
   ○ 자켓이 필요해서 추워요.
   ○ 자켓이 필요해서 정말 추워요.
   ○ 정말 추워서 자켓이 필요해요.

2. I can't read my text messages because my iPhone screen is broken.
   ○ 아이폰의 액정이 깨져서 문자를 못 읽어요.
   ○ 아이폰의 액정을 깨서 문자를 못 읽어요.
   ○ 문자를 못 읽어서 아이폰의 액정이 깨졌어요.

3. Because my friend bought me a Korean doll I am happy.
   ○ 친구가 저에게 한국 인형을 사 줘서 기뻐요.
   ○ 친구가 기뻐서 한국 인형을 사 주었어요.
   ○ 친구에게 저는 한국 인형을 사 줘서 기뻐요.

6 | Self Test Answers 연습 문제 정답

● A6-1. Sentence Jumble

1. 저는 돈이 없어서 여행을 할 수 없어요.
   저는 바빠서 여행을 할 수 없어요.
   저는 시간이 없어서 여행을 할 수 없어요.

2. 제 생일이라서 부모님이 저에게 차를 사 줬어요.
   생일에 엄마가 케이크를 만들어 줬어요.
   저는 친구에게 케이크를 줬어요.

3. 저는 바빠서 별로 못 잤어요.
   이번 주에 별로 못 자서 피곤해요.
   이번 주 일이 많아서 힘들어요.

● A6-2. Fill in the blanks

1. 저는 친구에게 재미있는 책을 사주었어요.
2. 제 컴퓨터의 액정이 깨졌어요.
3. 숙제가 어려워서 힘들어요.
4. 학생이 학교의 규칙을 많이 깼어요.
5. 우리 딸에게 인형을 만들어 줬어요.

● A5-3. Best Sentence Search

1. I need a jacket because it's so cold.
   ○ 자켓이 필요해서 추워요.
   ○ 자켓이 필요해서 정말 추워요.
   ✓ 정말 추워서 자켓이 필요해요.

2. I can't read my text messages because my iPhone screen is broken.
   ✓ 아이폰의 액정이 깨져서 문자를 못 읽어요.
   ○ 아이폰의 액정을 깨서 문자를 못 읽어요.
   ○ 문자를 못 읽어서 아이폰의 액정이 깨졌어요.

3. Because my friend bought me a Korean doll I am happy.
   ✓ 친구가 저에게 한국 인형을 사 줘서 기뻐요.
   ○ 친구가 기뻐서 한국 인형을 사 주었어요.
   ○ 친구에게 저는 한국 인형을 사 줘서 기뻐요.

6 | **Vocabulary Builder** 단어 구축

Although we don't recommend binging on learning words as unused words are easily forgotten, it's a good idea to learn new words as some of them will stick.

■ **Group B: Animals** 동물

학	crane
사자	lion
기린	giraffe
올빼미	owl
돌고래	dolphin
고래	whale
늑대	wolf
소	cow
앵무새	parrot
여우	fox
동물원	zoo

■ **Vocabulary Sentences**

The following sentences might contain words and concepts not yet taught. Focus on the new vocabulary more than the grammar.

1. 흰색 학은 예뻐요.
   White cranes are pretty.

2. 사자 다섯 마리가 동물원에 있었어요
   There were 5 lions in the zoo.

3. 기린의 목은 길어요.
   Giraffe's necks are long.

4. 올빼미는 야행성 동물이에요.
   Owls are nocturnal animals.

5. 돌고래는 똑똑한 동물이에요.
   Dolphins are smart animals.

6. 고래 고기를 먹어 봤어요?
Have you eaten whale meat?

7. 늑대는 개와 달라요.
Wolves are different from dogs.

8. 소는 개보다 똑똑해요.
Cows are smarter than dogs.

9. 앵무새는 시끄러워요.
Parrots are noisy.

10. 여우는 어떻게 울어요?
How does the fox cry?
(equivalent to "What does the fox say?")

11. 동물원에는 동물이 많아요.
There are many animals at the zoo.

7 Lesson 7: Introduction to Adverbs

7 New Vocabulary 새로운 단어

New Nouns etc.

왜	why?
가수	singer
얼음	ice
근육	muscles
번데기	silkworm
나비	butterfly

New Verbs

되다	to become
달리다	to run
운전하다	to drive

7 Grammar and Usage 문법과 사용법

● 7-1. What is an adverb?

An adverb is a word that modifies an adjective or verb by changing the manner, place, time, degree, or frequency of the adjective or verb.

Adverb Examples
1. 빨리 가요. (manner)   Go quickly.
2. 멀리 가요. (place)   Go far away.
3. 일찍 가요. (time)   Go early.
4. 조금 가요. (degree)   Go a little.
5. 가끔 가요. (frequency)   Go sometimes.

Korean adverbs must ALWAYS come BEFORE the verb or verb phrase.
In English you can say, "I quickly ran" or "I ran quickly", however in Korean, the adverb is always first and it must be 빨리 달렸어요 (I quickly ran).

● 7-2. 20 powerful and useful adverbs

Adverbs are the "spice" of any language. The flavor of the sentence can completely shift just by adding any of these adverbs.

Adverb		Usage Example
항상	always	항상 10 시에 일어나요. *Always* wake at 10:00.
자주	often	자주 10 시에 일어나요. *Often* wake at 10:00.
가끔	sometimes	가끔 10 시에 일어나요. *Sometimes* wake at 10:00.
보통	normally	보통 10 시에 일어나요. *Normally* wake at 10:00.
절대로	never ever	절대로 10 시에 안 일어나요. *Never* wake at 10:00.
갑자기	suddenly	갑자기 10 시에 일어났어요. *Suddenly* woke at 10:00.
완전히	completely	책을 완전히 읽었어요. *Completely* read the book.
조금, 좀	a little	책을 조금 읽었어요. *Read* the book *a little*.
꼭	definitely	책을 꼭 읽을 거예요. Will *definitely* read the book.
다	all	친구들은 다 왔어요. *All* friends came.
많이	a lot, many	친구들은 많이 왔어요. *Many* friends came.
약간	slightly	약간 재미있어요. *Slightly* interesting.
점점	gradually	점점 재미있어졌어요. *Gradually* getting interesting.
이미	already	이미 잤어요. *Already* slept.
별로	not much	별로 안 잤어요. Did *not* sleep *much*. (use with neg.)
아직	not yet	아직 안 잤어요. Have *not yet* slept.
빨리	quickly, right away	빨리 걸었어요. *Quickly* walked.
천천히	slowly	천천히 걸었어요. *Slowly* walked.
조용히	quietly	조용히 걸었어요. *Quietly* walked.
거의	almost~	거의 매일 걸었어요. Walked *almost* everyday.

● 7-3. More and Most (더~ and 제일~)

These are just adverbs really, but they have such a huge impact on the word they are modifying we decided to give them a special section.

더~	more~, ~er
제일~	most~, ~est

Adding 더 or 제일 in front of ANY adjective is like adding "er" or "est" respectively to the end of the adjective.

-er	
더 크다	bigger
더 달다	sweeter
더 춥다	colder
더 예쁘다	prettier
더 작다	smaller
더 짜다	saltier
더 덥다	hotter
더 깨끗하다	cleaner

-est	
제일 크다	biggest
제일 달다	sweetest
제일 춥다	coldest
제일 예쁘다	prettiest
제일 작다	smallest
제일 짜다	saltiest
제일 덥다	hottest
제일 깨끗하다	cleanest

–er and –est can't be attached to every English word, so when it sounds more natural you can translate 더 as "more" and 제일 as "most".

more-	
더 필요하다	need more
더 재미있다	more interesting
더 아프다	hurts more
더 어렵다	more difficult
더 다르다	more different
더 맛있다	more delicious

most-	
제일 필요하다	need most
제일 재미있다	most interesting
제일 아프다	hurts most
제일 어렵다	most difficult
제일 다르다	most different
제일 맛있다	most delicious

Example sentences
1. 이 차가 제일 빨라요.   This car is the fastest.
2. 이 차가 더 빨라요.   This car is faster.
3. 저 사과가 제일 싸요.   That apple is the cheapest.
4. 저 사과가 더 싸요.   That apple is cheaper.

1. Conversation at a restaurant.
A: 국이 어때요?
B: 소금이 더 필요해요.

A: How is the soup?
B: I need more salt.

2. Conversation at a used music shop.
A: 어떤 음악을 좋아해요?
B: 클래식 록을 제일 좋아해요.

A: What type of music do you like?
B: I like classic rock the most.

3. Conversation at a medical clinic.
A: 다리가 아파요?
B: 아니요, 팔이 더 아파요.

A: Do your legs hurt?
B: No, my arm hurts more.

● **7-4. Becoming cold, expensive etc. (~지다)**
Using ~지다 you can show that something has changed from one state to another. ~지다 follows the BASIC form of the adjective.

> **(adjective BASIC form) + 지다**
> **to become (adjective)**

Examples
1. 크다 (big)   커지다 (to get big)
2. 비싸다 (expensive) 비싸지다 (to become expensive)
3. 춥다 (cold)   추워지다 (to get cold)
4. 덥다 (hot)   더워지다 (to get hot)
5. 예쁘다 (pretty)   예뻐지다 (to become pretty)

Once you have created the new adjective, now you can conjugate it using all of the prior patterns and tenses you have learned.

Example sentences
1. 근육이 커졌어요.   Muscles got big.
2. 컴퓨터가 비싸질 거예요.   Computers will become expensive.
3. 오늘은 추워질 거예요.   Today will get cold.
4. 여름에는 날씨가 더워져요.   In summer it gets hot.

1. Conversation at an apple store.
A: 새로운 아이폰은 어때요?
B: 액정이 더 커졌어요.

A: How is the new iPhone?
B: The screen got bigger.

2. Conversation at a week long high school reunion event.
A: 어제 누구랑 만났어요?
B: 박지윤 씨랑 만났어요. 진짜 예뻐졌어요.

A: Who did you meet with yesterday?
B: I met with Jiyun Park. She really got pretty.

3. Conversation on a camping trip.
A: 내일 날씨가 추울까요?
B: 아마 밤에는 추워 질 거예요.

> 에는 stresses "in the evening".
> It will be cold in the EVENING
> compared to other times.

A: Will the weather be cold tomorrow?
B: Maybe it will get cold in the evening.

● 7-5. –만 (only-)

만 is added after nouns and counter words to say things such as 개만 (only a dog) or 3 명만 (only 3 people) etc.

Example sentences
1. 어제 5 시간만 잤어요.   I slept only 5 hours yesterday.
2. 맥주 3 병만 마시자.   Let's drink only 3 bottles of beer.
3. 저는 야채만 먹어요.   I only eat vegetables.
4. 조금만 먹었어요.   I only at a little.
5. 고양이가 한 마리만 있어요.   There is only one cat.
6. 영어만 할 수 있어요.   I can only speak English.

Example conversation
A: 준호 씨, 영어를 할 수 있어요?
B: 아니요, 한국어만 할 수 있어요.

Notice that the 를 is replaced by the 만.

A: Junho, can you speak English?
B: No, I can only speak Korean.

● 7-6. 되다 (to become)

TYPE	regular verb	BASIC FORM	되어 (돼)

The result that the topic "becomes" is marked with subject marker 이/가.
You have learned that words and their markers can be moved around.

Example sentences
1. 식당에서 김밥을 먹었어요.
   At the restaurant I ate gimbap.
2. 김밥을 식당에서 먹었어요.
   I ate gimbap at the restaurant.

되다 (to become) is an exception to the "order can change" rule.
The CLOSEST noun to 되다 is ALWAYS what the topic becomes.

The item positioned closest to 되다 is always the RESULT.

topic 은/는 result 이/가 되다

topic becomes result

Example sentences
1. 저는 선생님이 되고 싶어요.
   I want to become a teacher.

2. 물은 얼음이 됐어요.
   Water became ice.

3. 우리는 친구가 됐어요.
   We became friends.

4. 번데기는 나비가 될 거예요.
   The larva will become a butterfly.

● **7-7. 왜 (why?)**

The answer to "why?" is always a reason. You can answer a "why" question with 그래서 (because...) or the previously learned BASIC + 서 pattern.

---

1. Conversation between a mother and son.
A: 왜 돈이 없어요?
B: 학생이라서요.

A: Why don't you have money?
B: Because I am a student.

2. Conversation between a mother and son.
A: 오늘 학교에 가고 싶지 않아요.
B: 왜요?
A: 몸이 아파서요.

A: Today I don't want to go to school.
B: Why?
A: Because my body hurts...

● **7-8. 달리다 (to run)**

TYPE	regular verb	BASIC FORM	달려

Example sentences
1. 늦게 일어나서 학교까지 빨리 달렸어요.
   Because I woke up late, I ran fast all the way to school.

2. 우리 학교에서 김준호 씨가 제일 빨리 달릴 수 있어요.
   At our school Junho Kim can run the fastest.

3. 길에서 달리지 마세요.
   Don't run in the street.

4. 발이 아파서 잘 못 달려요.
   Because my legs hurt, I can't run so well.

5. 강아지가 아침에 많이 달렸어요.
   In the morning the puppy ran a lot.

● 7-9. (으) form

In this series, we have introduced grammar patterns such as
BASIC + *something* and **STEM** + *something*. From this point forward we will
introduce **(으)** + *something* patterns. (으) form for regular verbs is easy, but
some irregular verbs and adjectives have special change rules.

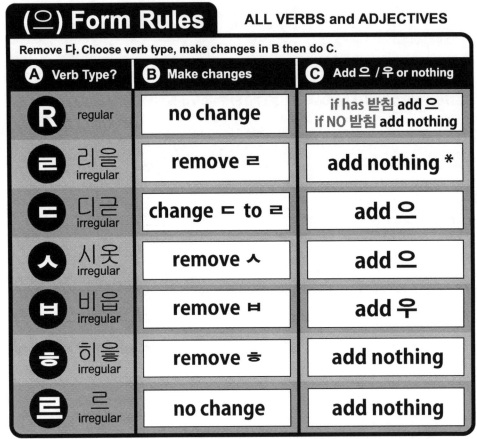

(으) Form Rules	ALL VERBS and ADJECTIVES
Remove 다. Choose verb type, make changes in B then do C.	

Ⓐ Verb Type?	Ⓑ Make changes	Ⓒ Add 으 / 우 or nothing
R regular	no change	if has 받침 add 으 / if NO 받침 add nothing
ㄹ 리을 irregular	remove ㄹ	add nothing *
ㄷ 디귿 irregular	change ㄷ to ㄹ	add 으
ㅅ 시옷 irregular	remove ㅅ	add 으
ㅂ 비읍 irregular	remove ㅂ	add 우
ㅎ 히읗 irregular	remove ㅎ	add nothing
르 르 irregular	no change	add nothing

* ㄹ exception: In some grammar structures the ㄹ is not removed.

Example change into 으 form

to go	가다 (regular)	→ 가~
to eat	먹다 (regular)	→ 먹으~
to do	하다 (하다)	→ 하~
to sell	팔다 (ㄹ irregular)	→ 팔~
to listen	듣다 (ㄷ irregular)	→ 들으~
to build	짓다 (ㅅ irregular)	→ 지으
to be cold	춥다 (ㅂ irregular)	→ 추우~
to be red	빨갛다 (ㅎ irregular)	→ 빨가~
to not know	모르다 (르 irregular)	→ 모르~

NOTE: (으) form by itself has no meaning. It's just used in other grammar.

● 7-10. Polite command form ~(으)세요

If you want to tell someone to do something, ~(으)세요 is a very polite way to do it. This is handy for kindly telling a taxi driver where to go or when telling an acquaintance what to do. Use the (으) from from section 7-9 + 세요.

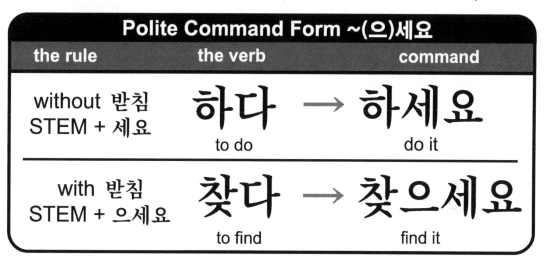

NOTE: In book 1 we learned **BASIC + 주세요** means "please do" etc. This is VERY similar to **STEM + (으)세요** however the main difference being that **BASIC + 주세요** is a request and **STEM + (으)세요** is a command.

1. 찾아 주세요.   Please find it.
2. 찾으세요.   Find it.

NOTE: Both of the statements above are the same level of politeness.

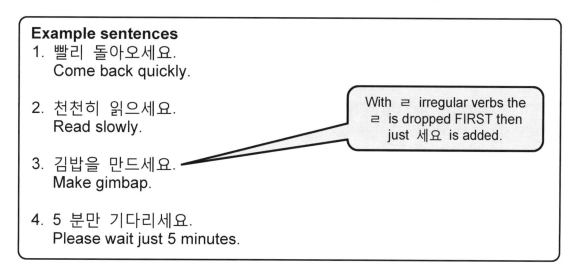

Example sentences
1. 빨리 돌아오세요.
   Come back quickly.

2. 천천히 읽으세요.
   Read slowly.

3. 김밥을 만드세요.
   Make gimbap.

With ㄹ irregular verbs the ㄹ is dropped FIRST then just 세요 is added.

4. 5 분만 기다리세요.
   Please wait just 5 minutes.

● 7-11. (으)세요 future, present tense

It's common to use ~(으)세요 as a polite command as taught in section 7-10.
~(으)세요 functions much like BASIC form. (section 6-4 in book 1)

Standard polite (BASIC)
1. 지금 뭐 해요?
   Are you studying?

2. 가요?
   Will you go?

3. 알아요?
   Do you know?

High level polite (~(으)세요)
공부하세요?
Are you studying?

가세요?
Will you go?

아세요?
Do you know?

NOTE: ㄹ irregulars for (으)세요 grammar just do not follow the (으) form rules but instead you must remove the ㄹ then add 세요.

Just like BASIC form, ~(으)세요 form can be a command, present tense, and even future tense depending on the context of the sentence.

Present Tense	Future Tense	Polite Command
지금 뭐 하세요? What are you doing now?	내일 뭐 하세요? What are you doing tomorrow?	빨리 하세요. Do it fast.

● 7-12. 운전하다 (to drive)

TYPE	하다 regular verb	BASIC FORM	운전해

The vehicle that you are driving is marked with 을/를.

Example sentences
1. 운전을 할 수 있어요?
   Can you drive?

2. 미국에서 몇 살부터 운전했어요?
   From what age do you drive in America?

3. 여기는 경찰이 많아서 천천히 운전할 거예요.
   I will drive slowly because there are a lot of police here.

7 | Q&A 질문과 대답

1. 아침밥을 먹었어요?
네. 저는 항상 아침밥을 먹어요.
아니요. 보통 아침밥을 먹지 않아요.
네. 아침에 자주 김밥을 먹어요.

Did you eat your breakfast?
Yes. I always eat breakfast.
No. Normally I don't eat breakfast.
Yes. In the morning I often eat gimbap.

2. 왜 새로운 컴퓨터를 샀어요?
제일 빠른 컴퓨터가 필요했어요.
더 조용한 컴퓨터를 사고 싶었어요.

Why did you buy a new computer?
I needed the fastest computer.
I wanted to buy a quieter computer.

3. 어제 여자친구를 만났어요?
네. 여자친구가 더 예뻐져서 기분이 좋았어요.
아니요. 돈이 별로 없어서 안 만났어요.

Did you meet your girlfriend yesterday?
Yes. I felt really good because my girlfriend got prettier.
No. I didn't meet her because I don't have so much money.

4. 주말에 술을 많이 마셨어요?
한 병만 마셨어요.
조금만 마셨어요.
거의 안 마셨어요.

Did you drink a lot of alcohol on the weekend?
I drank just one bottle.
I drank just a little.
I didn't drink almost anything.

5. 어떤 차를 사고 싶으세요?
제일 싼 차를 사고 싶어요.
운전을 잘 못 해서 좀 작은 차를 사고 싶어요.

What type of car do you want to buy?
I want to buy the cheapest car.
Because I can't drive well, I want to buy a small car.

7 | Test Yourself Activities 연습 문제

● **A7-1. Sentence Jumble**
Using ONLY the words provided, create Korean sentences that match the English translation. <u>You can freely add ANY required particle or pronoun</u> in your sentences as needed. Also conjugate and reuse items as needed.

1. 가수, 왜, 되다, 선생님, 언제, 제일, 더, 좋아하다, 어떤

   _____
   Why do you want to be a singer?

   _____
   When did you become a teacher?

   _____
   Which singer do you like the most?

2. 더럽다, 어떤, 작다, 제일, 너무, 천천히, 더, 귀엽다, 인형, 이, 그

   _____
   Which doll is the cutest?

   _____
   This doll is smaller.

   _____
   That doll is very dirty.

3. 춥다, 점점, 갑자기, 약간, 덥다, 날씨, 되다

   _____
   The weather suddenly got cold.

   _____
   The weather is slightly hot.

   _____
   The weather is gradually getting colder.

● **A7-2. Fill in the blanks**
Fill in the missing word based on the English sentence.

1. 남편의 자켓이 점점 _____요.
   My husband's jacket has gradually gotten dirty.

2. 저는 _____ 매년 중국에 여행을 가요.
   I go on a trip to China almost every year.

3. 우리 회사는 _____ 빠른 컴퓨터가 필요해요.
   Our company needs faster computers.

4. 음식이 _____ 매워서 다 못 먹어요.
   The food is slightly spicy so I can't eat all of it.

5. 노래방에서 _____ 노래해서 목이 아파요.
   My throat hurts since I sang a lot at karaoke.

● **A7-3. Select and Translate**
Mark the Korean sentence without mistakes then translate it.

1. ○ 오늘 날씨가 진짜 춥었어요!
   ○ 오늘 날씨가 찐자 추웠어요!
   ○ 오늘 날씨가 약간 추웠어요!

   Translation:_____

2. ○ 우리 학교어서 제일 빠른 학생은 박지윤 씨 입니다.
   ○ 우리 학교에서 제일 빠른 학생은 박지윤 씨 입니다.
   ○ 우리 학교예서 제일 빠른 학생은 박지윤 씨 입니다.

   Translation:_____

3. ○ 여름이라서 날씨가 점점 더워지고 있어요.
   ○ 겨울이서 날씨가 점점 더워지고 있어요.
   ○ 언제부터 날시가 선생님이 돼써요?

   Translation:_____

7 | Self Test Answers 연습 문제 정답

● A7-1. Sentence Jumble
1. 왜 가수가 되고 싶어요?
   언제 선생님이 됐어요.
   어떤 가수를 제일 좋아해요?

2. 어떤 인형이 제일 귀여워요?
   이 인형은 더 작아요.
   그 인형은 너무 더러워요.

2. 날씨가 갑자기 추워졌어요.
   날씨가 약간 더워요.
   날씨가 점점 추워져요. / 추워지고 있어요.

● A7-2. Fill in the blanks
1. 남편의 자켓이 점점 <u>더러워졌어요</u>.
2. 저는 <u>거의</u> 매년 중국에 여행을 가요.
3. 우리 회사는 <u>더</u> 빠른 컴퓨터가 필요해요.
4. 음식이 <u>약간</u> 매워서 다 못 먹어요.
5. 노래방에서 <u>많이</u> 노래해서 목이 아파요.

● A7-3. Select and Translate
1. ○ 오늘 날씨가 진짜 춥었어요!
   ○ 오늘 날씨가 찐자 추웠어요!
   ✓ 오늘 날씨가 약간 추웠어요!
   Translation: Today the weather is slightly cold.

2. ○ 우리 학교어서 제일 빠른 학생은 박지윤 씨 입니다.
   ✓ 우리 학교에서 제일 빠른 학생은 박지윤 씨 입니다.
   ○ 우리 학교예서 제일 빠른 학생은 박지윤 씨 입니다.
   Translation: The fastest student at our school is Jiyun Park.

3. ✓ 여름이라서 날씨가 점점 더워지고 있어요.
   ○ 겨울이서 날씨가 점점 더워지고 있어요.
   ○ 언제부터 날시가 선생님이 돼써요?
   Translation: Because it's summer, the weather is gradually getting hot.

7 | Vocabulary Builder 단어 구축

Although we don't recommend binging on learning words as unused words are easily forgotten, it's a good idea to learn new words as some of them will stick.

■ Group C: Nature 자연

번개	lightning
천둥	thunder
구름	clouds
개울	stream, brook
일몰	sunset
일출	sunrise
숲	forest
봄	spring
여름	summer
가을	autumn
겨울	winter

■ Vocabulary Sentences

The following sentences might contain words and concepts not yet taught. Focus on the new vocabulary more than the grammar.

1. 번개가 쳐서 놀랐어요.
   I was surprised because the lightning struck.

2. 천둥이 쳐서 아이가 놀랐어요.
   The child was startled by the thunder.

3. 하늘에 구름이 많아요.
   There are many clouds in the sky.

4. 개울에 올챙이가 살아요.
   Tadpoles live in streams.

5. 사람들은 새해에 일출을 봐요.
   People watch the sunrise on New Year's Day.

6. 오늘 일몰이 예뻐요.
   Today's sunset is pretty.

7. 겨울에는 따뜻한 옷을 입어야 돼요.
   You must wear warm clothes during winter.

8. 봄에는 꽃가루가 많아요.
   There is a lot of pollen during the spring.

9. 우리는 이번 여름에 바다로 가요.
   We are going to the beach this summer.

10. 나는 가을을 제일 좋아해요.
    I like autumn the most.

11. 숲에는 동물과 식물이 많아요.
    There are a lot of animals and plants in the forest.

8 Lesson 8: Counting Time

8 | New Vocabulary 새로운 단어

New Nouns etc.

얼마나	how many, how much
감옥	prison
캘리포니아	California
대도시	big city, metropolis
오랫동안	for a long time
무릎	knee(s)
사촌	cousin
~동안	period of time
~쯤	around~
~정도	about~

New Counters

~시간	hours
~분	minutes
~일	days
~주	weeks
~달	months (Korean)
~개월	months (Chinese)
~년	years
~번	times

New Verbs

걸리다	to take time
살다	to live
빌리다	to loan, to borrow, to rent
쉬다	to rest, to take a break

8 | Grammar and Usage 문법과 사용법

● 8-1. Time related counters

Let's look at some time related counters. Depending on the time span the
number system used is different. We will start with counters that use the
Korean based numbers.

hours 시간		months 달		times 번	
한 시간	1 hour	한 달	1 month	한 번	1 time
두 시간	2 hours	두 달	2 months	두 번	2 times
세 시간	3 hours	세 달	3 months	세 번	3 times
네 시간	4 hours	네 달	4 months	네 번	4 times
다섯 시간	5 hours	다섯 달	5 months	다섯 번	5 times
여섯 시간	6 hours	여섯 달	6 months	여섯 번	6 times
일곱 시간	7 hours	일곱 달	7 months	일곱 번	7 times
여덟 시간	8 hours	여덟 달	8 months	여덟 번	8 times
아홉 시간	9 hours	아홉 달	9 months	아홉 번	9 times
열 시간	10 hours	열 달	10 months	열 번	10 times
열한 시간	11 hours	열한 달	11 months	열한 번	11 times
열두 시간	12 hours	열두 달	12 months	열두 번	12 times
몇 시간? How many hours?		몇 달? How many months?		몇 번? How many times?	

The pattern for the numbers continue up to 99. If you need to go higher than
99 then you will use the Chinese-Korean number system.

NOTE: If something is open 24 hours, then it's common to say 이십사 시간
and not 스물네 시간.

minutes 분		days 일		weeks 주	
일 분	1 minute	일 일	1 day	일 주	1 week
이 분	2 minutes	이 일	2 days	이 주	2 weeks
삼 분	3 minutes	삼 일	3 days	삼 주	3 weeks
사 분	4 minutes	사 일	4 days	사 주	4 weeks
오 분	5 minutes	오 일	5 days	오 주	5 weeks
육 분	6 minutes	육 일	6 days	육 주	6 weeks
칠 분	7 minutes	칠 일	7 days	칠 주	7 weeks
팔 분	8 minutes	팔 일	8 days	팔 주	8 weeks
구 분	9 minutes	구 일	9 days	구 주	9 weeks
십 분	10 minutes	십 일	10 days	십 주	10 weeks
십일 분	11 minutes	십일 일	11 days	십일 주	11 weeks
십이 분	12 minutes	십이 일	12 days	십이 주	12 weeks
몇 분? How many minutes?		며칠? (not 몇 일) How many days?		몇 주? How many weeks?	

There is a second counter for months that uses the Chinese-Korean numbers using ~개월 (일 개월, 이 개월, 삼 개월 etc). There is no difference in meaning between the two versions.

Years use Chinese-Korean numbers using ~년 (일 년, 이 년, 삼 년 etc).

Special Information 특별 정보

In addition to 세 달 (3 months) and 네 달 (4 months), you will most likely hear and see these additional ways to say 3 and 4 months. 석달 (3 months) and 넉달 (4 months).

● 8-2. 동안 (period of time)

When saying something occurred for "a period of~" you will put 동안 after the time counter. The time marker 에 is not required after or before 동안.

Example sentences

1. 이 년 <u>동안</u> 서울에 있었어요.
   I was in Seoul <u>for</u> 2 years.

2. 한 달 <u>동안</u> 학교에 안 갔어요.
   <u>For</u> one month I didn't go to school.

3. 30 분 <u>동안</u> 기다렸어요.
   I waited <u>for</u> 30 minutes.

4. 다섯 달 <u>동안</u> 한국어를 공부했어요.
   I studied Korean <u>for</u> 5 months.

5. 남동생은 십 년 <u>동안</u> 감옥에 있었어요.
   My younger brother was in prison <u>for</u> 10 years.

● 8-3. 걸리다 (to take time)

TYPE	regular verb	BASIC FORM	걸려

The thing that takes time is marked with 이/가 or 은/는. 동안 is not used with 걸리다. 이/가 can also come after the time it took, however it's commonly dropped.

Example sentences

1. 시간이 많이 걸려요.
   It takes a lot of time.

2. 시험은 오 분 걸렸어요.
   The test took 5 minutes.

3. 얼마나 걸려요?
   How long will it take?

4. 우리 회사의 미팅이 두 시간 걸렸어요.
   Our company meeting took 2 hours.

5. 친구의 집까지 사십오 분 걸렸어요.
   It took 45 minutes to (get to) my friend's house.

● 8-4. 살다 (to live)

TYPE	ㄹ irregular verb	BASIC FORM	살아

The place that you live is marked with the location marker 에. However, it's important to note 살다 is special because the place you live can also be marked with the event location marker 에서.

Example sentences
1. 런던에 살아요.
   I live in London.

2. 도쿄에 육 개월 동안 살았어요.
   I lived in Tokyo for 6 months.

3. 언제부터 언제까지 부산에 살았어요?
   From when until when did you live in Pusan?

4. 여동생은 아직 우리 부모님과 같이 살아요.
   My younger sister still lives with our parents.

5. 날씨가 좋아서 캘리포니아에 살고 싶어요.
   I want to live in California because the weather is nice.

● 8-5. 빌리다 (to loan, borrow, rent)

TYPE	regular verb	BASIC FORM	빌려

In English we have different words for "loan" and "borrow" but in Korean it's just 빌리다. The item being loaned, or borrowed, is marked with the object marker 을/를.

Example sentences
1. 일곱 달 동안 아파트를 빌렸어요.
   I rented an apartment for 7 months.

2. 친구가 저에게 차를 빌려 줬어요.
   My friend loaned his car to me.

3. 너무 비싸서 대도시에서 아파트를 빌리고 싶지 않아요.
   I don't want to rent an apartment in a big city because it's too expensive.

4. 부모님한테서 백만 원을 빌릴 거예요.
   I will borrow 1,000,000 won from my parents.

● 8-6. 쉬다 (to rest, to take a break)

TYPE	regular verb	BASIC FORM	쉬어

The activity that you are resting from is marked with 을/를.

Example sentences

1. 5일 동안 일을 쉬었어요.
   I took a break from work for 5 days.

2. 무릎이 아파서 오랫동안 일을 쉴 겁니다.
   I will take a break for a long time from work since my knee hurts.

3. 숙제가 힘들어서 조금만 쉬고 싶어요.
   Because my homework is tough, I want to rest just a little.

4. 시간이 별로 없어서 쉴 수 없어요.
   Because there isn't a lot of time, we can't take a break.

5. 나무앞에서 쉬자!
   Let's rest in front of the tree.

● 8-7. The "not even" marker 도

Previously you have learned that 도 means "too" or "also". For example, 친구도 갔어요 (My friend *also* went.).

도 can also mean "even", especially when used in negative sentences.

Example sentences

1. 한 시간도 안 잤어요.
   I didn't <u>even</u> sleep one hour.

2. 저 편의점은 우유도 없어요.
   That convenient store doesn't <u>even</u> have milk.

3. 여자친구랑 키스도 안 해봤어요.
   I haven't <u>even</u> tried to kiss my girlfriend.

4. 미국에 한 번도 안 갔어요.
   I haven't gone to America <u>even</u> one time.

5. 친구가 천 원도 빌려 주지 않았어요.
   My friend wouldn't loan me <u>even</u> 1000 won.

● **8-8. A half of time and amounts using 반**

Adding 반 after any time or amount is like saying "and a half" in English.

Examples

1. 오 년 반	Five and a half years
2. 사 주 반	Four and a half weeks
3. 한 시간 반	One hour and a half
4. 이 분 반	Two and a half minutes
5. 한 잔 반	One and a half cups
6. 삼 인분 반	Three and half servings
7. 일곱 병 반	Send and a half bottles.

● **8-9. Making times and spans less specific (쯤, 정도)**

You can make any specific time or amount less specific using 쯤 and 정도. Both words are added to after the words they are making less specific.

Examples

1. 우리 다음 주 3 시쯤에 만날까요?
   Shall we meet next week at around 3 o'clock?

2. 2 년 정도 호주에 살았어요.
   I lived in Australia for about 2 years.

> Notice that 정도 has a space while 쯤 attaches directly.

3. 25 명쯤 부산에서 돌아왔어요.
   About 25 people returned from Pusan.

4. 50 분 정도 걸릴 거예요.
   It will take about 50 minutes.

Special Information 특별 정보

For counting days, Korean has a special counting system.

하루	1 day
이틀	2 days
사흘	3 days

These numbers continue higher, however Koreans nowadays typically only use 하루 (1 day) and 이틀 (2 days). Above 2 days it's more common to say 삼 일 (3 days), 사 일 (4 days), 오 일 (5 days) etc.

8 | Q&A 질문과 대답

1. 새 차를 샀어요?
아니요. 이 년 동안 친구에게 빌렸어요.
네. 새 차는 천 만원 정도 더 비쌌어요.
네. 아빠가 사줬어요.

Did you buy a new car?
No. For 2 years I borrowed (one) from a friend.
Yes. A new car was about 10 million won more expensive.
Yes. My father bought it for me.

2. 어디 살아요?
서울에 5 년 정도 살았어요.
캘리포니아에 오랫동안 살았어요.

Where do you live?
I have lived in Seoul for about 5 years.
I lived in California for a long time.

3. 집에서 식당까지 얼마나 걸려요?
집이 멀어서 한 시간 반 정도 걸려요.
버스로 오 분도 안 걸려요.

How long does it take from your house to the restaurant.
Because my house is far, It takes about an hour and a half.
It doesn't take even 5 minutes by bus.

4. 얼마나 공부했어요?
세 시간 반 공부했어요.
여섯 시간 동안 공부해서 쉬고 싶어요.
전혀 공부하지 않았어요.

How long did you study?
I studied for 3 and a half hours.
I want to take a break because I studied for a period of 6 hours.
I didn't study at all.

5. 대도시에 가 봤어요?
아니요. 한 번도 안 가 봤어요.
네. 대도시에서 삼 개월쯤 살았어요.

Have you ever been to a big city?
No. I haven't gone even once.
Yes. I lived in a big city for about 3 months.

8 | Test Yourself Activities 연습 문제

● A8-1. Sentence Jumble

Using ONLY the words provided, create Korean sentences that match the English translation. <u>You can freely add ANY required particle or pronoun</u> in your sentences as needed. Also conjugate and reuse items as needed.

1. 동안, 며칠, 살다, 한 번, 캐나다, 있다, 몇 달, 걸리다

_____

How many days were you in Canada?

_____

How many months did you live in Canada?

_____

How many months will it take?

2. 걸리다, 동안, 감옥, 살다, 십 년, 십 분, 있다

_____

It didn't even take 10 minutes.

_____

I was in jail for 10 years.

_____

It won't take even 10 minutes.

3. 사촌, 있다, 주다, 동안, 아파트, 살다, 어디, 언제, 삼 주, 빌리다, 차

_____

I rented a car for 3 weeks.

_____

I loaned my apartment to my cousin.

_____

Where were you for 3 weeks?

● **A8-2. Fill in the blanks**
Fill in the missing word based on the English sentence.

1. 삼촌이 자전거를 _____요.
   My cousin loaned me a bicycle.

2. 오월부터 칠월까지 일본에 _____요.
   I lived in Japan from May to July.

3. _____ 동안 운전했어요.
   I drove for 3 and a half hours.

4. 비행기가 12_____에 출발했어요.
   The plane departed around 12:00.

5. _____ 한국을 여행했어요?
   How many times have you travelled to Korea?

● **A8-3. Mark and Translate**
Mark the Korean sentence without mistakes then translate it.

1. ○ 한국에 동안 한달 있었어요.
   ○ 한국에 한 달 동안 살았어요.
   ○ 한국에 한 동안 달 빌렸어요.

   Translation:_____

2. ○ 버스로 갔어요. 30 분쯤 걸렸어요.
   ○ 버섯으로 갔어요. 30 분쯤 걸렸어요.
   ○ 버스더 갔어요. 30 분쯤 걸렸어요.

   Translation:_____

3. ○ 2 주 동안 일을 쉬었어요.
   ○ 2 주 동안 일를 쉬었어요.
   ○ 2 쥬 동안 일을 쉬었어요.

   Translation:_____

8 | Self Test Answers 연습 문제 정답

● **A8-1. Sentence Jumble**

1. 캐나다에 며칠 (동안) 있었어요?
   캐나다에 몇 달 (동안) 살았어요?
   몇 달 걸릴 거예요?

2. 십 분도 안 걸렸어요.
   저는 감옥에 십 년 동안 있었어요.
   십 분도 안 걸릴 거예요.

3. 삼 주 동안 차를 빌렸어요.
   사촌에게 제 아파트를 빌려 주었어요.
   삼 주 동안 어디에 있었어요?

● **A8-2. Fill in the blanks**

1. 삼촌이 자전거를 빌렸어요.

2. 오월부터 칠월까지 일본에 살았어요.

3. 3 시간 반 동안 운전했어요.

4. 비행기가 (<u>12 시쯤</u> / <u>12 시 정도</u>)에 출발했어요.

5. 몇 번 한국을 여행했어요?

● **A8-3. Best Sentence Search**

1. ○ 한국에 동안 한달 있었어요.
   ✓ 한국에 한 달 동안 살았어요.
   ○ 한국에 한 동안 달 빌렸어요.
   Translation: I lived in Korea for 1 month.

2. ✓ 버스로 갔어요. 30 분쯤 걸렸어요.
   ○ 버섯으로 갔어요. 30 분쯤 걸렸어요.
   ○ 버스더 갔어요. 30 분쯤 걸렸어요.
   Translation: I went by bus. It took about 30 minutes.

3. ✓ 2 주 동안 일을 쉬었어요.
   ○ 2 주 동안 일를 쉬었어요.
   ○ 2 쥬 동안 일을 쉬었어요.
   Translation: For 2 weeks I took a break from work.

8 | Vocabulary Builder 단어 구축

Even if you don't remember all of these words, review them and try to put them in your memory. One day you might be surprised that you randomly recalled one at the right time.

■ Group D: Geography 지리학

대륙	continent
해변	beach
섬	island
호수	lake
사막	desert
산	mountain
초원	grasslands
계곡	valley
언덕	hill
강	river

■ Vocabulary Sentences

The following sentences might contain words and concepts not yet taught. Focus on the new vocabulary more than the grammar.

1. 아주 오래 전에는 모든 대륙이 하나였어요.
   A very long time ago, all the continents were one.

2. 오늘 우리는 해변에 가요.
   Today, we're going to the beach.

3. 저는 섬으로 가고 싶어요.
   I want to go to an island.

4. 호수에는 물고기가 많이 살아요.
   Many fish live in the lake.

5. 사막에는 오아시스가 있어요.
   There is an oasis in the desert.

6. 오늘은 산을 타고 싶어요.
   I want to climb a mountain today.

7. 말이 넓은 초원을 달리고 있어요.
   The horse is running on a large grassland.

8. 날씨가 더워서 계곡으로 갔어요.
   Because the weather is hot, we went to a valley.

9. 언덕이 많을 때 달리기 어려워요.
   When there are a lot of hills running is hard.

10. 한국에서 제일 유명한 강은 한강입니다.
    The most popular river in Korea is the Han river.

SR! Super Review and Quiz #1: Lessons 5-8

SR Conversation 대화 K-E

Hide the English and try to translate the Korean. Take notes on words or grammar patterns that confuse you then review them if necessary.

1. **A polite conversation between co-workers.**

   A: 같이 저녁을 먹을까요?

   B: 아니요, 오늘은 저녁을 안 먹을 거예요.

   A: 왜 저녁을 안 먹어요?

   B: 점심을 많이 먹어서 배가 안 고파요.

   A: Shall we eat dinner together?

   B: No, today I am not going to eat dinner.

   A: Why aren't you going to eat dinner?

   B: I ate a lot of lunch so I am not hungry.

2. **A polite conversation between friends.**

   A: 오늘 학교 앞에서 2 시간 기다렸어요. 왜 안 왔어요?

   B: 미안해요. 미국에서 갑자기 친구가 와서 못 왔어요.

   A: 그럼 왜 전화도 안 했어요?

   B: 전화를하고 싶었어요. 하지만 전화번호를 몰라서 전화를못했어요.

   A: Today, I waited 2 hours in front of the school. Why didn't you come?

   B: I'm sorry. My friend suddenly came from America, so I couldn't come.

   A: So why didn't you even call?

   B: I wanted to call. But I didn't know your phone number, so I couldn't call.

3. **A polite conversation between international friends.**

   A: 10 월에 한국 날씨가 어때요?

   B: 12 시쯤은 아주 따뜻해요.

   A: 그럼 밤에는 어때요?

   B: 조금 추워요.

A: How is Korea's weather in October?

B: It gets very warm around 12:00.

A: Well then, how about in the evening.

B: It's a little cold.

4. A polite conversation between friends.

미나: 제프 씨는 매운 음식을 잘 먹어요?

제프: 네, 매운 음식을 좋아해서 자주 먹어요.

미나: 지금 떡볶이를 만들 거예요. 먹을 거예요?

제프: 네, 하지만 별로 배가 고프지 않아서 조금만 먹을 거예요.

미나: 알겠어요. 30 분 정도 걸릴 거예요.

Mina: Do you eat spicy food well George? (Can you eat spicy food?)

Jeff: Yes, since I like spicy food, I often eat it.

Mina: Now I am going to make spicy rice cakes. Will you eat some?

Jeff: Yes, but since I'm not that hungry, I want to eat just a little.

Mina: Okay. It will take about 30 minutes.

SR | Quiz Yourself 퀴즈

● **1. Combine the Sentences**

Combine the following sentences into one sentence using BASIC + 서 form.

> **Example**
> Ex) 시간이 있어요. 그래서 영화를 봤어요.
>
> <u>시간이 있어서 영화를 봤어요.</u>

1. 피곤해요. 그래서 쉬고 있어요.

2. 머리가 아파요. 그래서 약을 먹었어요.

3. 어제 옆집 (next door)에서 파티를 했어요. 그래서 너무 시끄러웠어요.

4. 숙제가 너무 어려워요. 그래서 할 수 없어요.

_____

5. 회사에서 집까지 너무 멀어요. 그래서 힘들어요.

_____

● **2. Complete the Sentence**
Make full sentences using the BASIC 서 pattern. Choose the best ending of each sentence from the list provided below, then translate the full sentence.

> **Ex.** 주말에 바쁘다
>
> 주말에 바빠서 못 가요.
>
> Because I am busy on the weekend, I can't go.

Ending Choices	
● <s>못 가요.</s> (example choice)	● 친구를 만날 수 없어요.
● 더 못 먹어요.	● 두 번 봤어요.
● 에어컨이 필요 없어요.	● 학교에 안 갔어요.

1. 주말에 바쁘다

Korean_____

English_____

2. 영화가너무 재미있다

Korean_____

English_____

3. 배가 부르다

Korean_____

English_____

4. 수업이 없다

Korean_____

English_____

5. 날씨가 덥지 않다

Korean_____

English_____

● **3. Plausible Reason**
Fill in the blank with answer to the question, using the BASIC + 서 pattern.

> **Ex.** A: 주말에 영화를봤어요?
> B: 아니요, 영화관에 <u>사람이 너무 많아서</u> 못 봤어요.

1. A: 이번 여름 (this summer)에 여행을 갈 거예요?

   B: 아니요, _____ 갈 수 없어요.

2. A: 왜 아침을 안 먹었어요?

   B: _____ 먹을 수 없었어요.

3. A: 제프 씨를 만날 거예요?

   B: 아니요, _____ 만나지 않을 거예요.

4. A: 왜 친구 결혼식에 안 갔어요?

   B: _____ 안 갔어요.

5. A: 왜 늦게 왔어요?

   B: _____ 늦게 왔어요.

SR | Answer Key 해답

● **1. Combine the Sentences (Answers)**

1. 피곤해서 쉬고 있어요.
   I am resting because I am tired.
   I am tired, so I am resting.

2. 머리가 아파서 약을 먹었어요.
   I took some medicine because my head hurts.
   My head hurts, so I took some medicine.

3. 어제 옆집에서 파티를 해서 너무 시끄러웠어요.
   It was very loud because they had a party next door.
   They had a party next door, so it was very loud.

4. 숙제가 너무 어려워서 할 수 없어요.
   Because my homework is too hard, I can't do it.
   My homework is too hard so I can't do it.

5. 회사에서 집까지 너무 멀어서 힘들어요.
   Since it's very far from the company to my house, I'm exhausted.

● **2. Complete the Sentence (Answers)**
** English translations will vary due to the way English allows for reason and result to be in different positions. Korean should always have the reason first.

1. 주말에 바빠서 친구를 만날 수 없어요.
   Because I am busy on the weekend I can't meet my friend.

2. 영화가너무 재미있어서 두 번 봤어요.
   Because the movie was very interesting I watched it two times.

3. 배가 불러서 더 못 먹어요.
   Because I am full, I can't eat anymore.

4. 수업이 없어서 학교에 안 갔어요.
   I didn't go to school because there wasn't any classes.

5. 날씨가 덥지 않아서 에어컨이 필요 없어요.
   Because the weather isn't hot, I don't need air conditioning.

● 3. Plausible Reason (Answers)

1. A: Are you going on a trip this summer?
   B: No, _____ I can't go.

   Sample possible answers:
   시간이 없어서 because I don't have time
   돈이 없어서 because I don't have money
   바빠서 because I'm busy

2. A: Why didn't you eat breakfast?
   B: _____ I couldn't eat.

   Sample possible answers:
   늦게 일어나서 because I woke up late
   밥이 없어서 because there wasn't any rice

3. A: Will you meet Jeff?
   B: No, _____ I won't meet him.

   Sample possible answers:
   제프 씨를 만나고 싶지 않아서 because I don't want to meet Jeff
   제프 씨를 싫어해서 because I dislike Jeff

4. A: Why didn't you go to your friend's wedding?
   B: _____ I didn't go.

   Sample possible answers:
   다른 약속이 있어서 because I had another appointment
   회사에 일이 많아서 because I had a lot of work at the company

5. A: Why did you come late?
   B: _____ I came late.

   Sample possible answers:
   늦게 일어나서 because I woke up late
   버스를 못 타서 because I wasn't able to ride the bus

9 Lesson 9: This "or" That

9 | New Vocabulary 새로운 단어

New Nouns etc.

현금	cash
카드(신용카드)	card (credit card)
비용	fee, cost
학원	private education academy, academy
유럽	Europe
홍대	Hongdae (place in Seoul)
오른쪽	right (direction)
왼쪽	left (direction)

New Adverbs

곧	right away, immediately
이따가	later, after a short while
나중에	later

9 | Grammar and Usage 문법과 사용법

● **9-1. 곧 (soon), 이따가 (later), 나중에 (later)**
이따가 is when the "later" is within the same day, such as after the meeting.
나중에 is later, but can be several days or months later. 곧 is "soon".

> **Example sentences**
> 1. 곧 집에 돌아갈 거예요.   I will return home soon.
> 2. 우리는 이따가 만날 거예요.   We will meet later.
> 3. 나중에 같이 영화를보자.   Let's watch a movie together later.

● **9-2. The difference between ~겠다 and other future tenses**
So far we have learned two future tenses. One is 아/어/여 BASIC form and the second is with the STEM + (으)ㄹ 거예요 pattern.

When ~겠다 is used in "first person" (yourself) it's very certain that you WILL do or INTEND to do the action. However, when it's used in "third person" (other people) it's more of a "guess" or an "assumption" of the action.

All of the future tense sentences below mean "will go to Korea tomorrow".

❶ 내일 한국에 가요.
❷ 내일 한국에 갈 거예요.
❸ 내일 한국에 가겠어요.
❹ 내일 한국에 가겠습니다.

Here are the key differences between the various future tenses.

❶ 아/어/여 BASIC
The BASIC form can be future tense based on the context or surrounding words. It's just the simple fact, "I am going".

❷ STEM + (으)ㄹ 거예요
With this version, you "intend" on going. It's your plan to go.

❸ STEM + 겠어요.
This form is stronger in meaning. In many cases it includes a "promise" or "determination" that you will "go to Korea". When used with adjectives and talking about people other than yourself it is "assumptive" in nature.

❹ STEM + 겠습니다
This is the more formal version of ~겠다. It's common in news broadcasts, and when talking in more formal situations.

Example sentences
1. 일곱 시에 꼭 일어나겠어요.
   I will definitely wake at 7:00.

2. 이따가 은행에 가겠습니다.
   I will go to the bank later.

3. 5 시에 바빠서 수영장에 못 가겠어요.
   I'm busy at 5:00 so I can't go to the swimming pool.

4. 오늘 밤에 아버지에게 남자친구에 대해 말하겠어요.
   I will tell my father about my boyfriend tonight.

5. 금요일까지 공부만 하겠어요.
   I will do nothing but study until Friday.

6. 수요일은 비가 올 거예요.
   It will rain on Wednesday.

❺ STEM + 겠습니까?

This is the formal way to ask a future tense question for the ~겠다 form.
~겠어요? also works as a 요 form question.

Example conversation
1. A: 무슨 영화를 보겠습니까?
   B: '슈퍼맨'을 보겠습니다.

   A: Which movie are you going to see?
   B: I am going to see 'Superman'.

~겠다 with adjectives

When used with adjectives ~겠다 translates to "It seems~, it appears~, it looks~" or "I think it will be~". For example 춥겠어요 can be translated to "I think it's cold" or "it appears cold". It can be future AND present.

Example sentences
1. 맛있겠어요.   It looks delicious.
2. 좋겠어요.   I think it will be good. / It looks good.
3. 비싸겠어요.   It looks expensive.
4. 바쁘겠어요.   (You) look busy.
5. 슬프겠어요.   (They) look sad.

~겠다 with everyday expressions

There are some ~겠다 phrases that are built into everyday Korean life.

Example sentences
1. 잘 먹겠습니다.
   I will eat well.

   > This is a common phrase said before eating a meal.

2. 모르겠어요.
   I don't know.

3. 알겠어요.
   I got it.

● **9-3. This, last, and next summer (지난, 이번, 다음)**

You can change which season or even day of the week you are talking about with these modifiers:

지난   last~
이번   this~
다음   next~

Just add these words in front of the time frame you want to change.
Let's learn the seasons then use these words with them.

봄 (spring)   여름 (summer)
가을 (fall, autumn)   겨울 (winter)

Now let's change which season we are talking about.

Example sentences
1. **this ~**
   이번 봄 (this spring)   이번 여름 (this summer)
   이번 가을 (this fall)   이번 겨울 (this winter)

2. **last~**
   지난 봄 (last spring)   지난 여름 (last summer)
   지난 가을 (last fall)   지난 겨울 (last winter)

3. **last~**
   다음 봄 (next spring)   다음 여름 (next summer)
   다음 가을 (next fall)   다음 겨울 (next winter)

Use can also 지난, 이번, and 다음 with days of the week.

Example sentences

1. 지난 목요일에 미국에 돌아왔어요.
   I came back to America last Thursday.

2. 다음 주 토요일에 같이 스시를 먹자.
   Let's eat sushi together next Saturday.

3. 이번 월요일에 친구가 호주 요리를 만들어 줄 거예요.
   This Monday, my friend will make me Australian cuisine.

> Country + 요리 translates to "cuisine" or "cooking" for that country.

이번, 지난, and 다음 can also be used in front of many words.

Examples

1. 지난 수업   the prior class
2. 다음 비행기   the next airplane
3. 이번 시험   the current test (this test)
4. 지난 생일   last birthday
5. 다음 콘서트   the next concert
6. 이번 시합   the current match (this match)

● 9-4. 로 for directions

We previously learned that (으)로 is the "by which means" marker.
Additionally, (으)로 can mean "towards" some direction or destination.

If the direction / place has a 받침 then 으로 is attached. If the direction / place doesn't have a 받침 or has ㄹ for the 받침 then 로 is used.

Example sentences

1. 왼쪽으로 갔어요.
   I went towards the left.

2. 오른쪽으로 가 주세요.
   Please go to the right.

3. 어디로 가겠습니까?
   Where will you go to?

4. 준호 씨는 대전으로 돌아갔어요.
   Junho headed back to Daejon.

5. 서울로 갈 거예요.
   I'll go to Seoul.

> When the proceeding consonant is a ㄹ then just 로 is used.

● 9-5. The difference between 로 and 에

에 should be used when there is a specific place or destination. (으)로 is used when heading towards a direction such as "north", or "left".

1. 곧 학원에 가고 싶어요.
   I want to go to the academy soon.

2. 학원으로 가고 싶어요.
   I want to go towards the academy.

3. 육 개월 동안 대구에 못 갔어요.
   I haven't gone down to Daegu for 6 months.

> 대구 is south of 서울 so the English is changed to "gone down". If it were above, "gone up" would have been used.

4. 이번 봄에는 유럽으로 가고 싶지 않아요.
   I don't want to go to Europe this spring.

5. 오늘이 엄마 생일이라서 이따가 엄마 집에 갈 거예요.
   Since today is my mother's birthday I'm going to my mom's house later.

● 9-6. Cost of things (~비, ~료)

The Korean language originally used 한자 (Chinese characters) for all of its words until 한글 was invented by King 세종 in the 16th century.
Knowing the 한자 base of words will help you considerably in understanding the connection between words.

For example the suffixes 비 and 료 come from the original 한자 used in many Chinese and even Japanese words.

Many Korean words have 비 or 료 built into them.

택시비	taxi fare
버스비	bus fare
학비	school expenses, tuition
숙박비	lodging expenses

항공료	airfare
수업료	tuition
무료	free (no charge)
유료	fee based (to have a charge)

Example sentences

1. 학비가 얼마예요?
   How much are the school expenses?

> Often 에서 is shortened to just 서.

2. 여기 무료 WiFi (와이파이)가 있어요?
   Is there free WiFi here?

3. 버스비가 얼마였어요?
   How much was bus fare?

4. 한국은 학원 수업료가 정말 비쌉니다.
   In Korea tuition for private academies are expensive.

5. 강남역까지 택시비가 10,000 원쯤이에요.
   The taxi fare to Gangnam station is about ten thousand won.

● **9-7. ~(이)나 Using "or" with nouns**

(이)나 is the "or" particle in Korean. When (이)나 is used, it shows a choice between two things just like English "or". If the noun ends with a 받침 use 이나, if there is no 받침 use 나.

Example sentences

1. 피자나 햄버거를 먹고 싶어요.
   I want to eat pizza or a hamburger.

2. 오늘 밤에 홍대나 강남에 가자.
   Let's go to Hongdae or Gangnam tonight.

3. 민수 씨가 프랑스나 인도에 갈 거예요.
   Minsu will go to France or India.

4. 현금이나 카드가 있어요?
   Do you have cash or a card?

5. 요즘 외로워서 강아지나 고양이가 필요해요.
   I need a puppy or a cat because I am sad recently.

● 9-8. The past tense form ~ㅆ다

In book 1 you learned how to make the past tense of a verb by adding ㅆ to the bottom of the BASIC form then adding 어.

```
Example past tense conjugations
1. to eat              먹다 → 먹어 → 먹었어 (ate)
2. to do               하다 → 해 → 했어 (did)
3. to be cold          춥다 → 추워 → 추웠어 (was cold)
4. to live             살다 → 살아 → 살았어 (lived)
5. to loan, borrow     빌리다 → 빌려 → 빌렸어 (loaned)
```

The ㅆ + 어 conjugation is great to simple say ~였어요 (it was) or 했어요 (I did) but sometimes you just need the *past tense stem*. This is just past tense form without the 어.

```
Example past tense STEMS only
1. to eat              먹다 → 먹어 → 먹었 (meaningless)
2. to do               하다 → 해 → 했 (meaningless)
3. to be cold          춥다 → 추워 → 추웠 (meaningless)
4. to live             살다 → 살아 → 살았 (meaningless)
5. to loan, borrow     빌리다 → 빌려 → 빌렸 (meaningless)
```

The examples above are labeled as "meaningless" because you can't just say 했 or 먹었 etc. by themselves. Instead the *past tense stem* is integrated into many different grammar patterns as past tense.

● 9-9. ~거나 Using "or" with verbs and adjectives.

With verbs and adjectives ~거나 is used to show a choice. To make ~거나 you can use the STEM or PAST TENSE STEM plus 거나.

```
Example sentences
1. 이따가 공부를 하거나 운동을 할 거예요..
   I will study or exercise later.

2. 내일 엄마는 쇼핑을 하거나 요리를 할 거예요.
   Mom will shop or cook tomorrow.
```

Notice that the LAST verb in the choices determines the tense of the FIRST verb also.

Example sentences

1. 술을 마시거나 노래방에 가자.
   Let's drink some alcohol or go to a karaoke room.

2. 티비를 보거나 책을 읽고 싶어요?
   Do you want to watch TV or read a book?

   > This is not a "Which one?" question. The answer should be YES or NO.

3. 누가 왔거나 전화했어요?
   Did anyone come or call?

   > This could also be 오거나 전화했어요? Since the last verb determines the tense.

4. 학원까지 걷거나 운전해서 갈 수 있어요.
   You can walk or drive to academy.

5. 쉬거나 자지 마세요.
   Don't rest or sleep.

6. 이 식당의 음식은 항상 너무 맵거나 달아요.
   This restaurant's food is always too spicy or sweet.

7. 다음 주 일요일 날씨가 따뜻하거나 조금 추울 거예요.
   Next Sunday's weather will be warm or a bit cold.

9 | Q&A 질문과 대답

1. 언제 한국에 갈 거예요?
곧 갈 거예요.
잘 모르겠어요.
이번 봄이나 다음 봄에 가고 싶어요.

When are you going to Korea?
I will go soon.
I don't really know. (I don't know well)
I want to go this spring or next spring.

2. 이번에 학비는 얼마예요?
이번에 학비는 백만 원 정도예요.
몰라요. 지난번에는 팔십만 원쯤이었어요.

How much is tuition this time?
This time the tuition is about 1 million won.
I don't know. Last time it was around 800,000 won.

3. 언제 만날 거예요?
오늘은 바빠요. 나중에 만나요.
이따가 홍대에서 만나요.

When will we meet?
I am busy today. We'll meet later.
We will meet later at Hongdae.

4. 현금 있어요?
아니요. 현금이 전혀 없어요.
네. 하지만 별로 없어요.
아니요. 하지만 카드가 있어요.

Do you have cash?
No. I don't have any cash.
Yes. But I don't have much.
No. But I have a card.

5. 오늘 저녁에 어디가요?
오늘이 제 생일이라서 가족과 생일파티를 할 거예요.
한국어 학원에 갈 거예요.

Where are you going this evening.
Because today is my birthday, I will have a birthday party with my family.
I'm going to the Korean language academy.

9 | Test Yourself Activities 연습 문제

● **A9-1. Sentence Jumble**
With the words provided, make Korean sentences that match the English. You can freely add particles, pronouns and conjugate verbs as needed.

1. 봄, 서울, 먹다, 마시다, 가다, 이번, 물, 다음, 런던, 바나나, 사과

_____
This spring I will go to Seoul or London.

_____
I will eat an apple or drink water.

_____
I want to drink water, or eat an apple.

2. 매일, 매달, 다음, 꼭, 지난, 항상, 수요일, 목요일, 가다, 거의, 부산

_____
I will definitely go to Pusan next Wednesday. (use 겠다)

_____
I go to Pusan almost every month.

_____
I always go to Pusan on Wednesday or Thursday.

3. 이따가, 가다, 왼쪽, 오른쪽, 있다, 집, 곧, 준호

_____
My house is on the right side.

_____
Please go left.

_____
I will go to Junho's house soon.

● **A9-2. Fill in the blanks**
Fill in the missing word based on the English sentence.

1. 피자가 _____요.
   It seems like the pizza is hot.

2. 우리 학교의 _____가 너무 비싸요.
   Our school's tuition is too expensive.

3. _____ 여름에 유럽이나 중국으로 여행을 가겠어요.
   I will go on a trip to Europe or China next summer.

4. 지난 여름과 이번 여름의 날씨가 _____달라요.
   Last summer and this summer's weather is completely different.

5. 여기부터 한국까지 몇 시간 _____ 걸려요?
   About how many hours does it take to get from here to Korea?

● **A9-3. Mark and Translate**
Mark the Korean sentence without mistakes then translate it.

1. ○ 김밥을 삼겹살이나 먹겠어요.
   ○ 김밥나 삼겹살나 먹겠어요.
   ○ 김밥이나 삼겹살을 먹겠어요.

   Translation:_____

2. ○ 다음 화요일에 서울로 갈 거예요.
   ○ 지난 화요일에 서울로 갈 거예요.
   ○ 이번 화요일로 서울에 갈 거예요.

   Translation:_____

3. ○ 커피나 콜라를 같이 마시자.
   ○ 커피이나 콜라를 같이 마시자.
   ○ 커피나 콜라가 같이 마시자.

   Translation:_____

9 | Self Test Answers 연습 문제 정답

● **A9-1. Sentence Jumble**
1. 이번 봄에 서울이나 런던에 갈 거예요.
   사과를 먹거나 물을 마실 거예요.
   물을 마시거나 사과를 먹고 싶어요.

2. 다음 수요일에 부산에 꼭 가겠어요.
   거의 매달 부산에 가요.
   항상 수요일이나 목요일에 부산에 가요.

3. 제 집은 오른쪽에 있어요.
   왼쪽으로 가 주세요.
   준호 씨의 집에 곧 갈 거예요 / 가겠어요.

● **A9-2. Fill in the blanks**
1. 피자가 <u>뜨겁겠어요.</u>
2. 우리 학교의 <u>수업료</u>가 너무 비싸요.
3. <u>다음</u> 여름에 유럽이나 중국으로 여행을 가겠어요.
4. 지난 여름과 이번 여름의 날씨가 <u>완전히</u> 달라요.
5. 여기부터 한국까지 몇 시간쯤 걸려요?

● **A9-3. Best Sentence Search**

1. ○ 김밥을 삼겹살이나 먹겠어요.
   ○ 김밥나 삼겹살나 먹겠어요.
   ✓ 김밥이나 삼겹살을 먹겠어요.
   Translation: I will eat Gimbap or Samgyeopsal.

2. ✓ 다음 화요일에 서울로 갈 거예요.
   ○ 지난 화요일에 서울로 갈 거예요.
   ○ 이번 화요일로 서울에 갈 거예요.
   Translation: I am going to Seoul next Tuesday.

3. ✓ 커피나 콜라를 같이 마시자.
   ○ 커피이나 콜라를 같이 마시자.
   ○ 커피나 콜라가 같이 마시자.
   Translation: Let's drink coffee or cola.

9 | Vocabulary Builder 단어 구축

Grammar will not trip you up as much as a word. Nothing stops a conversation like a missing word! But grammar you can work around.

■ Group E: In the house 집안에

쓰레기	garbage, trash
쓰레기통	garbage can
콘센트	power outlet
벽	wall
소파	sofa
계단	stairs
담요	blanket
베개	pillow
책장	bookcase
냉장고	refrigerator
냉동고	freezer
전자레인지	microwave
램프	lamp
식탁	dinner table

■ Vocabulary Sentences

The following sentences might contain words and concepts not yet taught. Focus on the new vocabulary more than the grammar.

1. 쓰레기는 꼭 쓰레기통에 넣어야 돼요.
   You must put trash in the trash can.

2. 당장 콘센트를 찾아야 돼요.
   I need to find the outlet right now.

3. 사진이 벽에 걸려 있어요.
   The picture is hanging on the wall.

4. 강아지가 소파에 앉아 있어요.
   The dog is sitting on the sofa.

5. 계단이 너무 많아요.

There are too many stairs.

6. 담요 하나만 주세요.
Give me just one blanket please.

7. 베개가 너무 높아요.
The pillow is too high.

8. 책은 책장에 넣어 주세요.
Please place the book in the bookshelf.

9. 저는 냉장고에 있는 사과를 먹고 있어요.
I am eating the apple in the refrigerator.

10. 만두는 냉동고에 넣어 주세요.
Please put the pot sticker in the freezer.

11. 새로운 전자레인지를 샀어요.
I bought a new microwave.

12. 잠을 잘 때에는 램프를 끄세요.
Turn off the lamp when you are sleeping.

13. 밥은 식탁에서 먹어야 해요.
You must eat food at the dinner table.

10 Lesson 10: Promises and Appointments

10 | New Vocabulary 새로운 단어

New Nouns etc.

비서	secretary
손님	customer, guest
사장님	boss, president
세금	taxes
월급	monthly pay
약속	promise
표	ticket
보고서	report
휴가	day off

New Adjectives

부끄럽다	to be shy, embarrassed, bashful

New Verbs

내다	to pay, to put out
약속하다	to make a promise
지키다	to keep, to protect
취소하다	to cancel
계속하다	to continue
이야기하다	to talk, to chat

10 | Grammar and Usage 문법과 사용법

● **10-1. 약속 (promise, appointment, plans)**

The meaning of 약속 can mean, "promise", "plans", or "appointment" depending on the context of the sentence.

The person you have the "appointment" or "plans" with is marked with any of the "with" markers (하고, 랑/이랑, 와/과).

[person]랑 약속이 있다 / 없다
To **have** / **not have** an appointment **with** a person.

Example sentences

1. 오늘 친구하고 약속이 있어요.
   I have plans with my friend today.

2. 요즘 약속이 많아서 친구를 만날 수 없어요.
   These days, I have many appointments so I can't meet with friends.

3. 오늘 준호 씨랑 약속이 있어서 일찍 출발해요.
   I'm leaving early because I have an appointment with Junho.

4. 이번 주 아주 중요한 약속이 있어요.
   I have a very important appointment this week.

5. 누구랑 약속이 있어요?
   Who do you have an appointment with?

Example conversation

1. A: 오늘 바빠요?
   B: 아니요. 오늘 약속이 없어요. 그래서 안 바빠요.

   A: Are you busy today?
   B: No. I don't have any appointments today. So, I am not busy.

● 10-2. 손님 (customer, guest)

Depending on if you are referring to a customer at work or talking about a friend coming to your house, Korean uses 손님 to mean either.

Example sentences
1. 엄마! 손님이 왔어요!
   Mom! A guest has come!

2. 손님, 몇 분 이세요?
   Customer, how many people are there?

> In a restaurant, a waitress will often directly call the customer 손님 when the name is not known.

3. 어제는 손님 두 명이 갑자기 왔어요.
   Yesterday two customers suddenly came.

4. 그 손님이 가게에서 제일 비싼 것을 샀어요.
   That customer bought the most expensive thing in the store.

● 10-3. 내다 (to pay, to put out)

TYPE	regular verb	BASIC FORM	내

The thing you are paying or putting out is marked with 을/를 and the method you use to pay is marked with (으)로.

Example sentences (to pay)
1. 보통 남자친구가 돈을 내요.
   Normally the boyfriend pays the money.

2. 어머니가 택시비를 냈어요.
   My mother paid the taxi fare.

3. 돈이 있어요. 하지만 세금을 내고 싶지 않아요.
   I have money. However, I don't want to pay taxes.

Example sentences (to put out)
1. 선생님에게 숙제를 냈어요.
   I turned in my homework to my teacher.

> To say "I put out my homework" isn't natural in English. So we used "turned in".

2. 보고서를 언제 낼 거예요?
   When will you put out the report?

Example conversation
1. 종업원: 손님, 현금으로 낼 거예요?
   손님: 아니요, 카드로 낼 거예요.

   Waitress: Customer, will you be paying with cash?
   Customer: No, I will pay with a card.

● **10-4. 약속하다 (to make a promise, appointment)**

TYPE	하다 verb	BASIC FORM	약속해

The person you are making the promise with is marked with any of the "with" markers 랑/이랑, 하고, or 와,과.

Example sentences
1. 3 시에 약속을 했습니다.
   I made an appointment at 3 o'clock.

   > 했습니다 is more formal and not typically used with friends.

2. 친구하고 약속을 했어요.
   I made a promise/appointment with my friend.

3. 오늘 친구 생일파티가 있어서 약속을 못 해요.
   Today is my friend's birthday party, so I can't make any appointments.

Example conversation
1. 비서: 사장님이랑 약속을 했어요?
   손님: 네, 어제 전화로 약속을 했어요.

   A: Did you make an appointment with the president?
   B: Yes, yesterday I made an appointment by phone.

Special Information 특별 정보

As you learn more Korean, you should learn to be flexible with how some Korean words translate into English. For example, 약속 can mean "promise", "appointment", and "engagement". But it also can mean "a commitment" or "a plan" depending on what sounds good in English.

Some Korean words will split into many nuanced English words and there are cases where one English word splits into more than one Korean word such as how "to be" turns into 있다, 없다, and 계시다.

● 10-5. 지키다 (to keep, to protect)

TYPE	regular verb	BASIC FORM	지켜

지키다 is used for keeping rules, and promises etc. The thing you are protecting or following / keeping is marked with the object marker, 을/를.

Example sentences

1. 규칙을 지킵시다.
   Let's follow the rules.

2. 친구가 약속을 지키지 않았어요.
   My friend didn't keep their promise.

3. 수업을 10 시에 시작할 거예요. 시간을 지켜 주세요.
   Class will start at 10 o'clock. Please be on time.

> "follow time" or "keep time" doesn't sound natural in English so we used "be on time".

● 10-6. 취소하다 (to cancel)

TYPE	하다 verb	BASIC FORM	취소해

The item being canceled is marked with 을/를.

Example sentences

1. 약속을 취소했어요.
   I cancelled my appointment.

2. 회사에 일이 많아서 여행을 취소했어요.
   I have a lot of work at my company so I cancelled my trip.

3. 손님, 이 표는 취소할 수 없어요.
   Customer, you can't cancel this ticket.

Example conversation

1. 학생 1: 누가 수업을 취소했어요?
   학생 2: 어제 선생님이 전화로 수업을 취소했어요.

   Student 1: Who cancelled class?
   Student 2: Yesterday, teacher cancelled the class by phone.

● 10-7. Putting it all together for 약속

This lesson is heavy with big promises. So let's put what we learned in this and the prior lessons all together to make sure we don't miss anything.

Example sentences
1. 약속을 하다.   To make a promise / appointment.
2. 약속을 지키다.   To keep a promise / appointment.
3. 약속을 취소하다.   To cancel a promise / appointment.
4. 약속을 깨다.   To break a promise / appointment.
5. 약속이 깨지다.   To have a promise / appointment broken.

NOTE: Sentences 1~4 use 을 particle because the verbs are all "action" verbs. Sentence 5's verb is a "state" verb, so 이 or 가 will be used.

Also verbs 깨다 (to break, to shatter) and 깨지다 (to be broken, to be shattered) are from a prior lesson but they are commonly used with 약속.

Example sentences
1. 갑자기 집에 손님이 왔어. 그래서 오늘 약속을 깼어.
   Suddenly a guest came to my house. So today I broke my appointment.

2. 오늘 약속이 깨졌어요. 그래서 시간이 많아요.
   Today my appointment got broken. So, I have a lot of time.

3. 너는 나와의 약속을 깼어.
   You broke a promise with me.

● 10-8. 계속하다 (to continue)

TYPE	하다 verb	BASIC FORM	계속해

The item being continued is marked with 을/를.

Example sentences
1. 선생님이 수업을 계속했어요.
   The teacher continued the class.

2. 일본어 공부를 계속하고 싶어요.
   I want to continue my Japanese studies.

3. 여기가 시끄러워서 공부를 계속할 수 없어요.
   Because it's loud here, I can't continue my studies.

● 10-9. 이야기하다 (to talk, to chat)

TYPE	하다 verb	BASIC FORM	이야기해

말하다 means "to talk" or "to speak" but it is used to say "I said" or "he said" etc. 이야기하다 is a back and forth conversation. It's common for 이야기 to be shortened to 얘기.

Example sentences
1. 친구 생일파티에서 이야기를 많이 했어요.
   We talked a lot at my friend's birthday party.

2. 학교에 대해 부모님과 이야기했어요.
   I talked with my parents about school.

3. 여자들하고 이야기를 못 해요.
   I can't talk with girls.

4. 친구랑 재미있는 이야기를 많이 했어요.
   I talked about a lot of interesting things with my friend.

> Adverbs can come before the 하다 or before the entire verb phrase as in sentence 1.

● 10-10. 계속 + VERB (to continue verb)

계속 can be added in front of any verb to make sentences like 계속 먹었어요 (I continued to eat) etc. The action is non-stop.

Example sentences
1. 아침까지 계속 운전을 했어요.
   I continued to drive until morning.

2. 배불렀어요. 하지만 계속 먹었어요.
   I was full. But I continued eating.

3. 우리는 학교에 대해 계속 이야기했어요.
   We continued to talk about school.

4. 비가 계속 오고 있어요.
   It's continuing to rain.

5. 제 딸은 숙제가 많아요. 하지만 티비를 계속 보고 있어요.
   My daughter has a lot of homework. But she is continuing to watch TV.

● 10-11. 부끄럽다 (to be shy, embarrased, bashful)

TYPE	ㅂ irregular adjective	BASIC FORM	부끄러워

Example sentences

1. 저는 예쁜 여자 앞에서 항상 부끄러워요.
   I am always shy in front of beautiful girls.

2. 어제 한국 사람들하고 처음으로 한국말을 했어요.
   진짜 부끄러웠어요.
   I spoke Korean with Koreans for the first time yesterday.
   I was really embarrassed.

3. 부끄러워서 여자들하고 이야기 못 했어요.
   Because I was shy I couldn't talk with girls.

● 10-12. The many ways to say "what" in Korean

In book 1 we learned two ways to say "what".

뭐 is the typical "what" used in a wide range of Korean sentences. It can also be used alone to just ask simply "what?" when you couldn't hear something.

무슨 is a direct modifier. In other words, it comes directly in front of nouns.

Example sentences (using 뭐)

1. **뭐**를 좋아해요?   What do you like?
2. **뭐**가 재미있어요?   What is interesting?

Example sentences (using 무슨)

1. **무슨** 음식을 좋아해요?   What foods do you like?
2. **무슨** 영화가재미있어요?   What movie is interesting?

무엇 is another way to say "what". 무엇 can NEVER be used alone. It must always be followed by a particle EVEN in casual speech. 무엇 was the original "what" for Korean, but over time the variation 뭐 developed.

Example sentences (using 무엇)

1. **무엇**을 좋아해요?   What do you like?
2. **무엇**이 재미있어요?   What is interesting?

10 | Q&A 질문과 대답

1. **오늘 저녁에 약속이 있어요?**
   친구와 영화를 볼 거예요.
   아니요. 너무 피곤해서 약속을 취소했어요.
   비가 계속 와서 약속이 깨졌어요.

   Do you have any plans this evening?
   I am going to watch a movie with a friend.
   No. Because I am so tired I cancelled my plans.
   My plans got cancelled because it's continually raining.

2. **이번 달 월급을 받았어요?**
   아니요. 사장님이 약속을 안 지켜서 월급을 받지 못했어요.
   네. 하지만 학원 수업료를 내서 벌써 돈이 없어졌어요.

   Did you get your salary this month?
   No. My boss didn't keep his promise, so I wasn't able to get my salary.
   Yes. But, since I paid my academy tuition I already am out of money.

3. **누가 택시비를 낼 거예요?**
   보통 남자친구가 택시비를 내요.
   택시비가 비싸서 버스로 갈 거예요.

   Who is going to pay the taxi fare?
   Normally my boyfriend pays the taxi fare.
   I am going to ride the bus since taxi fare is expensive.

4. **왜 오늘 집에 있어요?**
   엄마랑 약속했어요.
   손님이 집에 올 거예요.

   Why are you at home today?
   I made plans with my mother.
   There are guests coming to my house.

5. **보고서를 언제 낼 거예요?**
   내일까지 비서에게 낼 거예요.
   약속을 지키지 못해서 죄송합니다. 다음 주까지 낼게요.

   When can you turn in the report?
   I will turn it in to the secretary by tomorrow.
   I am sorry I wasn't able to keep my promise. I will turn it in by next week.

10 | Test Yourself Activities 연습 문제

● A10-1. Sentence Jumble
With the words provided, make Korean sentences that match the English.
You can freely add particles, pronouns and conjugate verbs as needed.

1. 약속, 깨다, 깨지다, 지키다, 친구, 할머니, 할아버지, 있다, 하다

_____

I made a promise with my grandfather.

_____

My friend broke their promise.

_____

I have a promise with my grandmother and grandfather.

2. 깨지다, 최소하다, 약속, 깨다, 지키다

_____

I cancelled the appointment.

_____

I kept my promise.

_____

The promise was broken.

3. 이야기하다, 월급, 손님, 내다, 사장님, 세금, 보고서, 계속, 곧

_____

The customer continually talked.

_____

My boss paid taxes.

_____

I will put out the salary report soon.

● **A10-2. Fill in the blanks**
Fill in the missing word based on the English sentence.

1. 박지윤 씨는 항상 약속을 _____요.
   Jiyoon Park always keeps promises.

2. 눈이 많이 와서 선생님이 수업을 _____했어요.
   Because it snowed a lot, teacher cancelled class.

3. 제 친구가 _____ 약속을 깨요.
   My friend continually breaks promises.

4. 파티에서 아주 귀여운 여자랑 두 시간 동안 _____했어요.
   At the party I talked to a very cute girl for 2 hours.

5. 부산까지는 3 시간 걸려서 3 시 _____에 못 가요.
   Because it takes 3 hours to Pusan, I won't make my 3:00 appointment.

● **A10-3. Mark and Translate**
Mark the Korean sentence without mistakes then translate it.

1. ○ 약속을 깨졌어요.
   ○ 약속이 깨졌어요.
   ○ 약속이 깨어요.

   Translation:_____

2. ○ 비서는 3 개월 동안 휴가가 없었어요.
   ○ 보고서가 3 개월 동안 휴가를 없었어요.
   ○ 비서가 3 달월 동안 휴가가 없었어요.

   Translation:_____

3. ○ 택시비가 비싸서 보통 사장님이 내요.
   ○ 택시비를 비싸서 보통 사장님이 내요.
   ○ 택시비가 비쌌어서 보통 사장님이 냈었어요.

   Translation:_____

10 | Self Test Answers 연습 문제 정답

● A10-1. Sentence Jumble

1. 할버지랑 약속을 했어요.
   친구가 약속을 깼어요.
   할머니랑 할아버지랑 약속이 있어요.

2. 약속을 최소했어요.
   약속을 지켰어요.
   약속이 깨졌어요.

3. 손님이 계속 이야기했어요.
   사장님이 세금을 냈어요.
   곧 월급 보고서를 낼 거예요.

● A10-2. Fill in the blanks

1. 박지윤 씨는 항상 약속을 <u>지켜</u>요.
2. 눈이 많이 와서 선생님이 수업을 <u>취소</u>했어요.
3. 제 친구가 <u>계속</u> 약속을 깨요.
4. 파티에서 아주 귀여운 여자랑 두 시간 동안 <u>이야기</u>했어요.
5. 부산까지는 3 시간 걸려서 3 시 <u>약속</u>에 못 가요.

● A10-3. Best Sentence Search

1. ○ 약속을 깨쪘어요.
   ✓ 약속이 깨졌어요.
   ○ 약속이 깨어요.
   Translation: The promise was (got) broken.

2. ✓ 비서는 3 개월 동안 휴가가 없었어요.
   ○ 보고서가 3 개월 동안 휴가를 없었어요.
   ○ 비서가 3 달월 동안 휴가가 없었어요.
   Translation: The secretary didn't have a day off for 3 months.

3. ✓ 택시비가 비싸서 보통 사장님이 내요.
   ○ 택시비를 비싸서 보통 사장님이 내요.
   ○ 택시비가 비쌌어서 보통 사장님이 냈었어요.
   Translation: Because the taxi is expensive the boss normally pays.

10 | Vocabulary Builder 단어 구축

Words. Words. Words. The weird thing is you never hear these words until you learn them. Then they seem to be everywhere as if they KNOW you just learned them.

■ Group F: In the bathroom 화장실에서

향기	scent, perfume
변기(통)	toilet
수건	towel
치약	toothpaste
칫솔	toothbrush
비누	soap
샴푸	shampoo
싱크대	sink
화장지	toilet paper
면도기	razor

■ Vocabulary Sentences

The following sentences might contain words and concepts not yet taught. Focus on the new vocabulary more than the grammar.

1. 꽃에서 좋은 향기가 나요.
   A pleasant scent is coming from the flower.

2. 개가 변기통의 물을 마셔요.
   The dog is drinking toilet water.

3. 오래된 수건을 버렸어요.
   I threw away the old towel.

4. 이 치약은 마음에 안 들어요.
   I don't like this toothpaste.

5. 제 칫솔이 변기통에 떨어졌어요.
   My toothbrush fell in the toilet.

6. 비누를 떨어뜨리지 마세요.
   Don't drop the soap.

7. 샴푸가 눈에 들어갔어요.
   The shampoo got into my eyes.

8. 싱크대에 반지가 떨어졌어요.
   The ring fell into the sink.

9. 화장지가 없어요!
   This isn't any toilet paper!

10. 오늘은 면도기가 필요 없어요.
    Today, I don't need a razer.

11 Lesson 11: Expressing Emotion

11 New Vocabulary 새로운 단어

New Nouns etc.

혼자	alone, myself
결혼생활	married life
하루	one day, day
귀신	ghost, spirit
공포영화	horror movie
점수	score
전쟁	war
전쟁터	battlefield
잘못	mistake, error

New Adjectives

외롭다	to be sad, lonely
행복하다	to be fulfilled, to be happy
우울하다	to be depressed
무섭다	to be scared
화가나다	to be mad
화를내다	to express anger

New Adverbs

이유 없이	without reason, for no reason
생각 없이	without thinking, without thought

New Verbs

싸우다	to fight
화해하다	to make up
사과하다	to apologize

11 | Grammar and Usage 문법과 사용법

● 11-1. Other people's emotions and intentions (BASIC + 하다)

Since you can never truly know how someone feels, or their true intentions,
you can't directly say they are "sad" or "happy". When talking about other
people's feelings or intentions you must use the BASIC + 하다 form.

1. 저는 슬퍼요.   I am sad. (1st person)
2. 슬퍼요?   Are you sad? (2nd person)
3. 준호 씨가 슬퍼해요?   Is Junho sad? (3rd person)
4. 준호 씨가 슬퍼해요.   Junho is sad. (3rd person)

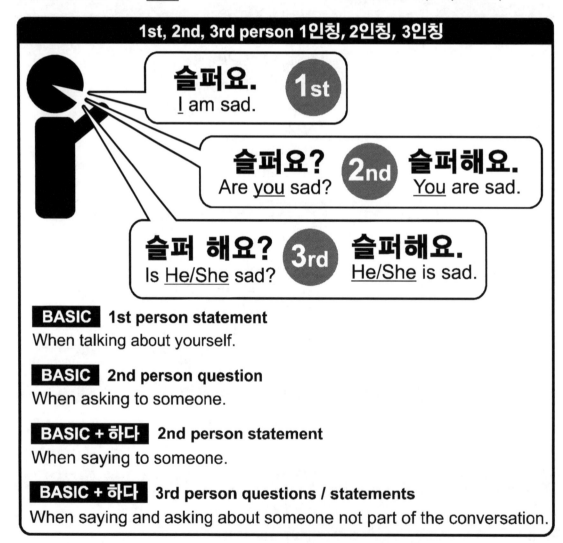

1st, 2nd, 3rd person 1인칭, 2인칭, 3인칭

슬퍼요. **1st** I am sad.

슬퍼요? **2nd** 슬퍼해요.
Are you sad?   You are sad.

슬퍼 해요? **3rd** 슬퍼해요.
Is He/She sad?   He/She is sad.

BASIC **1st person statement**
When talking about yourself.

BASIC **2nd person question**
When asking to someone.

BASIC + 하다 **2nd person statement**
When saying to someone.

BASIC + 하다 **3rd person questions / statements**
When saying and asking about someone not part of the conversation.

Not only does this rule apply for emotions but it also applies for a person's "intentions" such as with ~고 싶다 (want to~). When you are talking about another person's intentions you have to use say ~고 싶어하다 form.

Example sentences

1. 선생님은 미국에 가고 싶어해요.
   Teacher wants to go to America.

2. 제 아버지는 스시를 먹고 싶어해요.
   My father wants to eat sushi.

3. 준호 씨가 영어를 몰라서 영어를 공부 하고 싶어해요.
   Because Junho doesn't know English he wants to study English.

> 가고 싶어요 and 가고 싶어해요 both mean the same thing in English. The only difference is WHO wants to go.

● **11-2. 외롭다   (to be lonely, sad)**

TYPE	ㅂ irregular adjective	BASIC FORM	외로워

Example sentences

1. 혼자는 외로워요.
   I am sad alone.

2. 여자친구가 없어서 외로워요.
   I am lonely because I don't have a girlfriend.

3. 박지윤 씨는 별로 친구가 없어서 외로워해요.
   Because Jiyoon Park doesn't have many friends, she is lonely.

4. 밥을 혼자 먹어서 외로워요.
   I ate dinner alone so I am sad.

5. 제 친구들이 다 미국에 돌아가서 외로워요.
   Because all of my friends returned to America I am sad.

● **11-3. 행복하다   (to be fufilled, to be happy)**

TYPE	하다 adjective	BASIC FORM	행복해

Example sentences

1. 우리 가족은 행복해요.
   My (our) family is happy.

2. 남편과의 결혼생활은 행복했어요.
   Married life with my husband was happy.

> Oh! How sad! It seems they got divorced.

3. 맛있는 음식을 먹어서 행복해요.
   I am happy because I had delicious food.

4. 좋은 음악을 들어서 행복해요.
   I am happy because I listened to good music.

> This might look like a mistake, but 행복해해요 is correct.

5. 그녀는 항상 행복해해요.
   She is always happy.

Special Information 특별 정보

What is the difference between 행복하다 and 기쁘다?
Both of these words translate to "happy". But 기쁘다 is a much more casual form of happy. 행복하다 includes *satisfaction* as part of the happiness. When you are happy with life or are happy overall, as opposed to a "happy right now" feeling, then use 행복하다.

● **11-4. 우울하다 (to be depressed)**

TYPE	하다 adjective	BASIC FORM	부끄러워

Example sentences

1. 우울한 하루였어요.
   It was a depressing day.

2. 이번 주에 비가 매일 와서 점점 우울해졌어요.
   I'm gradually getting depressed because it's rained everyday this week.

3. 요즘 날씨가 추워서 우울했어요.
   I was depressed because the weather is cold these days.

● 11-5. 무섭다 (to be scared, to be scary)

TYPE	ㅂ irregular adjective	BASIC FORM	무서워

Depending on the usage 무섭다 can mean "scared" or "scary". Carefully look at each of the examples and see how the particle usage shifts depending on what is being said in English.

Example sentences

1. 지윤 씨가 선생님을 무서워해요.
   Jiyoon is scared of the teacher.

2. 저는 선생님이 무서워요.
   I am scared of the teacher.

3. 이 선생님은 무서워요.
   This teacher is scary.

4. 남동생이 귀신을 무서워해요.
   My younger brother is scared of ghosts.

5. 귀신을 무서워하지 마세요.
   Don't be scared of ghosts!

6. 귀신이 무서워요.
   Ghosts are scary.

7. 아이가 동물을 무서워해요.
   The child is scared of animals.

8. 동물이 무서워요.
   The animal is scary.

9. 동물이 무서워해요.
   The animal is scared.

10. 친구가 공포영화를무서워해요.
    My friend is scared of horror movies.

11. 공포영화는 무서워요.
    Horror movies are scary.

12. 전쟁은 무서워요.
    War is scary.

Special Information 특별 정보

Scary mistakes with 무섭다

What if a small child cries when you come in the room? In English you can say "I am not scary!". But since 무섭다 means "to be scary", and also "to be scared", if you want to say "I am not scary" you need to say 저는 무서운 사람이 아니에요 (I am not a scary person). Because if you just say 무섭지 않아요 it just means "I am not scared".

Furthermore, maybe you want to tell a child not to be scared. But if you say 무섭지 마세요 you just told them "don't be scary". Instead you need to say 무서워 하지 마세요 (don't be scared).

● 11-6. 화가나다 (to be mad)

TYPE	regular adjective	BASIC FORM	화가나

화 means "anger" and 나다 means "to come out". 화가나다 means that your anger "came out". It isn't something you can control.

Example sentences

1. 나는 시험 점수가 나빠서 화가났어요.
   I got mad because my test score was bad.

2. 그와 데이트를 하지 못해서 화가났어요.
   I am mad because I'm unable to date him.

   장난감 = toy

3. 부모님이 아이에게 장난감을 사 주지 않아서 아이가 화가났어요.
   Because the parents didn't buy the toy for the child, the child got mad.

4. 숙제를 안 해서 부모님이 화가났어요.
   Because I didn't do my homework, my parents got mad.

● 11-7. 화를내다 (to express anger)

TYPE	regular adjective	BASIC FORM	화를내

화를내다 is different from 화가나다 because 내다 means "to express" or "to put out". You are actually *releasing* your anger and not just *getting* mad. You can tell someone to NOT get mad with 화를내지 마세요 but it would be weird to say 화가나지 마세요 because it would literally mean "don't come out your anger" which doesn't make sense.

It can be confusing because in English we can say "don't be angry" or "don't get mad" and we don't typically separate the usage.

The person you are mad at is marked with 에게.

Example sentences

1. 그는 나에게 화를 냈어요.
   He is mad at me.

2. 친구에게 이유 없이 화를냈어요.
   I got mad at my friend for no reason.

3. 사장님은 매일 화를내요.
   The teacher is mad every day.

4. 아침에 여동생이 진짜 시끄러워서 화를냈어요.
   I got mad because my younger sister was really loud in the morning.

● 11-8. 싸우다 (to fight)

TYPE	regular verb	BASIC FORM	싸워

The person who you are fighting with is marked with any of the "with" markers. This can be a physical fight or just a fight of words.

Example sentences

1. 그녀와 자주 싸워요.
   I often fight with her.

2. 어제 누나랑 싸웠어요.
   Yesterday I fought with my older sister.

> 누나 is what a boy calls his older sister. A girl calls her older sister 언니.

3. 내 고양이와 개는 매일 싸워요.
   My cat and dog fight everyday.

4. 남자들은 전쟁터에서 싸웠어요.
   The men fought on the battlefield.

5. 너랑 싸우고 싶지 않아!
   I don't want to fight with you!

● 11-9. 화해하다 (to make up, to reconcile)

TYPE	하다 verb	BASIC FORM	화해해

The person who you make up with is marked with any of the "with" markers.

Example sentences

1. 남편과 화해했어요.
   I made up with my husband.

2. 사촌과 화해할 거예요.
   I am going to make up with my cousin.

3. 빨리 화해하고 싶어요. 하지만 아내가 아직 화를내요.
   I want to make up quickly. But my wife is still mad.

4. 친구가 아내랑 싸웠어요. 하지만 곧 화해하고 싶어해요.
   My friend fought with his wife. But he wants to make up soon.

● 11-10. 사과하다 (to apologize)

TYPE	하다 verb	BASIC FORM	사과해

The person you apologize to is marked with the "to-for" marker 에게 or 한태.
The thing you apologize for is marked with the object marker 을/를.

Example sentences

1. 제 잘못을 사과했어요.
   I apologized for my mistake.

> 오빠 is what a girl calls her older brother. A boy calls his older brother 형.

2. 오빠에게 사과할 거예요.
   I will apologize to my brother.

3. 약속을 지키지 못해서 사과했어요.
   I apologized because I couldn't keep my promise.

4. 너무 늦어서 사과했어요.
   I apologized for being too late.

5. 어젯밤에 아버지가 저에게 화를 냈어요. 하지만 오늘 사과했어요.
   Yesterday night my father got really mad at me.
   But today he apologized.

11 Q&A 질문과 대답

1. 준호 씨가 슬퍼해요?
네. 친구가 별로 없어서 외로워해요.
아니요. 여자친구와 화해해서 행복해 해요
어제 만났어요. 하지만 슬퍼하지 않았어요.

Is Junho sad?
Yes. He is sad because he doesn't have many friends.
No. He is happy because he made up with his girlfriend.
I met him yesterday. However, he wasn't sad.

2. 내일 뭘 하고 싶어요?
혼자 생각 없이 걷고 싶어요.
준호 씨와 공포영화를 보고 싶어요.

What do you want to do tomorrow?
I want to walk alone without thinking. (without any thoughts)
I want to watch a horror movie with Junho.

3. 그는 왜 항상 화를내요?
모르겠어요. 항상 이유 없이 화를내요.
제가 매번 약속을 깨서 항상 화를내요.

How come he is always mad?
I don't know. He is always mad for no reason.
He is always made because I break every appointment.

4. 귀신이 무서워요?
아니요. 제 남동생이 귀신을 무서워해요.
네. 저는 귀신이 제일 무서워요.

Are you scared of ghosts?
No. My younger brother is scared of ghosts.
Yes. I am most scared of ghosts.

5. 오빠랑 싸웠어요?
네. 하지만 빨리 화해하고 싶어요.
네. 사과하고 싶어요.

Did you fight with your older brother?
Yes. But I want to make up fast.
Yes. I want to apologize.

11 | Test Yourself Activities 연습 문제

● A11-1. Sentence Jumble

With the words provided, make Korean sentences that match the English.
You can freely add particles, pronouns and conjugate verbs as needed.

1. 우울하다, 친구, 가끔

_____

I am sometimes depressed.

_____

Sometimes my friend is depressed.

_____

Are you sometimes depressed?

2. 갑자기, 화를내다, 화가나다, 싸우다, 이유 없이, 화해하다, 아내, 남편

_____

My husband suddenly got mad.

_____

I fought with my wife. But we made up.

_____

I got mad without reason.

3. 먹다, 화해하다, 사과하다, 싸우다, 빨리, 일찍, 여자친구, 사과, 먹다

_____

I fought with my girlfriend. But since I wanted to make up fast I apologized.

_____

I will eat an apple or apologize to my girlfriend.

_____

I fought with my girlfriend because my girlfriend ate my apple.

● **A11-2. Fill in the blanks**
Fill in the missing word based on the English sentence.

1. 결혼생활이 힘들어서 우리는 자주 _____요.
Because married life is hard we often fight.

2. 여자친구가 없어서 친구가 _____요.
Because he has no girlfiend, my friend is sad.

3. 왜 갑자기 _____요?
Why did you get mad all of a sudden?

4. 남자 친구가 유럽에 3주 동안 있어서 _____요.
I am lonely because my boyfriend is in Europe for 3 weeks.

5. 결혼생활이 _____요?
How is married life?

● **A11-3. Mark and Translate**
Mark the Korean sentence without mistakes then translate it.

1. ○ 저는 화를났어요.
   ○ 저는 화해가 났어요.
   ○ 저는 화가났어요.

Translation:_____

2. ○ 다음 금요일에 남동생이에게 화해했어요.
   ○ 지난 금요일에 남동생이랑 화해했어요.
   ○ 지난 금요일에 남동생이랑 화해하고 싶어요.

Translation:_____

3. ○ 언제부터 누나가 슬퍼했어요?
   ○ 언제부터 누나가 슬퍼요?
   ○ 언제부터 누나를 슬퍼요?

Translation:_____

11 | Self Test Answers 연습 문제 정답

● A11-1. Sentence Jumble
1. 저는 가끔 우울해요.
   친구는 가끔 우울해해요.
   가끔 우울해요?

2. 남편이 갑자기 화를 냈어요.
   아내와 싸웠어요, 하지만 화해했어요.
   나는 이유 없이 화가났어요.

3. 여자친구랑 싸웠어요. 하지만 빨리 화해하고 싶어서 사과했어요.
   사과를 먹거나 여자친구에게 사과 할 거예요.
   여자친구가 내 사과를 먹어서 싸웠어요.

● A11-2. Fill in the blanks
1. 결혼생활이 힘들어서 우리는 자주 <u>싸워</u>요.
2. 여자 친구가 없어서 친구가 <u>우울해</u>해요.
3. 왜 갑자기 <u>화를냈</u>어요?
4. 남자친구가 유럽에 3주 동안 있어서 <u>외로워</u>요.
5. 결혼생활이 <u>어때</u>요?

● A11-3. Best Sentence Search

1. ○ 저는 화를냈어요.
   ○ 저는 화해가 났어요.
   ✓ 저는 화가났어요.
   Translation: <u>I got mad.</u>

2. ○ 다음 금요일에 남동생이에게 화해했어요.
   ✓ 지난 금요일에 남동생이랑 화해했어요.
   ○ 지난 금요일에 남동생이랑 화해하고 싶어요.
   Translation: Last Friday I made up with my younger brother.

3. ✓ 언제부터 누나가 슬퍼했어요?
   ○ 언제부터 누나가 슬퍼요?
   ○ 언제부터 누나를 슬퍼요?
   Translation: Since when is (your) older sister sad?

11 | Vocabulary Builder 단어 구축

Even though the sentences might be above your grammar level try reading them anyway to see interesting ways the new words are used.

■ Group G: Food Words 음식

그릇	bowl
접시	plate
젓가락	chopsticks
숟가락	spoon
칼	knife
포크	fork
컵	cup
반찬	side dish
디저트	dessert
간식	snack

■ Vocabulary Sentences

The following sentences might contain words and concepts not yet taught. Focus on the new vocabulary more than the grammar.

1. 밥은 그릇에 담아 주세요.
   Please put the rice in the bowl.

2. 접시가 깨졌어요.
   The plate broke.

3. 젓가락은 사용하기 너무 어려워요.
   Chopsticks are too difficult to use.

4. 국은 숟가락으로 먹는 거예요.
   Soup is eaten with a spoon.

5. 이 칼은 날카로워서 조심해야 돼요.
   You must be careful since this knife is sharp.

6. 젓가락은 사용하기 어려워서 포크가 필요해요.
   Because chopsticks are hard to use I need a fork.

7. 아이가 컵을 깼어요.
The child broke a cup.

8. 반찬이 너무 많아요.
There are too many side dishes.

9. 어떤 디저트를 좋아하세요?
What kind of dessert do you like?

10. 저녁을 먹기 전에 간식을 먹지 마세요.
Don't eat snacks before you eat dinner.

12 Lesson 12: 하다 vs 되다

12 | New Vocabulary 새로운 단어

New Nouns etc.

결혼식장	wedding hall
노래	song
폭풍	storm
예약	reservations
준비	preparations
경찰	police
범죄	crime
범죄자	criminal
기계	machine
정부	government

New Verbs

잡다	to grab
보이다	to be seen, to appear
안다	to hug
준비하다	to prepare
준비되다	to be prepared
계속하다	to continue
계속되다	to be continued, continue on
예약하다	to reserve
예약되다	to be reserved

New Adjectives

새롭다	to be new
낡다	to be old, worn, beaten

● **12-1. Particle usage trick "Can you (VERB) it?" (을/를 vs 이/가)**

It's often a struggle to know when to mark a word with an object marker 을/를 or with a subject marker 이/가. There are a variety of ways to figure out which particle to use. For example:

ACTIVE / PASSIVE
#1 *Active* verbs **almost always** mark objects being acted on with 을/를.
#2 *Passive* verbs **almost always** mark subject being described with 이/가.

But in the heat of the moment it's often difficult to know if a verb is active or passive… and this topic has yet to have been taught in this series.

ACTION / STATE
#1 Action verbs mark the objects they are acting upon with 을/를.
#2 Adjectives use 이/가 to mark the item being discussed.

It's perhaps easy to think that you ALWAYS use 이/가 with adjectives and this is actually true.

However, there is a another quick (almost fool proof) way to know whether to use 을/를 or 이/가.

In the following sentence replace (VERB) with the English for the verb. The answer to the question tells you which particle to use.

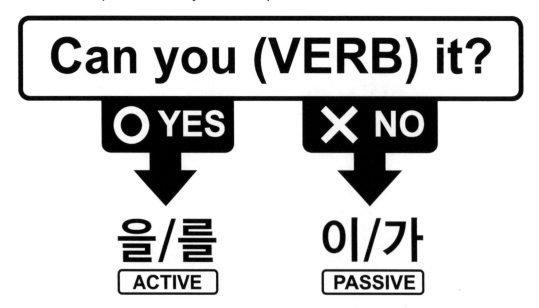

Let's try this trick to find out which verbs use 을/를 and which use 이/가.

1. 받다 (to receive) - Can you (receive) it?
   YES! 을/를 marks the thing being received.

2. 보다 (to see) - Can you (see) it?
   YES! 을/를 marks the thing you see.

> NEVER forget the "IT". Without "IT" "Can you (die)?" is a YES and you get the wrong answer.

3. 죽다 (to die) - Can you (die) it?
   NO! 이/가 marks the thing that dies.

4. 좋다 (to be good) - Can you (be good) it?
   NO! 이/가 marks the thing that is good.

5. 좋아하다 (to like) - Can you (like) it?
   YES! 을/를 marks the thing that is liked.

● 12-2. The exceptions to the rule

The "Can you (verb) it?" rule works pretty well for most verbs. Unfortunately for 있다 (to be, to have), 없다 (to not be, to not have) and 되다 (to become) it fails. All of these would appear to use 을/를 if you ask the "Can you (verb) it?" question, when in fact they use 이/가.

1. 서울에서 맛있는 식당이 있어요.
   There are delicious restaurants in Seoul.

2. 우리 집에 커피가 없어요.
   There isn't any coffee in our house.

3. 남동생이 선생님이 되고 싶어해요.
   My younger brother wants to be a teacher.

● 12-3. When to use 은/는 vs 이/가 vs 을/를

The prior section often leads to a commonly asked question.
When do you use 은/는 instead of 이/가?

은/는 has three primary functions.
1. Introducing new topics.
2. Comparing things (directly / indirectly).
3. Specifying or stressing an item.

은/는 can replace BOTH 을/를 AND 이/가 when any of the three functions above are being used.

Example sentences
1. 피자를 먹었어요. 하지만 스시는 안 먹었어요.
   I ate the pizza. But I didn't eat sushi.
   ("sushi" is being stressed)

2. 단 것을 좋아해요. 하지만 쓴 것은 싫어해요.
   I like sweet things. But I don't like bitter things.
   ("bitter things" are being stressed)

3. 오늘은 더워요.
   Today is hot.
   ("today" is being compared indirectly to other days)

4. 저는 미국 사람입니다.
   I am American.
   ("I" is a new topic)

● 12-4. 잡다 (to grab, catch)

잡다	TYPE	regular verb	BASIC FORM	잡아

Can you guess which particle to use to mark the thing that is grabbed?
Can you (grab) it? → YES! → Use 을/를 to mark the item being grabbed.

Example sentences (잡다) active
1. 여자친구의 손을 잡고 싶어요.
   I want to grab (hold) my girlfriend's hand.

2. 작은 고양이를 잡았어요.
   I caught the small cat.

3. 경찰이 범죄자를 잡았어요.
   The police caught the criminal.

4. 물고기를 많이 잡았어요.
   I caught many fish.

● 12-5. 보이다 (to be seen, to appear, to be visible)

보이다	**TYPE**	regular verb	**BASIC FORM**	보여

Let's again try the trick.

보이다
Can you (be seen) it? → NO! → Use 이/가 to mark the item being seen.

보이다 is not often used alone. It can be used used to say "is viewable" or "came into sight". The following grammar point (12-6) will explain one of the more common ways it's used.

Fxample sentences (보다) active

1. 산이 보였어요.
   The mountain came into sight.

   > The mountain didn't actually DO anything. The state of "being seen" happened passively.

2. 길에서 호수가 보여요.
   The lake is viewable from the road.

3. 산이 내 방에서 안 보여요.
   The mountain isn't visible from my room.

● 12-6. Doing more with 보이다
Using 보이다 we can make one very wide reaching Korean structure and one entirely new verb.

보여 주다 (to show)
First let's add 주다 to make 보여 주다 (to show). Even though 보이다 itself is passive and uses 이/가, 보여 주다 (to show) is active and therefore the thing you are showing is marked with 을/를.

Fxample sentences

1. 결혼식 사진을 보여 주세요.
   Show me your wedding pictures.

2. 친구에게 새로운 차를 보여 주었어요.
   I showed my friend my new car.

3. 김준호 씨에게 제 사진을 보여 주지 마세요.
   Don't show my picture to Junho Kim.

BASIC adjective + 보이다 (to appear or seem~)

In lesson 11, we talked about expressing the emotions of other people. Instead of saying 기뻐요 you should say 기뻐해요 for other people. Another way to talk about other's emotions is to use BASIC adjective + 보이다. As a matter of fact anytime you think something looks one way or another you can use this pattern.

Example sentences

1. 선생님은 행복해 보여요.
   Teacher looks happy.

2. 그 고기는 매워 보여요.
   That meat looks spicy.

3. 반지가 비싸 보여요.
   The ring looks expensive.

4. 영화가재미있어 보여요.
   The movie looks interesting.

5. 음식이 맛있어 보여요.
   The food looks delicious.

● **12-7. 안다 (to hug, embrace, hold)**

안다	TYPE	regular verb	BASIC FORM	안아

The object being hugged is marked with 을/를. Or you could have asked "Can you hug it?" and the answer would be "yes" so you use 을/를.

Example sentences

1. 제가 엄마를 안았어요.
   I hugged my mother.

2. 고양이를 안고 싶어요.
   I want to hold the cat.

3. 할머니가 아기를 안았어요.
   The grandmother embraced the child.

● **12-8. 준비하다 (to prepare), 준비되다 (to be prepared)**

준비하다	TYPE	하다 verb	BASIC FORM	준비해
준비되다	TYPE	regular verb	BASIC FORM	준비돼

All 하다 verbs are "active". An active verb is a verb in which someone has an active role in the verb. In other words, THEY did or will do the action.

Reversely, any verb containing 되다 (to become) is "passive". With passive verbs it isn't necessarily known WHO did the action. 되다 verbs merely show the state of the action.

This is easily understood by looking at 준비하다 and 준비되다.

Example sentences
1. 식사를 준비했어요. I prepared dinner.
2. 식사가 준비됐어요. Dinner is prepared.

In sentence 1, the speaker has completed the action of "preparing".
In sentence 2, we don't necessarily know who prepared dinner, but we do know that the state of dinner is "prepared".

3. 선생님은 시험을 준비했어요. The teacher prepared the test.
4. 학생들은 준비됐어요. The students were prepared.

5. 방을 준비했어요. I prepared the room.
6. 방이 준비됐어요. The room is prepared.

NOTE: When using 준비되다 to say something is "prepared" you have to use the past tense since the preparations are already done.

Special Information 특별 정보

The particle reality
Now that you have undoubtedly been speaking more Korean with actual Korean people, you might have noticed that Koreans ~~like~~ LOVE to drop particles. Instead of 피자를 먹었어요 they will say 피자 먹었어요.

While it's okay to drop particles when speaking or casually texting your friends, if you are writing reports at a company or in a school make sure you keep all the particles in their proper places.

● 12-9. 계속하다 (to continue), 계속되다 (to be continued)

계속하다	TYPE	하다 verb	BASIC FORM	계속해

계속되다	TYPE	regular verb	BASIC FORM	계속돼

If something "gets continued" or "continues going on" then 계속되다 is used.

> **Example sentences**
> 1. 정부가 전쟁을 계속했어요.
>   The government continued the war.
>
> 2. 전쟁이 계속됐어요.
>   The war continued on.
>
> 3. 폭풍이 계속될 거예요.
>   The storm will continue.
>
> 4. 이 수업은 한 달 동안 계속돼요.
>   This class continues for one month.

계속되다 show the STATE of something being continued. If we need to know WHO continued the action then 계속하다 is used.

● 12-10. 예약하다 (to reserve), 예약되다 (to be reserved)

예약하다	TYPE	하다 verb	BASIC FORM	예약해

예약되다	TYPE	regular verb	BASIC FORM	예약돼

Here is another common 하다 / 되다 combination. The thing you reserved is marked with 을/를 and that thing is reserved is marked with 이/가.

> **Example sentences**
> 1. 노래방에서 노래를 많이 예약했어요.
>   I reserved many songs at the karaoke room.
>
> 2. 이미 많은 노래가 예약됐어요.
>   Many songs were already reserved.
>
> 3. 다음 주에 스페인에 갈 거예요. 비싼 호텔을 예약했어요.
>   Next week I am going to Spain. I booked an expensive hotel.
>
> 4. 호텔 방은 다 예약됐어요.
>   All of the hotel rooms are booked.

● **12-11. ~같아 보이다 (to look like a~, to seem like a~)**

In section 12-6 we learned how to say "looks hot" or "looks expensive". If you want to just say something looks "looks like a cat" or any other now you can combine it with 같다 (to be the same).

> **[NOUN] 같다 보여요.**
> **It looks like a [NOUN]**

Example sentences
1. 우리 엄마가 학생 같아 보여요.
   Our mother looks like a student.

2. 그는 머리가 길어서 여자 같아 보여요.
   He looks like a girl because his hair is long.

3. 리드 씨는 미국 사람이에요. 하지만 프랑스사람 같아 보여요.
   Reed is American. But he looks French.

● **12-12. 새롭다 (to be new), 낡다 (to be old, battered, beat up)**

새롭다	TYPE	ㅂ irregular	BASIC FORM	새로워
낡다	TYPE	regular adjective	BASIC FORM	낡아

Since these are adjectives, the thing they describe is marked with 이/가.

Example sentences
1. 우리 학원의 책은 다 새로워요.
   All of our academy books are new.

2. 새로운 차를 사고 싶어요.
   I want to buy a new car.

3. 그 자전거는 정말 낡았어요.
   This bicycle is really old (beat up).

4. 이 도시에 낡은 차가 많아요.
   There are many old cars in this city.

Special Information 특별 정보

Other ways to say "old"

Usage of 낡다 is limited to physical objects. It is similar to saying "beat up". If you are saying "old" for non-physical things such as "ideas" or "songs" OR are saying that something is old due to age then you can use 오래되다 to say "old".

Example sentences

1. 이 노래는 오래됐어요.   This song is old.
2. 우리 엄마는 오래된 것을 좋아해요.   My mother likes old things.

12 | Q&A 질문과 대답

1. **결혼식장을 예약했어요?**
   당연하지요! 결혼식장은 이미 예약됐어요.
   아니요. 시간이 없어서 아직 못했어요.

   Did you reserve the wedding hall?
   Of course! The wedding hall has already been reserved.
   No. I couldn't do it since I haven't had time.

2. **저는 차를 샀어요. 어때요?**
   와! 차가 비싸 보여요!
   제 차가 낡아서 저도 새로운 차를 사고 싶어요.

   I bought a car. How is it?
   Wow! The car looks expensive!
   I also want to buy a new car since my car is old.

3. **여행 준비를 했어요?**
   네. 한달 동안 준비를 했어요.
   당연하죠!
   네. 다 준비했어요.

   Have you prepared for your trip?
   Yes. I prepared for a one month.
   Of course!
   Yes. I did all the preperations.

4. **호텔방을 언제 예약 할 거예요?**
   일 월에 이미 예약 했어요.
   다음 주까지 예약을 할 거예요.

   When are you going to reserve the hotel room?
   I already reserved it in January.
   I will reserve it by next week.

5. **제 남자친구 어때요?**
   너무 어려 보여서 남동생 같아 보여요.
   정말 착해 보여요.

   How is my boyfriend? (what do you think?)
   Because he looks so young, he looks like your younger brother.
   He really looks kind.

12 | Test Yourself Activities 연습 문제

● A12-1. Sentence Jumble
With the words provided, make Korean sentences that match the English. You can freely add particles, pronouns and conjugate verbs as needed.

1. 먹다, 오늘, 오래되다, 낡다, 집, 새롭다, 것, 맵다, 달다, 친구, 오다

   _____

   An old friend came to my house today.

   _____

   My house is beat up.

   _____

   My friend ate something spicy.

2. 범죄자, 보이다, 잡다, 빨리, 계속하다, 식사, 계속되다, 경찰, 똑똑하다

   _____

   The police quickly captured the criminal.

   _____

   The criminal looked smart.

   _____

   The criminal continued his meal.

3. 준비, 예약, 되다, 하다, 식사, 비행기표

   _____

   I reserved airplane tickets.

   _____

   The meal was prepared.

   _____

   I prepared the meal.

● **A12-2. Fill in the blanks**
Fill in the missing word or particle based on the English sentence.

1. 노래방_____ 준비됐어요.
   The karaoke room is prepared.

2. 영화가계속_____.
   The movie continued.

3. 작은 고양이_____ 잡았어요.
   I grabbed the small cat.

4. 친구가 노래_____ 많이 예약해서 저는 노래를 못했어요.
   My friends reserved many songs, so I couldn't sing.

5. 친구의 어머니가 _____요.
   My friend's mother looks sad.

● **A12-3. Mark and Translate**
Mark the Korean sentence without mistakes then translate it.

1. ○ 제일 비싼 차를 예약했어요.
   ○ 제일 빘안 차를 예약했어요.
   ○ 제일 비싼 차를 예약됐어요.

   Translation:_____

2. ○ 저는 빨리 식사가 준비되고 싶어요.
   ○ 저는 빨리 식사를 준비하고 싶어요.
   ○ 저는 빨리 식사를 준비 싶어요.

   Translation:_____

3. ○ 이 컴퓨터를 새로워 보여요.
   ○ 이 컴퓨터는 새롭 보여요.
   ○ 이 컴퓨터는 새로워 보여요.

   Translation:_____

12 | Self Test Answers 연습 문제 정답

● A12-1. Sentence Jumble

1. 오래된 친구가 우리 집에 왔어요.
   제 집은 낡았어요.
   제 친구가 매운 것을 먹었어요.

2. 경찰은 범죄자를 빨리 잡았어요.
   범죄자가 똑똑해 보여요.
   범죄자가 식사를 계속했어요.

3. 비행기표를 예약했어요.
   식사가 준비됐어요.
   저는 식사를 준비했어요.

● A12-2. Fill in the blanks

1. 노래방<u>이</u> 준비됐어요.
2. 영화가<u>계속됐어</u>요.
3. 작은 고양이<u>를</u> 잡았어요.
4. 친구가 노래<u>를</u> 많이 예약해서 저는 노래를 못했어요.
5. 친구의 어머니가 슬퍼 보여요.

● A12-3. Best Sentence Search

1. ✓ 제일 비싼 차를 예약했어요.
   ○ 제일 빗안 차를 예약했어요.
   ○ 제일 비싼 차를 예약됐어요.
   Translation: I reserved the most expensive car.

2. ○ 저는 빨리 식사가 준비되고 싶어요.
   ✓ 저는 빨리 식사를 준비하고 싶어요.
   ○ 저는 빨리 식사를 준비 싶어요.
   Translation: I want to prepare dinner fast.

3. ○ 이 컴퓨터를 새로워 보여요.
   ○ 이 컴퓨터는 새롭 보여요.
   ✓ 이 컴퓨터는 새로워 보여요.
   Translation: This computer looks new.

12 | Vocabulary Builder 단어 구축

Learning vocabulary is like taking medicine that doesn't taste good. It helps you but sometimes it isn't pleasant. Drink these following words.

■ Group H: Medicines 약

아스피린	aspirin
기침약	cough medicine
연고	cream, ointment
피임약	birth control
처방전	prescription
항생제	antibiotic
백신	vaccine
안약	eye drops
알약	pill
주사	injection, shot

■ Vocabulary Sentences

The following sentences might contain words and concepts not yet taught. Focus on the new vocabulary more than the grammar.

1. 머리가 아파서 아스피린을 먹었어요.
   I took an aspirin because my head hurts.

2. 기침이 많이 나서 기침약을 먹었어요.
   I was coughing a lot, so I took cough medicine.

3. 상처에는 연고를 발라 주세요.
   Please apply the ointment to the wound.

4. 이 피임약에는 부작용이 있어요?
   Are there any side effects with this birth control?

5. 제 처방전을 잃어버렸어요.
   I lost my prescription.

6. 새로운 항생제가 나왔어요.
   A new antibiotic came out.

7. 두 살 때 아이들은 어떤 백신이 필요해요?
    When children are 2 years old which vaccines are needed?

8. 안구건조증에는 안약이 좋아요.
    Eye drops are good for dry eye syndrome.

9. 우리 아이는 알약을 삼키기 힘들어 해요.
    My child is having difficulty swallowing the pill.

10. 주사는 무섭지만 필요해요.
    An injection is scary but is necessary.

SR! Super Review and Quiz #2: Lessons 9-12

SR | Question and Answer 질문과 대답

Hide the English and try to translate the Korean. Take notes on words or grammar patterns that confuse you then review them if necessary.

1. 내일 학원에 오겠습니까?
네, 9 시까지 오겠어요.
아니요, 내일은 약속이 있어요. 학원에 못 와요.
죄송해요. 내일은 올 수 없어요. 다음 주에 꼭 오겠습니다.

Are you coming to the academy tomorrow?
Yes, I will be there by 9 o'clock.
No, I have an appointment tomorrow. I can't come to the academy.
I'm sorry. Tomorrow I can't come. Next week I will definitely come.

2. 언제까지 돈을 내겠습니까?
내일까지 내겠습니다.
이번 주나 다음 주까지 꼭 내겠습니다.
이번 달은 돈이 없어요. 다음 달에 낼 수 있어요.

By when can you pay the money?
I can pay by tomorrow.
I will for sure pay by this week or next week.
I don't have money this month. I can pay next month.

3. 이번 휴가에 어디로 여행을 가고 싶어요?
중국으로 가고 싶어요.
하와이로 갈 거예요.
일본으로 가고 싶었어요. 하지만 비행기표가 비쌌어요. 그래서 못 가요.

On this break, where do you want to go for a trip?
I want to go to China.
I will go to Hawaii.
I wanted to go to Japan. But plane tickets were expensive. So, I can't go.

4. 보통 아침에 무엇을 먹어요?
김밥이나 샌드위치를 먹어요.
아침에는 먹지 않아요.
우유나 커피를 마셔요.

What do you normally eat in the morning?
I eat gimbap or a sandwich.
I don't eat in the morning.
I drink milk or coffee.

5. **우리 내일 만날까요?**
네, 제가 내일 1 시에 학교로 가겠습니다.
아니요. 내일은 바빠요. 이번 주말이나 다음 주에 전화하겠어요.

Shall we meet tomorrow?
Yes, I will go to school tomorrow at 1 o'clock.
No. Tomorrow I am busy. I will call you this weekend or next week.

6. **어디로 갈까?**
쇼핑을 하고 싶어. 명동으로 가자.
영화관이나 백화점으로 가자.
배가 고파. 스파게티나 스테이크를 먹자.

Where shall we go?
I want to shop. Let's go to Myeongdong.
Let's go to a movie theatre or a department store.
I am hungry. Let's eat spaghetti or steak.

SR | Conversation 대화 K-E

1. **Polite conversation between friends.**
준호: 미나 씨, 내일 시간이 있어요? 같이 영화 볼까요?
미나: 미안해요. 내일은 회사에 일이 많아요.
준호: 그럼, 주말에 만날 수 있어요?
미나: 네, 이번 주말에는 약속이 없어요.

A: Mina, Do you have a time tomorrow? Do you want to watch a movie?

B: I am sorry. I have a lot of work at my company.

A: Then, can we meet on the weekend?

B: Yes, I don't have any plans this weekend.

2. **Polite conversation between friends.**
조지: 선희 씨, 지금 어디예요?
선희: 미안해요. 집에서 늦게 출발했어요.
조지: 괜찮아요. 저는 지금 학교 앞에 있어요.
미나: 네, 지금 그쪽으로 가고 있어요.

A: Sunhee, Where are you now?

B: Sorry. I departed from home late.

A: It's okay. I am in front of the school.

B: Okay, I am going toward there now.

3. **Polite conversation between friends.**

준호: 미나 씨, 지금 미나 씨 회사 앞에 있어요.

미나: 그럼 3층으로 오세요. 기다리고 있겠습니다.

준호: 네, 지금 가겠습니다.

A: Mina, I am in front of your company now.

B: Then come to the 3rd floor. I am waiting for you.

A: Okay, I'll go now.

4. **Polite conversation between friends.**

조지: 어제 카페에서 선희 씨를 2시간 기다렸어요.

선희: 정말 미안해요. 어제 갑자기 미국에서 친구가 왔어요.

조지: 그럼 왜 전화를하지 않았어요?

선희: 문자를 보냈어요. 문자를 못 봤어요?

조지: 그래요? 못 봤어요.

선희: 어제 약속을 못 지켰어요. 그래서 오늘 제가 저녁을 사겠습니다.

조지: 좋아요. 그럼 6시에 선희 씨 회사 앞으로 가겠어요.

A: Yesterday, I waited for you (Sunhee) for 2 hours at the cafe.

B: I am really sorry. Yesterday, my friend suddenly came from Amarica.

A: Then why didn't you call me?

B: I sent you a text message. Didn't you see it?

A: Really? I didn't see it.

B: I broke a promise. Therefore I will buy dinner today.

A: Good. Then I will be (go) in front of your company at 6 o'clock.

SR | Quiz Yourself 퀴즈

● 1. Sentence completion
Using the ~겠다 form, fill in the blank parts. Use the schedule below.
다음 주에(10 월 5 일) 친구가 한국에 올 거예요. 뭐를 하겠습니까?

10 월 5 일(월)	한국 식당
10 월 6 일(화)	명동하고 인사동 구경
10 월 7 일(수)~8 일(목)	부산 여행
10 월 9 일(금)	박물관 (museum)
10 월 10 일(토)	백화점 (department store)

> **Sample**
> 월요일에 한국 식당에서 밥을 먹겠습니다.

1) 화요일에 _____.

2) 수요일부터 목요일까지 _____.

3) 금요일에 _____.

4) 토요일에 _____.

● 2. Translate and answer
대답하세요. Translate, then answer the question asked using the ~겠다 form. Answer as if you were directly asked. Answers can vary.

> **Sample**
> 돈이 1000 만 원 (10,000 달러)이 있어요. 뭐를 사겠습니까?
> **Translation:** You have 10,000,000 won ($10,000). What will you buy?
> **Answer:** 유럽 여행을 가겠습니다.

1. 여자(남자) 친구 생일이에요. 뭐를 선물하겠습니까?

Translation: _____.

Answer: _____.

2. 주말에 약속이 없어요. 뭐를 하겠습니까?

Translation: _____.

Answer: _____.

3. 유럽에 가요. 어느 나라에 가겠습니까?

Translation: _____.

Answer: _____.

4. 주말에 여자(남자) 친구를 만나요. 뭐를 하겠습니까?

Translation: _____.

Answer: _____.

5. 친구들이 집에 옵니다. 뭐를 하겠습니까?

Translation: _____.

Answer: _____.

6. 한국말 공부가 너무 어려워요. 한국말 공부를 계속 하겠습니까?

Translation: _____.

Answer: 네, _____.

● 3. More translate and answer
대답하세요. Translate then answer the question. Answers must contain:
A) (으)ㅂ시다 of ~자 (let's form) **B)** (으)로 particle **C)** provided location.

> **Sample**
> A: 배가 고파요. 어느 식당으로 갈까요?
> B: 피자헛으로 갑시다. (피자헛)

1. 눈이 와요. 어디로 갈까요?

   Translation: _____.

   Answer: (스키장)_____.

2. 다음 주부터 휴가예요. 어디로 갈까요?

   Translation: _____.

   Answer: (하와이)_____.

3. 오늘 날씨가 너무 좋아요. 어디로 갈까요?

   Translation: _____.

   Answer: (산)_____.

4. 커피를 마시고 싶어요. 어디로 갈까요?

   Translation: _____.

   Answer: (스타벅스)_____.

5. 예쁜 여자를 만나고 싶어요? 어디로 갈까요?

   Translation: _____.

   Answer: (서울)_____.

● **4. Picture perfect (nouns)**
Answer with (이)나 using the pictures.

Sample: 뭘 탈 거예요?

기차

비행기

Answer: <u>기차나 비행기를 탈 거예요.</u>

1. 점심에 뭘 먹을 거예요?

김밥

햄버거

Answer: _____

2. 이번 여름에 어디로 가고 싶어요?

바다

산

Answer: _____

3. 친구 생일에 뭘 선물하겠습니까?

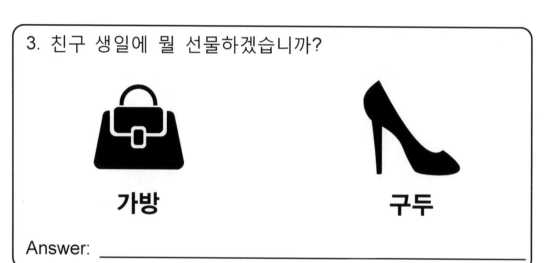

가방   구두

Answer: _____

4. 오늘밤 저녁에 뭘 만들 거예요?

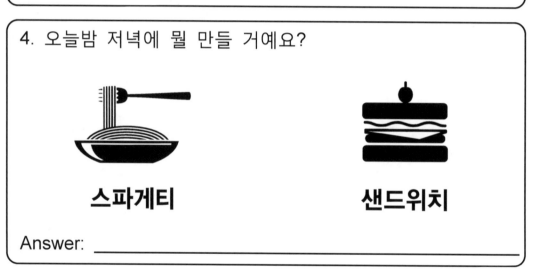

스파게티   샌드위치

Answer: _____

● **5. Picture perfect (verbs)**
Answer with ~거나 using the pictures.

Sample: 보통 책을 어디에서 사요?

도서관   서점

Answer: 책을 도서관에서 빌리거나 서점에서 사요.

1. 돈이 많이 있어요. 뭘 하고 싶어요?

놀이공원에 가다

여행을 하다

Answer: _____

2. 날씨가 너무 더워요. 뭘 하겠습니까?

수영을 하다

집에서 쉬다

Answer: _____

3. 머리가 너무 아파요. 어떻게 하겠습니까?

약을 먹다

병원에 가다

Answer: _____

4. 배가 고파요. 뭘 할 거예요?

식당에 가다

요리를 하다

Answer: _____

SR | Answer Key 해답

● **1. Sentence completion**
~겠습니다 and ~겠어요 are both acceptable.

1) 화요일에 명동하고 인사동을 구경하겠습니다.
    On Tuesday we will sightsee in Myeong-dong and Insa-dong.

2) 수요일부터 목요일까지 부산에서 여행을 하겠습니다.
    From Wednesday to Thursday we will travel in Busan.

3) 금요일에 박물관에 가겠습니다.
    On Friday we will go to a museum.

4) 토요일에 백화점에서 쇼핑을 하겠습니다.
    On Saturday we will shop at a department store.

● **2. Translate and answer (answers will vary)**
~겠습니다 and ~겠어요 are both acceptable.

1) It's your girl(boy)friend's birthday. What will you gift to them?
    가방/구두/옷을 선물하겠습니다.

2) You have no plans on the weekend. What will you do?
    집에서 쉬겠습니다. / 집에서 영화를보겠습니다.

3) You are going to Europe. What countries will you go to?
    영국/프랑스/독일에 가겠습니다.

4) You will meet your girl(boy)friend on the weekend. What will you do?
    저녁을 먹겠습니다. / 공원에서 자전거를 타겠습니다.
    노래방에 가겠습니다. / 쇼핑을 하겠습니다.

5) Friends are coming to your house. What will you do?
    스파게티를 만들겠습니다. / 친구들하고 게임을 하겠습니다.

6) Korean study is too hard. Will you continue studying Korean?
    네, 한국말을 계속 공부하겠습니다.

● **3. More translate and answer**
~자 is okay instead of (으)ㅂ시다.

1. It's snowing. Where shall we go?
스키장으로 갑시다. / 스키장으로 가자.

2. From next week you have days off (vacation). Where shall we go?
하와이로 갑시다.

3. Today the weather is really cold. Where shall we go?
산으로 갑시다.

4. I want to drink coffee. Where shall we go?
스타벅스로 갑시다.

5. Do you want to meet beautiful girls? Where shall we go?
서울로 갑시다.

● **4. Picture perfect (nouns)**
1. What will you eat for lunch?
김밥이나 햄버거를 먹을 거예요. (I will eat gimbap or a hamburger.)

2. This summer where do you want to go?
바다나 산으로 가고 싶어요. (I will go to the ocean or the mountains.)

3. It's your friend's birthday. What will you gift to them?
가방이나 구두를 선물하겠습니다. (I will give a bag or shoes.)

4. What will you make for dinner tonight?
스파게티나 샌드위치를 만들 거예요. (I will make spaghetti or a sandwich.)

● **5. Picture perfect (verbs)**
1. You have a lot of money. What do you want to do?
놀이공원에 가거나 여행을 하고 싶어요.

2. The weather is very hot. What are you going to do?
수영을 하거나 집에서 쉬겠습니다.

3. Your head hurts a lot. What will you do?
약을 먹거나 병원에 가겠습니다.

4. You are hungry. What will you do?
식당에 가거나 요리를 할 거예요.

13 Lesson 13:
But and However

13 | New Vocabulary 새로운 단어

New Nouns etc.

떡볶이	spicy rice cake (stir fried)
바위	rock, stone
날	day
옛날	long time ago; the old days
관심	interest
언어	language
정치	politics
팬	fan (of singer, tv show etc)
차 키	car keys
대한민국	Republic of Korea

Note: 한국 and 대한민국 are both used to say "Korea". 한국 is the general name for Korea, but Korea's official name is 대한민국.

북한	North Korea
~번 출구	No. ~ exit (train stations etc)
종업원	employee, worker

New Verbs

가르치다	to teach
늦다	to be late
잊어버리다	to forget

New Adjectives

가볍다	to be light
무겁다	to be heavy
친절하다	to be kind, friendly
불친절하다	to be not kind, unfriendly

13 | Grammar and Usage 문법과 사용법

● **13-1. 관심 (interest)**

By combining 관심 with 있다 (to have) and 없다 (to not have) you can relay interest. The thing you are interested in or not is marked with 에.

Example sentences

1. 저는 언어에 관심이 있어요.
   I have an interest in languages.

2. 저는 스포츠에 관심이 없어요.
   I have no interest in sports.

3. 제 아버지는 옛날부터 정치에 많은 관심이 있어요.
   My father has a lot of interest in politics from way back.

● **13-2. ~마다 (every~)**

By adding 마다 to the end of a time such as hours, minutes, days, and months, you can show the interval of a certain action.

Example sentences

1. 날마다 커피를 마셔요.
   I drink coffee every day.

2. 아침마다 공원에서 자전거를 타요.
   Every morning I ride my bicycle in the park.

3. 주말마다 집에서 야구를 봐요.
   Every weekend I watch baseball at my house.

4. 10 분마다 버스가 와요.
   The bus comes every 10 minutes.

5. 날마다 부모님한테 전화해요.
   I call my parents everyday.

   > 해마다 is another way to say 매년 (every year)

6. 해마다 일본 여행을 해요.
   I take a trip to Japan every year.

> **Example conversation**
> A: 요즘 왜 바빠요?
> B: 요즘 저녁마다 한국어를 배우고 있어서 시간이 없어요.
>
> A: Why are you busy these days?
> B: I don't have time, because these days I have been studying
>   Korean every evening.

● 13-3. ~지만 sentence connecting with "but" (verbs / adjectives)

In book 1 we learned the pattern:
SENTENCE 1. 하지만 (but, however) SENTENCE 2.

Using ~지만 directly with verbs and adjectives you can combine these into one sentence. First let's look at to make the first part of the sentence.

> **Examples (present tense) STEM + 지만**
> 1. 가지만…   I go but…
> 2. 춥지만…   It's cold but…
> 3. 피곤하지만…   I am tired but…
> 4. 비싸지만…   It's expensive but…
> 5. 더럽지만…   It's dirty but…
> 6. 아프지만…   It hurts but…
> 7. 공부하지만…   I study but…
>
> **Examples (past tense) PAST TENSE STEM + 지만**
> 1. 갔지만…   I went but…
> 2. 추웠지만…   It was cold but…
> 3. 피곤했지만…   I was tired but…
> 4. 비쌌지만…   It was expensive but…
> 5. 더러웠지만…   It was dirty but…
> 6. 아팠지만…   It hurt but…
> 7. 공부했지만…   I studied but…
>
> **Examples (other verb forms) STEM or PAST TENSE STEM + 지만**
> 1. 가고 싶지만…   I want to go but…
> 2. 춥지 않지만…   It's not cold but…
> 3. 피곤하겠지만…   I will be tired but…
> 4. 비싸지 않았지만…   It wasn't expensive but…
> 5. 더러워지지만…   It will get dirty but…
> 6. 아플 거지만…   It will hurt but…
> 7. 공부하고 싶지 않지만 I don't want to study but…

The second part of the sentence is the same as what would follow 하지만.

Example sentences

1. 좋은 대학교에 가고 싶지만 돈이 없어요.
   I want to go to a good college but I don't have any money.

2. 밥을 먹었지만 아직 배고파요.
   I ate rice, but I'm still hungry.

   > Notice the use of the past tense stem in 먹었지만.

3. 맛있는 음식이 많지만 먹지 않을 거예요.
   There is lots of delicious food but I'm not going to eat it.

4. 너를 사랑하지만 남자친구가 있어.
   I love you but I have a boyfriend.

   > Notice this is all casual, including 너 (you). Even the 를 particle was dropped.

5. 돈은 없지만 시간은 있어요.
   I don't have money, but I have time.

6. 작년에는 프랑스어를 공부하고 싶었지만 지금은 관심이 없어요.
   She is a nice person but doesn't have any friends.

7. 여자에는 관심이 없지만 차는 좋아해요.
   I'm not interested in girls but I like cars..

8. 음악에 관심이 있지만 노래방에 가고 싶지 않아요.
   I'm interested in music but I don't want to go to the karaoke room.

● 13-4. ~지만 sentence connecting with "but" (nouns)

For nouns you can use 이다 and 아니다 connected with ~지만.
The second part of the sentence is the same as what would follow 하지만.

Example sentences

1. 이것은 사탕이지만 별로 달지 않아요.
   It's candy, but it isn't that sweet.

   > Spell properly or the meaning changes:
   > 펜 = pen; 팬 = fan

2. 저는 싸이의 팬이 아니지만 가끔 싸이의 노래를 들어요.
   I am not a fan of Psy, but I sometimes listen to Psy's songs.

3. 그녀는 착한 사람이지만 친구가 없어요.
   She is a nice person but doesn't have any friends.

4. 오늘은 주말이 아니지만 일이 없어요.
   Today isn't the weekend, but I don't have work.

● 13-5. Directions

쪽 means "direction", "side", "way" etc. when combined with other words. Its English translation changes to match what sounds more natural in English. For example in English you can say "left <u>side</u> of the TV" or "turn to the left <u>direction</u>" but the Korean would still always be 왼쪽.

Direction words	Flexible English translations
이쪽	this way, side, direction; here
그쪽	that way, side, direction; there
저쪽	that way, side, direction; over there
오른쪽	to the right; right side; right direction
왼쪽	to the left; left side; left direction
동쪽	east; east side; east direction
서쪽	west; west side; west direction
남쪽	south; south side; south direction
북쪽	north; north side; north direction
어느 쪽	which side?, which direction?

In addition to the words above you can add 쪽 after any of the location words that you already learned in book 1.

Direction words	Flexible English translations
위쪽	on top, upper side, up direction
아래쪽	below, underneath, down direction, lower side
앞쪽	in front, front side, forward direction
뒤쪽	behind, back side, backward direction
옆쪽	the side, next

Example sentences
1. 차 키는 식탁 아래쪽에 있어요.
The car keys are under the dinner table.

2. 저는 북쪽에 살아요.
I live on the north side.

3. 북한은 한국 위쪽에 있어요.
North Korea is above South Korea.

4. 저쪽에 예쁜 꽃이 있어요.
There are beautiful flowers over there.

5. 집 앞쪽에 편의점이 두 개 있어요.
There are 2 convenience stores in front of my house.

6. 식당은 어느 쪽에 있어요?
Which direction is the restaurant.

The prior examples all use 에 to mark the direction. In the following examples we will use (으)로 to mark direction to mean "towards", and also we will use 에서 to mark "event location".

Example sentences
1. 오른쪽으로 가세요.
Go towards the right.

2. 서쪽으로 갔지만 바다가 없었어요.
I went toward the west but there weren't any beaches.

3. 뒤쪽에서 쉬세요.
Rest in the back.

4. 회사 앞쪽으로 맛있는 식당이 있어요.
There is a delicious restaurant in front of the company.

5. 서울쪽으로 운전하고 있어요.
I am driving towards Seoul.

6. 10 (십)번 출구 왼쪽에서 먹고 싶어요.
I want to eat on the left side of exit 10.

> ~번 출구 is the way train stations exits are numbered. It's used with Chinese numbers.

● 13-6. 가르치다 (to teach)

TYPE	regular verb	BASIC FORM	가르쳐

The person or thing you are teaching is marked with 을/를. If a sentence has two objects, the thing being taught to a person is marked with 에게/한테.

Example sentences

1. 선생님이 학생을 가르쳤어요.
   The teacher taught the student.

2. 전화번호를 가르쳐 주세요.
   Please give me your phone number.

   > Koreans say "teach me your number" instead of "give me your number".

3. 우리 선생님은 매일 한국어를 가르치고 있어요.
   Our teacher is teaching Korean everyday.

4. 이번 월요일에 호주 친구에게 한국어를 가르칠 거예요.
   This Monday I will teach my Australian friend Korean.

5. 영어를 가르쳐 줘요.
   Please teach me English.

● 13-7. 늦다 (to be late)

TYPE	regular verb	BASIC FORM	늦어

Example sentences

1. 시간이 늦었어요.
   The time has gotten late.

2. 오늘은 늦었지만 내일은 더 일찍 올 거예요.
   I was late today, but I will come earlier tomorrow.

3. 올해는 봄이 늦을 거예요.
   Spring will be late this year.

4. 시간이 늦어서 사람들이 별로 없어요.
   It's late so there aren't many people.

5. 제프가 늦었어요.
   Jeff was late.

● 13-8. 잊어버리다 (to forget)

TYPE	regular verb	BASIC FORM	잊어버려

The thing that is "forgot" is marked with the 을/를 object marker. NOTE: 잊어버리다 is not used to say "I forgot something at home". It's used for the mental process of forgetting. It is used to forget non-physical things.

Example sentences

1. 약속을 잊어버리지 마세요.
   Don't forget our appointment.

2. 그의 이름을 벌써 잊어버렸어요.
   I already forgot his name.

3. 저를 잊어버리세요.
   Forget me.

4. 박가영 씨랑 약속을 잊어버렸어요.
   I forgot about the appointment with Gayoung Park.

5. 친구의 생일을 잊어버려서 친구가 화가났어요.
   Since I forgot my friend's birthday, my friend got mad.

Special Information 특별 정보

Origins of 잊어버리다

잊다 means "to forget", but using the verb alone is not as common as using it in combination with 버리다 which means "to throw away". The addition of 버리다 doesn't change the meaning but changes the nuance. It can show that the action was *unintentional*, show *slight regret,* or show that the action was *completely* done. In Korea, out of habit most Koreans will use 잊어버리다 over just 잊다.

You will see BASIC verb form + 버리다 with other verbs also.

잃다 (to lose) → 잃어버리다 (to lose)
먹다 (to eat) → 먹어 버리다 (to eat)

Example sentences

1. 생각 없이 사탕을 다 먹어 버렸어요.
   Without thinking I ate all of the candy.

2. 지갑을 잃어버렸어요.
   I lost my wallet.

NOTE: 잃어버리다 and 잊어버리다 never have spaces as they are so commonly used, however other verb combinations will have a space before 버리다.

———— Special Information 특별 정보 ————

Koreans don't FORGET things!
In English we commonly say, "I forgot my wallet" or "I forgot my phone" but Koreans don't use 잊어버리다 to directly forget physical things.

잊어버리다 is used when you forgot to DO an action, or when you forgot a non-physical thing such as an appointment, a birthday, or name.

Example sentences
1. 친구랑 약속을 잊어버렸어요.
   I forgot the appointment with my friend.

2. 선생님 이름을 잊어버렸어요.
   I forgot the teacher's name.

NOTE: You can forget to "bring your wallet" but you can't just forget your "wallet".

~~지갑을 잊어버렸어요.~~
~~I forgot my wallet.~~

Instead you could say:

3. 지갑을 가져오는 것을 잊어버렸어요.
   I forgot to bring my wallet.

NOTE: We will learn how to make verb phrases like this in book 3 of this series.

Sometimes you learn how to say something that sounds perfectly proper, and the grammar itself is also 100% correct. However, often culture or history makes certain phrases unnatural. For example, even though it's grammatically correct to say **XXX 을 잊어버렸어요** (I forgot XXX), it's more natural that Koreans would say **XXX 을 놓고왔어요** (I left XXX).

1. 집에서 지갑을 놓고왔어요.
   I left my wallet at home.

● 13-9. 가볍다 (to be light)

TYPE	ㅂ irregular adjective	BASIC FORM	가벼워

Example sentences
1. 제 가방은 안 가벼워요.
   My bag is not light.

2. 이 아이가 진짜 가벼워요.
   This child is very light.

3. 이것은 정말 가벼워요.
   This is very light.

4. 더 가벼운 책이 없어요?
   You don't have a lighter book?

5. 빵이나 가벼운 음식을 먹고 싶어요.
   I want to eat bread or some light food.

> Just like in English, Koreans use the expression "light food" to mean something "small" and not "heavy".

● 13-10. 무겁다 (to be heavy)

TYPE	ㅂ irregular adjective	BASIC FORM	무거워

Example sentences
1. 아, 무거워!
   Ah, it's heavy!

2. 그 물고기가 무거워요.
   That fish is heavy.

3. 피자를 너무 많이 먹어서 몸이 무거워졌어요.
   My body got heavy because I ate too much pizza.

4. 눈이 무거워졌어요.
   My eyes became heavy.

> Just like English, this means "got tired".

5. 저 바위는 진짜 무거워요.
   That rock over there is really heavy.

● **13-11. 친절하다 (to be kind), 불친절하다 (to be unkind)**

TYPE	하다 adjective	BASIC FORM	(불)친절해

Example sentences

1. 민서 씨는 정말 친절한 사람이에요.
   Minseo is a very kind person.

2. 캐나다 사람들은 친절해요.
   Canadians are kind.

3. 친절한 선생님을 좋아해요.
   I like friendly teachers.

4. 그 사람이 불친절해요.
   That person is unfriendly.

5. 아빠가 저에게 불친절해요.
   Dad is unkind to me.

● **13-12. 보고 싶다 (to miss)**

보다 means "to see" and when it's changed to 보고 싶다 it means "I want to see". However, when this is used in relation to a friend or another person 보고 싶다 is better translated to "I miss you" instead. All the other rules for the verb 보다 are followed.

IMPORTANT NOTE: When verbs are in ~고 싶다 form you can use either 을/를 or 이/가 to mark the object or subject of the verb. This is a special rule for ~고 싶다 form.

Example sentences

1. 너를 보고 싶어!
   I miss you!

2. 저를 보고 싶지 않아요?
   Don't you miss me?

3. 남자친구가 보고 싶지만 시간이 없어요.
   I miss my boyfriend but I don't have time.

13 | Q&A 질문과 대답

1. 주말마다 뭐해요?
보통 집에서 티비를 봐요.
요즘 날씨가 따뜻해서 공원에서 농구를 해요.
주말마다 항상 피곤하지만 산에 가요.

What do you do every weekend?
I normally watch TV at my house.
These days since the weather is warm, I play basketball in the park.
Every weekend I am tired but I go to the mountain.

2. 무슨 스포츠에 관심이 있어요?
저는 스포츠에 관심이 없어요.
스포츠를 다 좋아해요.

What sports do you have interest in?
I don't have interest in sports.
I like all sports.

3. 사장님이 왜 화가났어요?
어제 미팅에 늦어서 화가났어요.
제가 우리 회사에서 제일 중요한 손님 이름을 잊어버렸어요.

What was the boss mad?
Because I was late to the meeting yesterday he was mad.
I forgot the name of our company's most important customer.

4. 차키는 어디에 있어요?
냉장고 오른쪽에 있어요.
어제 밤에 소파 위쪽에서 봤어요.

Where are the car keys?
There are on the right side of the refridgerator.
Last night I saw them on the top of the sofa.

5. 오늘 회사 앞 새로운 식당에 같이 가고 싶어요?
어제 갔었어요. 떡볶이가 맛있었어요.
아니요. 그 식당에는 맛없는 음식이 많아요.
종업원이 너무 불친절해서 가고 싶지 않아요.

Do you want to go together to the new restaurant in front of the company?
I went yesterday. The spicy rice cakes were delicious.
No. There are a lot of bad tasting food at that restaurant.
I don't want to go because the workers are too unfriendly.

13 | Test Yourself Activities 연습 문제

● **A13-1. Sentence Jumble**
With the words provided, make Korean sentences that match the English. You can freely add particles, pronouns and conjugate verbs as needed.

1. 왼쪽, 오른쪽, 식탁, 재미있다, 관심, 언어, 있다, 잃어버리다, 차 키

_____

Are you interested in languages?

_____

I lost my car keys.

_____

My car keys are on the left side of the table.

2. 내리다, 타다, 오분, 오번 출구, 늦다, 지하철, 친절하다,
   사촌, 다섯 시, 기다리다, 동안

_____

I got off of the subway at 5 o'clock.

_____

My cousin waited 5 minutes at exit 5.

_____

My cousin is kind.

3. 바위, 무겁다, 가볍다, 무섭다, 귀신, 정말, 이, 그, 저

_____

This rock is really heavy.

_____

I am not scared of ghosts.

_____

This rock is heavy, but that rock over there is light.

● A13-2. Fill in the blanks

Fill in the missing word or particle based on the English sentence.

1. 저는 정치_____ 관심이 없어요.
   I am not interested in politics.

2. 사촌은 언어를 _____요.
   My cousin teaches languages.

3. 대한민국 사람들은 진짜_____요.
   The people of South Korea are really kind.

4. 필요한 책을 _____ 새로운 책을 샀어요.
   I lost the book that I need, so I bought a new book.

5. 우리 학교에 _____ 사람이 많아요.
   There are many unkind people in my school.

● A13-3. Mark and Translate

Mark the Korean sentence without mistakes then translate it.

1. ○ 저는 프랑스어에 괌신이 없어요.
   ○ 저는 프랑스어에 관십이 있어요.
   ○ 저는 프랑스어에 관심이 없어요.

   Translation:_____

2. ○ 떡볶이가 많았지만 혼자서 먹을 수 있었어요.
   ○ 떡볶이가 많았지만 혼자서 머글 수 있었어요.
   ○ 떡볶이가 많읐지만 혼자서 먹을 수 있었어요.

   Translation:_____

3. ○ 저 바의들은 거위 다 무거워요.
   ○ 저 바위들은 거의 다 무겁아요.
   ○ 저 바위들은 거의 다 무거워요.

   Translation:_____

13 | Self Test Answers 연습 문제 정답

● **A13-1. Sentence Jumble**
  1. 언어에 관심이 있어요?
     차 키를 잃어버렸어요.
     제 차 키는 식탁 왼쪽에 있어요.

  2. 저는 다섯시에 지하철을 내렸어요.
     제 사촌은 오분 동안 오번 출구에서 기다렸어요.
     제 사촌은 친절해요.

  3. 이 바위는 정말 무거워요.
     저는 귀신이 무섭지 않아요.
     이 바위는 무겁지만 저 바위는 가벼워요.

● **A13-2. Fill in the blanks**
  1. 저는 정치<u>에</u> 관심이 없어요.
  2. 사촌은 언어를 (<u>가르치고 있어</u> or <u>가르쳐</u>)요.
  3. 대한민국 사람들은 진짜 <u>친절해</u>요.
  4. 필요한 책을 <u>잃어버려서</u> 새로운 책을 샀어요.
  5. 우리 학교에 <u>불친절한</u> 사람이 많아요.

● **A13-3. Best Sentence Search**
  1. ○ 저는 프랑스어에 괌신이 없어요.
     ○ 저는 프랑스어에 관십이 있어요.
     ✓ 저는 프랑스어에 관심이 없어요.
     Translation: I don't have interest in French.

  2. ✓ 떡볶이가 많았지만 혼자서 먹을 수 있었어요.
     ○ 떡볶이가 많았지만 혼자서 머글 수 있었어요.
     ○ 떡볶이가 많읐지만 혼자서 먹을 수 있었어요.
     Translation:
     There was a lot of spicy rice cakes, but I was able to eat them all by myself.

  3. ○ 저 바의들은 거위 다 무거워요.
     ○ 저 바위들은 거의 다 무겁아요.
     ✓ 저 바위들은 거의 다 무거워요.
     Translation: Almost all of those rocks over there are heavy.

13 | Vocabulary Builder 단어 구축

The more words you learn, the easier it becomes to learn more words. It's like working out in the gym. The more reps you do eventually you will be able to lift heavier weights.

■ Group I: Education 교육

교육	education
교수님	professor
학원	after school academy
학기	semester
점수	grade
전공	major
부전공	minor
유학	studying abroad
휴학	leave of absence from school
토익	TOEIC (a test of English proficiency)

■ Vocabulary Sentences

The following sentences might contain words and concepts not yet taught. Focus on the new vocabulary more than the grammar.

1. 우리 학생들은 어떤 교육을 받고 있어요?
   What kind of education are our students receiving?

2. 저는 교수님이 되기 위해서 열심히 공부하고 있어요.
   I am studying diligently to become a professor.

3. 학생들은 학원에 가기 싫어해요.
   Students do not want to go to after school academies.

4. 이번 학기에는 좋은 성적을 받기 어려워요.
   It's difficult to get good grades this semester.

5. 이번 시험에서 어떤 점수를 받았어요?
   What grade did you get on this test?

6. 많은 학생들이 유학을 가고 싶어 해요.
   Many students want to go study abroad.

7. 저는 잠시 휴학을 하고 싶어요.
    I want to have a short leave of absence from school.

8. 당신의 전공이 뭐예요?
    What is your major?

9. 빨리 졸업을 하고 싶으면 낙제를 하면 안 돼요.
    If you want to graduate early, you cannot fail (a class).

10. 저는 영어를 잘 못하지만 토익 점수가 높았어요.
     I can't speak English well, but my TOEIC score was high.

14 Lesson 14: And Combinations

14 New Vocabulary 새로운 단어

New Nouns etc.

안전벨트	safety belt (seat belt)
짐	luggage, baggage
회의	business meeting
편견	prejudice (against), bias (toward)
운전면허증	driver's license
국제	international
클럽	night club, club
목걸이	necklace
귀걸이	earrings
인터넷	internet
연결	connection

New Verbs

죽다	to die
돌아가시다	to pass away
태어나다	to be born
들다	to carry, to hold, to lift, to raise
가지다	to have, to hold
춤을 추다	to dance
노래를 부르다	to sing a song

New Adjectives

편하다	to be comfortable, convenient
불편하다	to be uncomfortable, inconvenient
아름답다	to be beautiful
느리다	to be slow

14 | Grammar and Usage 문법과 사용법

● **14-1. ~고 (and~) multiple actions**
When saying multiple actions in one sentence the actions are connected using ~고. Usage is similar to 그리고 (and)

Multiple actions 고	
to eat **먹다**	→	to eat and **먹고**
to go **가다**	→	to go and **가고**

Verb Tense
The tense (past, present, future) of the FINAL verb determines the tense of the every ~고 verb in the statement. This rule applies no matter how many verbs there are prior to the final verb.

In the sentences below notice that 먹고 (eat and~) never changes in Korean, however the English tense changes to match the final verb.

1. **먹고** 갈 거예요.	I will **eat and** go.
2. **먹고** 갔어요.	I **ate and** went.
3. **먹고** 가고 싶어요.	I want to **eat and** go.
4. **먹고** 가자.	Let's **eat and** go.

You can think of the ~고 as acting like the comma does in English. Just like in English the comma is important, so is the ~고 important in Korean.

5. 점심을 먹**고** 쇼핑을 하**고** 도서관에 갈 거예요
   I will eat lunch, go shopping, **and** go to the library.

6. 운동을 하**고** 물을 많이 마시**고** 아침을 먹**고** 학교에 갔어요.
   I exercised, drank a lot of water, ate breakfast, **and** went to school.

7. 매일 숙제를 하**고** 친구에게 문자를 보내**고** 학교에 가요.
   Everyday I do my homework, text my friends, **and** go to school.

Example sentences

1. 아침에 밥을 먹고 운동했어요.
   I ate and exercised in the morning.

2. 여자친구가 이유 없이 화를내고 약속을 깼어요.
   My girlfriend got mad for no reason and broke our plans (appointment).

3. 수업이 끝나고 친구를 기다리고 있어요.
   Class ended and I am waiting for my friends.

4. 저는 꼭 안전벨트를 하고 운전해요.
   I always (definitely) wear my seatbelt and drive.

   > 하다 can be used as "to wear". You shouldn't use 입다.

5. 남자친구랑 손을 잡고 걸었어요.
   I held my boyfriend's hand and walked.

6. 파티에 가지 않고 집에 돌아갔어요.
   I didn't go the party and returned home.

   > The actions here aren't successive and occur at the same time.

7. 다섯 시간 동안 쉬지 않고 친구랑 이야기했어요.
   Without taking a break for 5 hours I talked with my friend.

● 14-2. 죽다 (die), 돌아가시다 (pass away), 태어나다 (be born)

죽다	TYPE	regular verb	BASIC FORM	죽어

돌아가시다	TYPE	regular verb	BASIC FORM	돌라가셔

태어나다	TYPE	regular verb	BASIC FORM	태어나

English and Korean both have many ways to say "to die". English has "passed away" and Korean similarly has 돌아가시다 (to return) which is a very respectful version of 돌아가다 (to return). There are MANY more ways but we are going to focus on the simple and direct 죽다 (to die).

Example sentences

1. 우리 강아지가 죽어서 슬퍼요.
   Our puppy died so I am sad.

2. 우리 할아버지는 1998 년에 돌아가셨어요.
   My grandfather passed away in 1998.

3. 지난해 일월에 남동생이 태어났어요.
My younger brother was born last year in January.

4. 아이가 언제 태어날 거예요?
When will the baby be born?

> You should never use respectful verbs for yourself, so using 죽다 is best here.

5. 100 살까지 죽고 싶지 않아요.
I don't want to die until 100 years old.

● **14-3. 들다 (to carry, to hold, to lift, to raise)**

TYPE	ㄹ irregular verb	BASIC FORM	들어

The item that is being held or lifted is marked with 을/를 object marker.
NOTE: 들다 has MANY other meanings that we will introduce later.

Example sentences
1. 여자친구의 가방을 들고 있어요.
I am holding my girlfriend's bag.

2. 무거운 짐을 들고 싶지 않아요.
I don't want to carry heavy baggage.

> This is literally "hold your cards and come" but the English doesn't sound natural that way.

3. 회의에 명함을 들고 오세요.
Come with your business cards to the meeting.

4. 질문이 있어서 손을 들었어요.
Because I had a question I raised my hand.

5. 부끄러워서 얼굴을 못 들었어요.
I was so embarrassed that I couldn't raise my head (face).

Special Information 특별 정보

ㄹ irregular conjugation note
Normally to make future tense verb stems with a 받침 you just add 을 (받다 → 받을 and without a 받침 you add ㄹ (가다 → 갈). However, with ㄹ irregular since they already have ㄹ you just leave them as is and don't add 을 (들다 → 들)

1. 들 거예요.   I will carry it.
2. 들 수 없어요.   I can't carry it.

● **14-4. 가지다 (to hold / carry / possess)**

TYPE	regular verb	BASIC FORM	가져

가지다 can be used to say you "have" or are "carrying" something. It can be used to have physical and non-physical things such as prejudice.

가지다 is similar in many ways to 있다 except that 가지다 is used when expressing that the item you "have" is with you right now.

Example sentences
1. 운전면허증을 가지고 있어요?
   Are you carrying (do you have) your driver's license?

2. 저는 중국어에 관심을 가지고 있어요.
   I have an interest in Chinese.

3. 현금을 얼마 가지고 있어요?
   How much cash do you have on you?

4. 사장님은 처음에 저에게 편견을 가지고 있었어요.
   The president (of the company) had a prejudice against me at first.

5. 집에서 삼각김밥을 가지고 공원에 갔어요.
   I carried triangle-shaped gimbap from my house and went to the park.

● **14-5. 춤을 추다 (to dance)**

TYPE	regular verb	BASIC FORM	춤을 춰

춤을 추다 literally means "dance a dance". There are other interesting verbs like this in Korean such as 꿈을 꾸다 "dream a dream". The usage is simple.

Example sentences
1. 저와 같이 춤을 춰요.
   Dance with me.

2. 새벽 3시까지 클럽에서 춤을 췄어요.
   I danced in the club until 3 in the morning.

3. 춤을 잘 춰? (casual)
   Do you dance well?

● **14-6. 노래를 부르다 (to sing a song)**

TYPE	르 irregular verb	BASIC FORM	노래를 불러

In book 1 we learned 노래하다 (to sing). There isn't any difference in meaning, however most Koreans often 노래를 부르다. 부르다 literally means "to call, to call out".

Example sentences

1. 노래방에서 노래를 많이 불렀어요.
   I sang many songs at Karaoke.

> When you have a verb phrase that uses 을/를 it's more natural to put adverbs after the 을/를.

2. 박민수 씨와 같이 춤을 추고 노래를 부르고 싶어요.
   I want to dance and sing with Minsu Park.

3. 한국어를 아직 잘 못해서 한국어로 노래를 못 불러요.
   Because I still can't speak Korean well, I can't sing in Korean.

14-7. 편하다 (to be comfortable, convenient) 불편하다 (to be uncomfortable, inconvenient)

편하다	TYPE	하다 adjective	BASIC FORM	편해
불편하다	TYPE	하다 adjective	BASIC FORM	불편해

Example sentences

1. 이 의자는 편해요.
   This chair is comfortable.

2. 지난달에 편한 침대를 샀어요.
   Last month I bought a comfortable bed.

3. 어느 시간이 편하세요?
   Which time is convenient for you?

4. 지금 핸드폰이 없어서 진짜 불편해요.
   It's really inconvenient because I don't have a cell phone now.

5. 불편한 소파에서 자서 몸이 아파요.
   Because I slept on an uncomfortable sofa my body hurts.

● **14-8. Multiple adjectives in one sentence ~고 (and)**

If you want to describe an object with multiple adjectives then we can string them together using the ~고 (and) form. However, you shouldn't mix positive and negative adjectives. To mix positive and negative you should use ~지만 to say "slow but cheap" etc.

Example sentences
1. 떡볶이는 맵고 달아요.
   Spicy rice cakes are spicy and sweet.

2. 제 자전거는 빠르고 편해요.
   My bicycle is fast and comfortable.

3. 이 핸드폰은 비싸고 무거워요.
   This cell phone is expensive and heavy.

4. 한국의 지하철은 편하고 싸요.
   Korea's subway is convenient and cheap.

5. 이 노래방은 시끄럽고 비싸요.
   This karaoke room is loud and expensive.

6. 이 편의점은 편하고 가까워요.
   This convenience store is convenient and close.

● **14-9. 아름답다 (to be beautiful)**

TYPE	ㅂ irregular adjective	BASIC FORM	아름다워

You will hear 아름답다 in just about every KPOP song it seems. ㅋㅋㅋ
It's a ㅂ irregular adjective so remember the ㅂ changes to 워.

Example sentences
1. 한국 산은 아름다워요.
   Korean mountains are beautiful.

ㅋㅋㅋ is the sound of laughing like LOL in English.

2. 한국 여자가 제일 아름다워요.
   Korean girls are the most beautiful.

Sorry... but it's true.
- George Trombley

3. 남자 친구가 저에게 아주 아름다운 목걸이와 귀걸이를 사 주었어요.
   My boyfriend bought a very beautiful necklace and earrings for me.

● **14-10. 느리다 (to be slow)**

TYPE	regular adjective	BASIC FORM	느려

The opposite of 느리다 is 빠르다 (to be fast).

> **Example sentences**
> 1. 이 비행기는 너무 느려요.
>   This airplane is too slow.
>
> 2. 택시가 느렸지만 회의에 늦지 않았어요.
>   The taxi was slow but I wasn't late to the meeting.
>
> 3. 인터넷 연결이 느려서 일을 못 했어요.
>   Because the internet connection was slow I couldn't do my work.

● **14-11. Particle 도 review and expansion**

In simple usage we know that 도 is used to say "also" when coming after a noun. It can be used multiple times in a sentence to say things such as 이것도, 이것도, 이것 (this, this, and also this).

When you have a 하다 verb or a verb phrase that contains an 을/를 such as 노래를 부르다 then it's common to see 을/를 being replaced with 도. This is especially common in sentences with multiple actions.

> **Example sentences**
> 1. 밥도 먹고 아이스크림도 먹었어요.
>   I ate dinner and I also ate ice cream.
>
> 2. 노래도 부르고 공부도 했어요.
>   I sang songs and also studied.
>
> 3. 수영도 하고 맛있는 것도 많이 먹었어요.
>   I swam and also ate many delicious things.

14 | Q&A 질문과 대답

1. 오늘 어때요?
어제 노래방에서 5시간 동안 춤을 추고 노래를 불러서 몸이 아파요.
어제 할아버지가 돌아가셔서 마음이 너무 아파요.

How are you today?
Yesterday I danced and sang for 5 hours so my body hurts.
My heart hurts because yesterday my grandfather passed away.

2. 어제 잘 잤어요?
침대가 불편해서 잘 못잤어요.
꿈 속에서 빅뱅을 만나서 진짜 행복했어요.

> "Big Bang" is a popular Korean boy group.

Did you sleep well yesterday?
I didn't sleep well because my bed is uncomfortable.
I was really happy because I met Big Bang in my dream.

3. 운전면허증을 가지고 왔어요?
아니요. 어제 클럽에서 잃어버렸어요.
네. 하지만 국제 운전면허증이 아니에요.

> 가지고 오다 is literally "to hold AND come" but in English we just say "bring".

Do you bring your license?
No. Yesterday I lost it at the club.
Yes. However it's not an international driver's license.

4. 오늘 밤에 약속이 있어요?
여동생이 태어나서 병원에 가요.
밥을 먹고 쇼핑을 할 거예요. 귀걸이와 목걸이도 살 거예요.
우리 고양이가 죽어서 집에 돌아가요.

Do you have plans this evening?
My younger sister was born so I am going to the hospital.
I will eat and go shopping. I will buy earrings and a necklace.
Our cat died so I will return home.

5. 새로운 사무실에 인터넷을 연결했어요?
아직 연결하지 못했어요. 그래서 너무 불편해요.
이미 연결도 하고 돈도 냈어요. 하지만 너무 느려요.

Did you connect the new office to the internet?
I haven't been able to connect it yet. So it's really inconvenient.
I already connected it and also paid the money. However, it's really slow.

14 | Test Yourself Activities 연습 문제

● A14-1. Sentence Jumble

With the words provided, make Korean sentences that match the English.
You can freely add particles, pronouns and conjugate verbs as needed.

1. 클럽, 무겁다, 운전면허증, 가지다, 짐, 돌아가시다, 편견, 한국사람들

   _____

   I had my driver's license at the club.

   _____

   Don't have prejudice towards Koreans. (command)

   _____

   I was holding heavy luggage.

2. 아름답다, 꽃, 비싸다, 이, 좋아하다, 화가나다, 배고프다, 아버지

   _____

   I am hungry and mad.

   _____

   This flower is beautiful but inexpensive.

   _____

   I like beautiful and inexpensive flowers.

3. 학교, 오늘, 어젯밤, 김밥, 타고, 자전거, 먹다, 노래를 부르다, 같이, 버스, 내리다, 강남역, 서울역, 친구, 가다

   _____

   I got on at Gangnam station and got off at Seoul station.

   _____

   Last night I sang with friends and went to Seoul.

   _____

   I ate gimbap and went to school by bicycle.

● **A14-2. Fill in the blanks**

Fill in the missing word or particle based on the English sentence.

1. 오늘 나의 인터넷 _____이 안 좋아.
   Today, my internet connection isn't good.

2. 신용카드를 몇 개_____ 있어요?
   How many credit cards are you carrying?

3. 우리 할머니가 이번 주에 _____요.
   Our grandmother passed away this week.

4. 이 목거리는 비싸_____ 아름다워요.
   This necklace is not expensive and is beautiful.

5. 다른 나라에서 국제 _____이 필요해요.
   In other countries you need an international driver's license.

● **A14-3. Mark and Translate**

Mark the Korean sentence without mistakes then translate it.

1. ○ 저는 1992 년에 태어났었어요.
   ○ 저는 1992 년이 태어났어요.
   ○ 저는 1992 년에 태어났어요.

   Translation:_____

2. ○ 짐이 무거워서 들 수 없어요.
   ○ 짐이 무겁지만 들 수 없어요.
   ○ 짐이 무거워서 들을 수 없어요.

   Translation:_____

3. ○ 어젯밤에 노래방에서 노래를 많이 불었어요.
   ○ 어젯밤에 노래방에서 노래를 많이 불렀어요.
   ○ 어젯밤에 노래방에서 노래를 많은 불었어요.

   Translation:_____

14 | Self Test Answers 연습 문제 정답

● A14-1. Sentence Jumble

1. 저는 클럽에서 운전면허증을 가지고 있었어요.
   한국사람들(한테 / 에게) 편견을 가지지 마세요.
   저는 무거운 짐을 가지고 있었어요.

2. 저는 배고프고 화가나요.
   이 꽃은 아름답지만 (비싸지 않아요 / 안 비싸요).
   저는 아름답고 (비싸지 않은 / 안 비싼) 꽃을 좋아해요.

3. 저는 강남역에서 타고 서울역에서 내렸어요.
   어젯밤에 친구랑 노래를 부르고 서울에 갔어요.
   저는 김밥을 먹고 자전거로 학교에 갔어요.

● A14-2. Fill in the blanks

1. 오늘 나의 인터넷 <u>연결</u>이 안 좋아요.
2. 신용카드를 몇 개 <u>가지고</u> 있어요?
3. 우리 할머니가 이번주에 <u>돌아가셨어</u>요.
4. 이 목거리는 비싸<u>지 않고</u> 아름다워요.
5. 다른 나라에서 국제 <u>운전면허증</u>이 필요해요.

● A14-3. Best Sentence Search

1. ○ 저는 1992 년에 태어났었어요.
   ○ 저는 1992 년이 태어났어요.
   ✓ 저는 1992 년에 태어났어요.
   Translation: I was born in 1992.

2. ✓ 짐이 무거워서 들 수 없어요.
   ○ 짐이 무겁지만 들 수 없어요.
   ○ 짐이 무거워서 들을 수 없어요.
   Translation: Because the luggage is heavy I can't (carry / lift) it.

3. ○ 어젯밤에 노래방에서 노래를 많이 불었어요.
   ✓ 어젯밤에 노래방에서 노래를 많이 불렀어요.
   ○ 어젯밤에 노래방에서 노래를 많은 불었어요.
   Translation: Last night I sang many songs at a karaoke room.

14 | Vocabulary Builder 단어 구축

Learning new words should be your hobby. Co-authors Reed and George often carry small notebooks containing hundreds of Korean vocabulary to review during free time. A good list on your phone will also do the job.

■ Group J: Hobbies 취미

취미	hobby
기타	guitar
예술	art
연극	play (theater)
낚시	fishing
등산	hiking
만화책	comics
골프	golf
스쿠버 다이빙	scuba diving
캠핑	camping

■ Group K: Foreign names 외국인의 이름
In the following lessons we will be using more names.

리드	Reed
제시	Jessie
조지	George
대니	Danny
제니퍼	Jennifer
요코	Yoko
에밀리	Emily

■ Vocabulary Sentences
The following sentences might contain words and concepts not yet taught. Focus on the new vocabulary more than the grammar.

1. 무슨 취미를 가지고 있어요?
   What kind of hobbies do you have?

2. 조지 씨는 기타를 칠 줄 몰라요.
   George doesn't know how to play guitar.

3. 제시 씨는 예술에 관심이 없어요.
   Jessie doesn't have interest in art.

4. 저랑 같이 연극을 보러 갈래요?
   Do you want to go watch a play with me?

5. 제니퍼는 낚시를 싫어해요.
   Jennifer doesn't like to fish.

6. 등산은 몸에 좋아요.
   Hiking is good for your body.

7. 요코는 만화책을 많이 봐요.
   Yoko looks at (reads) a lot of comics.

8. 최근에는 골프를 배우고 있어요.
   Recently, I have been learning golf.

9. 어제 처음으로 스쿠버 다이빙을 했어요.
   I scuba dived for the first time yesterday.

10. 에밀리의 아버지는 캠핑을 좋아해요.
    Emily's father likes camping.

15 Lesson 15: Korean Contractions

15 New Vocabulary 새로운 단어

New Nouns etc.

술	alcohol, liquor
낮잠	nap
아르바이트	part time job
빵	bread
빵집	bakery
고깃집	barbecue restaurant
회사원	employee, company worker
티켓	tickets (concerts, movies)
농담	joke
아이고	oh my!, goodness!, ouch! (sigh...)
와!	wow!

New Verbs

아르바이트하다	to do a part-time job
구경하다	to go sightseeing, to watch, to see
잠을 자다	to sleep
울다	to cry
웃다	to laugh
없어지다	to disappear, to run out

New Adjectives

키가 작다	to be short
키가 크다	to be tall

15 | New Expressions 새로운 표현

1. 그래요?
Is that so? / Really?

2. 그래요.
That's right. / Okay. / Yes.

15 | Grammar and Usage 문법과 사용법

● **15-1. Common Korean contractions**
Koreans like to shorten things when possible. The most common type of shortening is the combining of words and the following particle.

Full	Contracted	Meaning
무엇을	뭘	what
뭐를	뭘	what
저는	전	I (polite)
나는	난	I (casual)
너는	넌	you (casual)
에는	엔	to (stressed)
에서는	에선	in, on, at (stressed)
이것은	이건	this
그것은	그건	that
이것이	이게	this
그것이	그게	that
것이	게	thing (many uses in grammar)
것을	걸	thing
에서	서	in, on, at (shortened form)
우리는	우린	us

Example sentences

1. 뭘 먹고 싶어요?	What do you want to eat?
2. 전 내년에 한국에 가고 싶어요.	I want to go to Korea next year.
3. 이게 뭐예요?	What is this?
4. 어디를 구경하고 싶어요?	Where do you want to sightsee?
5. 한국에는 차가 많아요.	In Korea there are many cars.
6. 이건 얼마예요?	How much is this?
7. 그걸 저에게 사 주세요.	Buy this for me.

● 15-2. 아르바이트하다 (to do a part-time job)

TYPE	하다 adjective	BASIC FORM	아르바이트해

아르바이트 comes from the German word "Arbeit" which means "work". In Korea 아르바이트 just means part-time work. Remember that 하다 verbs can sometimes have the 을/를 particle, but it's not always necessary.

Example sentences

1. 박민수 씨는 편의점에서 아르바이트를 해요.
   Minsoo Park is doing a part-time job at a convenience store.

2. 옛날에 전 빵집에서 아르바이트했어요.
   A long time ago I did part-time work at a bakery.

● 15-3. 구경하다 (to go sightseeing, to watch, to see)

TYPE	하다 verb	BASIC FORM	구경해

The place you will sight-see is marked with object marker 을/를. 구경 by itself means "sightseeing".

Example sentences

1. 우리는 라스베가스를 구경하고 싶어요.
   We want to go sightseeing in Las Vegas.

   > 만리장성 is "the great wall of China"

2. 중국에 가서 만리장성을 구경했어요.
   I went to China and went sightseeing at the great wall.

3. 넌 어디를 구경하고 싶어?
   Where do you want to go sightseeing?

구경하다 is also used to for watching, sports events, and concerts etc. It's not just limited to "sightseeing".

Example sentences

1. 집에서 코서트를 구경할 거예요.
   I will watch the concert at my house.

2. 2012 년에 런던에서 가족이랑 올림픽을 구경했어요.
   In 2012 I watched the Olympics with my family in London.

3. 야구 시합을 구경하고 싶지만 티켓이 너무 빗아요.
   I want to watch a baseball game but the tickets are too expensive.

4. 매년 십이월에 친구랑 스키장에 가고 눈을 구경해요.
   Every December I go to the ski area and look at the snow with a friend.

● 15-4. 잠을 자다 (to sleep)

TYPE	regular verb	BASIC FORM	잠을 자

잠 itself means "sleep" so it's sort of weird to say "sleep a sleep". It's maybe just as weird as "sing a song" but nonetheless, 잠을 자다 is used in the same way as 자다 (to sleep) is. Other words can replace 잠 in the phrase to make other verbs:

낮잠을 자다   to take a nap
늦잠을 자다   to oversleep

Look at that! Three verbs for the price of one!

Example sentences

1. 전 피곤해서 낮잠을 잤어요.
   Because I was tired I took a nap.

2. 어젯밤에 너무 늦게 자서 오늘 늦잠을 잤어요.
   Because I slept too late yesterday night, today I overslept.

3. 보통 몇 시에 잠을 자요?
   What time do you normally sleep?

● 15-5. 울다 (to cry), 웃다 (to laugh)

울다	TYPE	regular verb	BASIC FORM	울어

웃다	TYPE	regular verb	BASIC FORM	웃어

Example sentences

1. 왜 울어요?
   Why are you crying?

2. 울지 마세요!
   Don't cry!

3. 영화가재미있어서 계속 웃었어요.
   Because the movie was funny, I laughed continuously.

4. 너무 많이 웃어서 배가 아파요.
   I laughed so much my stomach hurts.

● 15-6. 없어지다 (to disappear, be missing, to run out)

TYPE	regular verb	BASIC FORM	없어져

In section 7-4 we learned how to combine adjectives with ~지다 to say "becoming cold" or "becoming hot" etc. 없어지다 is similar in that it means something has "become not there" or "It's gone now." 없어지다 is also used to just to say "there is no more".

Example sentences

1. 어제 책상위에 펜이 있었지만 오늘 없어졌어요.
   There was a pen on the desk yesterday, but today it's gone.

2. 오늘 아침에 제 지갑이 없어졌어요.
   This morning, my wallet was missing.

3. 우리 개가 없어진 제 가방을 찾았어요.
   Our dog found my missing bag.

4. 배고 파서 힘이 없어졌어요.
   Because I am hungry I have no more power.

● **15-7. 키가 작다 (to be short), 키가 크다 (to be tall)**

키가 작다	**TYPE**	regular adjective	**BASIC FORM**	키가 작아

키가 크다	**TYPE**	regular adjective	**BASIC FORM**	키가 커

> **Example sentences**
> 1. 농구 선수는 거의 다 키가 커요.
>   Almost all basketball players are tall.
>
>   선수 = player (sports)
>
> 2. 우리 남동생은 키가 작아요.
>   My younger brother is short.
>
>   부딪히다 means to "bump" or "crash".
>
> 3. 저는 키가 커서 자주 머리를 부딪혀요.
>   Since I am tall I often bump my head.
>
> 4. 키가 작은 남자랑 데이트를 하고 싶지 않아요.
>   I don't want to date short men.

● **15-8. Korean sentence ending ~네요**

By now you have most likely already heard a phrase ending with ~네요. If you say even one Korean phrase many Koreans will response with 한국어 잘 하시네요! (Your Korean is good!).

This phrase is made with 하다 in a high level polite form (taught in book 3) plus the ~네요 ending. ~네요 can have the following nuances:

1. ~네요 shows the speaker is surprised at the situation.

2. ~네요 is used when the speaker realizes, hears, or feels a certain situation. For example they walk outside and realize it's cold.
   They would say: 춥네요! (Wow it's cold!)

3. ~네요 is used to soften how a sound feels. It's similar to saying "It sure is cold." instead of just "It's cold".

To make this form you just add 네요 to the normal, past tense, or future tense verb stem.

Example sentences

1. 오늘은 덥네요.
   Today sure is hot.

   > 덥네요 is much softer than just 더워요.

2. 그는 키가 크네요.
   He sure is tall.

3. 보통은 한 시간 걸리지만 오늘은 두 시간 걸렸네요!
   Normally it takes 1 hour, but it took 2 hours!

4. 올해부터 학비가 비싸지네요!
   From this year tuition really got expensive.

5. 갑자기 비가 왔네요.
   All of a sudden it started raining.

6. 한국어는 정말 어렵네요.
   Korean is so difficult.

7. 선생님, 오늘 예쁘네요.
   Teacher, you are so pretty today.

● 15-9. (으)ㄹ 게요 I'll do it!

We will use 하다 (to do) as the sample verb to make this explanation easier. 할게요 is similar to 할 거예요 in the fact that you use it to say "I will do".

Unique Features of 할게요.

1. 할게요 is more definite and often includes a "promise" that it will be done.

2. You only use 할게요 about an action that you will do. * never other people

3. You can't make 할게요 into a question. Read rule #2.

4. 할게요 is said in response to a situation and isn't said as an opening line.
   Ex 1) Someone is washing dishes. You offer to help. "I'll do them".
   Ex 2) Someone needs a drink. You offer to buy one. "I'll buy one".

5. 할게요 is often used when saying you will do something for someone else's benefit. It's also often used with ~주다 verbs (section 6-3) to say 해줄게. In some cases, 해줄게 sounds more natural. Everyone will understand if you use 할게 instead 해줄게 as the meaning is similar.

Example conversation
1. A: 아이고... 숙제가 어려워서 못 하겠어요!
    B: 제가 같이 해 줄게요!
    A: 진짜요? 고마워요!

    A: Oh... I can't do the homework because it's hard.
    B: I'll do it with you!
    A: Really? Thank you!

2. A: 현금과 카드를 잃어버렸어요.
    B: 제가 내 줄게요.
    A: 와! 너무 친절하네요!

    A: I lost my cash and cards.
    B: I'll pay for you.
    A: Wow! You are so kind!

3. A: 우린 언제 저녁을 같이 먹을까요?
    B: 다음 주는 어때요?
    A: 내일 연락할게요.

    A: When shall we eat dinner together?
    B: What about next week?
    A: I'll contact you tomorrow.

NOTE: Example 3 doesn't use 연락해줄게 since the person isn't doing that action on someone's behalf.

15 | Q&A 질문과 대답

1. **언제부터 아르바이트를 시작했어요?**
   지난달부터 시작했어요.
   빵집 아르바이트는 오늘부터 시작했어요.

   From when did you start your part time job?
   I started it from last month.
   I started my bakery part time job from today.

2. **이번 콘서트에 갔어요?**
   티켓이 없어서 티비로 구경했어요.
   네. 가수의 키가 정말 컸어요.
   당연하죠! 너무 좋아서 계속 울었어요.

   Did you go to the concert this time?
   Since there weren't tickets, I saw it on TV.
   Of course! It was so good I kept on crying.

   > 계속 doesn't have to always translate to "continue". "kept on" sounds better in English.

3. **오늘 낮잠을 잤어요?**
   너무 피곤해서 3 시간 동안 낮잠을 잤어요.
   아니요. 숙제가 많아서 안 잤어요.

   Did you take a nap today?
   Because I was so tired, I napped for 3 hours.
   No. I didn't sleep because I had a lot of homework.

4. **오늘 저녁 같이 먹고 싶어요?**
   그래요. 가벼운 음식이 좋아요.
   아이고! 오늘은 약속이 이미 있어요.
   좋아요. 고깃집에 갑시다.

   Tonight do you want to eat together?
   Ok. Light food would be good.
   Oh man! I already have plans tonight.
   Good. Let's go to a barbecue restaurant.

5. **저 여자는 왜 울어요?**
   아침에 강아지가 없어져서 울어요.
   아버지가 돌아가셔서 어제부터 계속 울었어요.

   Why is that girl over there crying?
   In the morning her dog disappeared so she is crying.
   She's been continually crying since yesterday since her father passed away.

15 | Test Yourself Activities 연습 문제

● A15-1. Contractions and Translations
Rewrite each sentence. Change the underlined items into their contracted form. Then translate the sentence into English.

1. <u>너는</u> <u>무엇을</u> 들고 있어?

   Contracted:_____

   English: _____

2. <u>저는</u> 2000 년에 태어났어요.

   Contracted:_____

   English: _____

3. 중국<u>에는</u> 친절한 사람이 많아요.

   Contracted:_____

   English: _____

4. <u>이것은</u> 아주 매워서 못 먹어요.

   Contracted:_____

   English: _____

5. <u>나는</u> 사탕을 좋아해서 매일 먹고 싶어.

   Contracted:_____

   English: _____

● A15-2. Fill in the blanks

Fill in the missing word or particle based on the English sentence.

1. 박민수가 편의점에서 _____를 해요.
   Minsoo Park is doing a part-time job at a convenience store.

2. 어젯밤에 너무 늦게 자서 오늘 _____을 잤어요.
   Because I slept too late yesterday night, today I overslept.

3. 영화가재미있어서 _____ 웃었어요.
   Because the movie was funny, I laughed continuously.

4. 사진을 찍고 싶지만 카메라가 _____요.
   I want to take a picture but the camera is gone.

5. 키가 _____ 여자와 데이트를 하고 싶지 않아요.
   I don't want to date a tall woman.

● A15-3. Mark and Translate

Mark the Korean sentence without mistakes then translate it.

1. ○ 어제밤엔 뭘 먹았아요?
   ○ 어제밤엘 뭔 먹었어요?
   ○ 어젯밤엔 뭘 먹었어요?

   Translation:_____

2. ○ 제 친구의 친구는 키가 아주 커요.
   ○ 나위 친구위 친구는 키가 아주 커.
   ○ 제 친구의 친구는 키가 아주 코요.

   Translation:_____

3. ○ 한국어는 정말 어렵네요.
   ○ 한국어는 정말 어려워네요.
   ○ 한국어는 정말 어렵내요.

   Translation:_____

15 | Self Test Answers 연습 문제 정답

● A15-1. Sentence Jumble

1. <u>넌</u> 뭘 들고 있어?
   What are you holding?

2. <u>전</u> 2000 년에 태어났어요.
   I was born in 2000.

3. 중국<u>엔</u> 친절한 사람이 많아요.
   In China there are many kind people.

4. <u>이건</u> 아주 매워서 못 먹어요.
   Since this is very spicy I can't eat it.

5. <u>난</u> 사탕을 좋아해서 매일 먹고 싶어.
   Since I like sweet things I want to eat them every day.

● A15-2. Fill in the blanks

1. 박민수가 편의점에서 <u>아르바이트</u>를 해요.

2. 어젯밤에 너무 늦게 자서 오늘 <u>늦잠</u>을 잤어요.

3. 영화가재미있어서 <u>계속</u> 웃었어요.

4. 사진을 찍고 싶지만 카메라가 없어졌어요.

5. 키가 <u>큰</u> 여자와 데이트를 하고 싶지 않아요.

● A15-3. Best Sentence Search

1. ○ 어제밤엔 뭘 먹았아요?
   ○ 어제밤엘 뭔 먹었어요?
   ✓ 어젯밤엔 뭘 먹었어요?
   Translation: What did you eat yesterday night?

2. ✓ 제 친구의 친구는 키가 아주 커요.
   ○ 나위 친구위 친구는 키가 아주 커.
   ○ 제 친구의 친구는 키가 아주 코요.
   Translation: My friend's friend is very tall.

3. ✓ 한국어는 정말 어렵네요.
   ○ 한국어는 정말 어려워네요.
   ○ 한국어는 정말 어렵내요.
   Translation: Korean sure is very hard. / Wow, Korean is hard.

15 | Vocabulary Builder 단어 구축

How is your vocabulary shaping up? Keep up the good work!

■ Group L: Shapes 모양

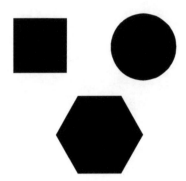

모양	shape
원	circle
삼각(형)	triangle
사각(형)	square
오각형	pentagon
육각형	hexagon
직사각형	rectangle

■ Vocabulary Sentences

The following sentences might contain words and concepts not yet taught. Focus on the new vocabulary more than the grammar.

1. 그 컴퓨터의 모양이 이상해요.
   That computer's shape is odd.

2. 원을 제대로 그리세요.
   Properly draw a circle.

3. 삼각김밥은 삼각형이에요.
   Samgak gimbap's shape is triangle.

4. 저기에 있는 사각형 물건은 책이에요.
   That square object over there is a book.

5. 종이를 오각형으로 접으세요
   Fold the paper into a pentagon.

6. 벌은 집을 육각형으로 만들어요.
   Bees make their hives by making hexagons.

7. 우리 집 텔레비전은 직사각형이에요.
   The television in our house is a rectangle.

SR! Super Review and Quiz #3:
Lessons 13-15

SR | Question and Answer 질문과 대답

Hide the English and try to translate the Korean. Take notes on words or grammar patterns that confuse you then review them if necessary.

1. 한국 음식이 어때요?
한국 음식은 싸고 맛있어요.
한국 음식은 맛있지만 좀 매워요.
한국 음식을 안 먹어 봐서 잘 몰라요.

How is Korean food?
Korean food is cheap and tasty.
Korean food is tasty but a little spicy.
I've never eaten Korean food before so I don't know.

2. 어제 싸이 콘서트에 갔어요?
네, 갔어요. 싸이는 춤도 잘 추고 노래도 잘 불러요.
아니요, 표를 샀지만 시간이 없어서 갈 수 없었어요.
아니요, 가고 싶었지만 표를 못 샀어요.

Did you go to the PSY concert yesterday?
Yes, I went. PSY dances well and sings well too.
No, I bought a ticket but since I didn't have time I couldn't go.
No, I wanted to go but I wasn't able to buy a ticket.

3. 왜 숙제를 안 했어요?
숙제가 너무 어렵고 많았어요.
한국어 공부는 재미있지만 숙제는 재미없어요.
요즘 회사에 일도 많고 친구들하고 약속도 많아서 할 수 없었어요.

Why didn't you do your homework?
The homework is too hard and there was a lot of it.
Studying Korean is fun but doing homework is not fun.
Lately I have lots of work at the company and meetings with friends, so I couldn't do it.

4. **휴가에 어디로 갈 거예요?**
   제주도로 갈 거예요. 제주도는 바다도 아름답고 맛있는 음식도 많아요.
   호주로 가고 싶어요. 호주에서 친구도 만나고 구경도 할 거예요.
   하와이에 가요. 하와이는 멀지만 바다가 정말 예뻐요.

   Where are you going to go on vacation?
   I'm going to Jeju Island. Jeju Island's beaches are beautiful and it also has a lot of tasty food.
   I want to go to Australia. I'll meet my friends in Australia and go sightseeing.
   I'm going to Hawaii. Hawaii is far away but the ocean is very pretty.

5. **보통 몇 시에 일어나요?**
   아침마다 운동을 해서 6 시에 일어나요.
   보통 7 시에 일어나지만 주말에는 늦게 일어나요.
   날마다 6 시에 일어나. 나는 항상 일찍 자고 일찍 일어나. (casual)

   What time do you normally get up?
   Since I work out every morning, I get up at 6.
   Usually I get up at 7 but on the weekends I get up late.
   Everyday I get up at 6. I always go to bed early and get up early.

6. **여행이 어땠어요?**
   산도 아름답고 바다도 너무 예뻤어요.
   날씨가 좋지 않았지만 정말 재미있었어요.
   날마다 비가 와서 구경을 별로 못 했어요.

   How was the trip?
   The mountain was beautiful and the ocean was also very pretty.
   The weather was not good but it was very fun.
   It rained everyday so we couldn't really do that much sightseeing.

SR Conversation 대화 K-E

1. **Co-workers are discussing plans.**
   A: 오늘 영화를보고 뭘 할까요?
   B: 영화를보고 술을 마셔요.
   A: 전 영화는 보고 싶지만 술은 마시고 싶지 않아요.
   B: 그래요? 그럼 영화만 봅시다.

   A: Today you are going to watch a movie and do what?
   B: I'll watch a movie and drink alcohol.
   A: I want to watch a movie but I don't want to drink alcohol.
   B: Really? Alright then, let's watch a movie.

2. **Classmates are talking before class starts.**

   A: 어제 수업이 끝나고 어디에 갔어요?

   B: 수업이 끝나고 저녁마다 아르바이트를 하고 있어요.

   A: 무슨 일을 해요?

   B: 빵집에서 케이크를 만들어요.

   A: Yesterday class finished and you went somewhere?

   B: Class finishes and every night I work a part-time job.

   A: What work do you do?

   B: I make cakes at a bakery.

3. **Friends are talking on the phone.**

   A: 오늘 서울 날씨가 어때요?

   B: 비가 오고 추워요. 뉴욕은 어때요?

   A: 비가 오지만 춥지 않아요. 오늘 뭘 할 거예요?

   B: 추워서 집에 있을 거예요.

   A: How is the weather in Seoul today?

   B: It is raining and it's cold. How about New York?

   A: It's raining but its not cold. What will you do today?

   B: It's cold so I'm going to stay home.

4. **A girlfriend is a bit upset with her boyfriend. (casual)**

   A: 어제 왜 전화 안 했어?

   B: 머리도 아프고 시간도 없었어.

   A: 그럼 오늘은 왜 전화 안 했어? 오늘도 머리가 아파?

   B: 아니, 머리는 아프지 않지만 오늘은 배가 아파.

   A: 너는 왜 날마다 아파?

   A: Why didn't you call yesterday?

   B: My head was hurting and I didn't have any time.

   A: So why didn't you call today? Does your head hurt today too?

   B: No, today my head doesn't hurt but my stomach hurts.

   A: Why are you sick everyday?

SR | Quiz Yourself 퀴즈

● **1. Sentence combining**

Combine the two provided sentences using the ~고 pattern. On the second line translate the new sentence into English.

> Sample
> Ex. 조지 씨는 공부를 해요. 제니퍼 씨는 컴퓨터를 해요.
> Combined: 조지 씨는 공부를 하고 제니퍼 씨는 컴퓨터를 해요.
> Translation: George is studying and Jennifer is on the computer.

1. 제시 씨는 음악을 듣고 있어요. 리드 씨는 텔레비전을 보고 있어요.

   Combined: _____

   _____

   Translation:_____

   _____

2. 조지 씨는 일본어를 배우고 있어요. 제니퍼 씨는 프랑스어를 배워요.

   Combined: _____

   _____

   Translation:_____

   _____

3. 에밀리 씨는 친절해요. 예뻐요.

   Combined: _____

   _____

   Translation:_____

   _____

4. 저 식당은 깨끗해요. 맛있어요.

Combined: _____

_____

Translation:_____

_____

5. 대니 씨는 회사원이에요. 요코 씨는 학생이에요.

Combined: _____

_____

Translation:_____

_____

● **2. Sentence completion**
Using the ~지만 connector combine the best matching sentences using the provided sentences. Then translate the new sentence on the following line.

Choose the best match:	
저는 키가 작다	영화를못 봤다
제 친구는 일하다	동생은 놀고 있다
선물을 못 받았다	한국말을 못하다
아보카도는 비싸다	

> **Sample**
> Ex. 바나나는 싸다
> Combined: 바나나는 싸고 아보카도는 비싸요.
> Translation: Bananas are cheap and avacados are expensive.

1. 저는 쉬다

Combined: _____

Translation:_____

2. 저는 공부하고 있다

   Combined: _____

   Translation: _____

3. 조지 씨는 일본말을 잘하다

   Combined: _____

   Translation: _____

4. 동생은 키가 크다

   Combined: _____

   Translation: _____

5. 영화관에 갔다

   Combined: _____

   Translation: _____

6. 생일이다

   Combined: _____

   Translation: _____

● 3. Sentence completion ~고

Combine the descriptive words (adjectives) into one sentence using the ~고 connector then translate on the following line.

> **Sample**
> Ex. 요코 씨 / 아름답다 / 친절하다
> Combined: 요코 씨는 아름답고 친절해요.
> Translation: Yoko is beautiful and kind.

1. 그 식당 / 깨끗하다 / 음식이 맛있다

   Combined: _____

   Translation: _____

2. 이 음식 / 맛없다 / 비싸다

   Combined: _____

   Translation: _____

3. 우리 집 / 깨끗하다 / 좋다

   Combined: _____

   Translation: _____

4. 백화점 / 크다 / 사람이 많다

   Combined: _____

   Translation: _____

5. 이 원피스 / 예쁘다 / 싸다

   Combined: _____

   Translation: _____

6. 이 케이크 / 크다 / 맛있다

   Combined: _____

   Translation: _____

● 4. Connector choice ~지만, ~고

Using ~지만 or ~고 create sentences using the provided text. The sentences must make logical sense. For example you should use ~지만 only when showing a negative and positive aspect in the same sentence. If the aspects are **BOTH** positive or **BOTH** negative you can use ~고 to combine them.

When the aspects can be either negative or positive based on your opinion then choose the appropriate connector.

Sample
Ex. 그 가방이 작다 / 가볍다
Combined: 그 가방이 작지만 가벼워요.
Translation: <u>That bag is small but light.</u>

---

1. Subways are fast and comfortable.

_____

Subways are fast but uncomfortable.

_____

2. Mina is pretty and kind.

_____

Mina is pretty but not kind.

_____

3. My company work is exhausting but interesting.

_____

My company work is exhausting and tiring.

_____

4. Our house is loud and dirty.

_____

Our house is loud but interesting.

_____

● 5. Reading comprehension
Read the following selection then answer the questions.

저는 지난 주말에 미나 씨하고 같이 공원에 갔어요. 미나 씨는 운동을 좋아해서 공원에서 자전거를 탔어요. 저도 자전거를 타고 싶었지만 다리가 아파서 자전거를 못 탔어요. 미나 씨하고 점심을 먹고 혼자 영화관에서 영화를봤어요. 그 영화는 조금 길었지만 재미있었어요.

1. 이 사람은 지난 주말에 어디에 갔어요?

_____

2. 미나 씨가 공원에서 뭘 했어요?

_____

3. 이 사람은 운동을 싫어해요?

_____

4. 이 사람은 미나 씨하고 같이 영화를봤어요?

_____

SR | Answer Key 해답

● 1. Sentence combining
1. 제시 씨는 음악을 듣고 있고 리드 씨는 텔레비전을 보고 있어요.
   Jessie is listening to music and Reed is watching TV.

2. 조지 씨는 일본어를 가르치고 제니퍼 씨는 프랑스어를 가르쳐요.
   George is learning Japanese and Jennifer is learning French.

3. 에밀리 씨는 친절하고 예뻐요.
   Emily is kind and pretty.

4. 저 식당은 깨끗하고 맛있어요.
That restaurant is clean and delicious.

5. 대니 씨는 회사원이고 요코 씨는 학생이에요.
Danny is a company worker and Yoko is a student.

● 2. Sentence completion

1. 저는 쉬지만 제 친구는 일해요.
I am resting, but my friend is working.

2. 저는 공부하고 있지만 동생은 놀고 있어요.
I'm studying, but my younger brother (sister) is playing.

3. 조지 씨는 일본말을 잘하지만 한국말을 못해요.
George is good at Japanese, but can't speak (do) Korean well.

4. 동생은 키가 크지만 저는 키가 작아요.
My younger sister (brother) is tall, but I am short.

5. 영화관에 갔지만 영화를못 봤어요.
I went to the movie theatre but I was unable to watch a movie.

6. 생일이지만 선물을 못 받았어요.
It's my birthday but I didn't get any presents.

● 3. Sentence completion ~고

1. 그 식당은 깨끗하고 음식이 맛있어요.
This restaurant is clean and the food is delicious.

2. 이 음식은 맛없고 비싸요.
This food tastes bad and is expensive.

3. 우리 집은 깨끗하고 좋아요.
Our house is clean and good.

4. 백화점은 크고 사람이 많아요.
Department stores are big and there are many people.

5. 이 원피스는 예쁘고 싸요.
This one piece dress is pretty and cheap.

6. 이 케이크는 크고 맛있어요.
   This cake is big and delicious.

● 4. Connector choice ~지만, ~고

1. 지하철이 빠르고 편해요.
   지하철이 빠르지만 불편해요.

2. 미나 씨가 예쁘고 친절해요.
   미나 씨가 예쁘지만 불친절해요.

3. 회사 일이 힘들지만 재미있어요.
   회사 일이 힘들고 피곤해요.

4. 우리 집은 시끄럽고 더러워요.
   우리 집은 시끄럽지만 재미있어요.

● 5. Reading comprehension

Last weekend I went to the park with Mina. Because Mina likes exercise (physical activity) she rode her bicycle in the park. I also wanted to ride my bicycle but since my legs hurt I wasn't able to ride my bike. Mina ate lunch and I watched a movie by myself at the movie theatre. That movie was a bit long but it was interesting.

1. Where did this person go last weekend?
   (이 사람은 지난 주말에) 공원에 갔어요.

2. What did Mina do at the park?
   (미나 씨가 공원에서) 자전거를 탔어요.

3. Does this person dislike physical activity?
   아니요, 이 사람은 운동을 좋아해요.

4. Did this person watch a movie with Mina?
   아니요, (이 사람은) 혼자 영화를 봤어요.

16

Lesson 16:
Directly Modifying

16 New Vocabulary 새로운 단어

New Nouns etc.

물건	item; product
제목	title, name
지난번	last time
이번	this time
다음 번	next time
방법	method
그런데	but, however
근데	(short for 그런데)
선수	player
그날	that day

New Adjectives

유명하다	to be famous

New Verbs

팔다	to sell
나오다	to come out
찾다	to find, to look for, to search for
찾아보다	to look for, to search
입다	to wear, to put on
유행하다	to be in fashion, trending
찍다	to take a picture or film, to dip

16 | Grammar and Usage 문법과 사용법

● **16-1. Overview of directly modifying with verbs**

Directly modifying with verbs is one of the most powerful grammar stuctures. It's important to know how English works to understand what we are trying to accomplish in Korean. In English with two sentences we can say:

> *I watched a movie yesterday. It was interesting.*

We have "indirectly described" the movie in the second sentence.
We can "directly modify" in just one powerful sentence.

> *The movie **that** I watched yesterday was interesting.*

English uses "that" immediately after the item we are directly modifying.

(past)   The movie **that** I *watched* is interesting.
(present)   The movie **that** I *am watching* is interesting.
(future)   The movie **that** I *will watch* is interesting.

Korean and English change the verb tense, but in Korean the verb always comes IMMEDIATELY before the item. In English it would look like this:

(past)   The *watched* movie is interesting.
(present)   The *am watching* movie is interesting.
(future)   The *will watch* movie is interesting.

Now that you understand direct modifying we can learn it in Korean.

● **16-2. (으)ㄹ Directly modifying verbs (future tense)**

We will start with future tense as you know it so well. Simply remove 거예요 from future tense then add a noun after it.

Future direct modifier form

할 거예요   →   할
먹을 거예요 →   먹을

먹을 음식	the food I will eat
갈 도시	the city I will go
운전할 차	the car I will drive
쓸 핸드폰	the cell phone I will use
읽을 책	the book I will read

Once we have a directly modified noun we can plug it into any sentence as if it was a simple noun.

Example sentences

1. 오늘 먹을 음식은 불고기예요.
   The food we will eat is bulgogi.

2. 제가 갈 도시는 커요.
   The city I will go to is big.

3. 제가 운전할 차는 빨라요.
   The car I will drive is fast.

4. 제가 쓸 핸드폰은 내일 도착해요.
   The cell phone I will use arrives tomorrow.

5. 제가 읽을 책은 어려워요.
   The book I will read is difficult.

Let's look at some more involved sentences.

1. 이건 여자 친구에게 줄 선물이에요.
   This is the gift I will give to my girlfriend.

2. 만날 사람이 있어서 명동에 가요.
   I'm going to Myeong-dong because there is someone I'm going to meet.

3. 도서관에는 읽을 책이 많아요.
   There are lots of books I'll read in the library.

4. 내일 아침에 먹을 빵을 이미 샀어요.
   I already bought the bread that I'll eat tomorrow morning.

5. 같이 놀 친구가 없어요.
   I don't have a friend who will hang out with me.

● 16-3. ~는 Directly modifying verbs (present tense)
VERB STEM + 는 is how you make the present tense direct modifier.

Present tense direct modifier form

하다　　→　하는
먹다　　→　먹는

Let's reuse the items from the last section to see how they change.

먹는 음식	the food I am eating
가는 도시	the city I am on the way to
운전하는 차	the car I am driving
쓰는 핸드폰	the cell phone I am using
읽는 책	the book I am reading

Example sentences
1. 제가 먹는 음식은 짜요.
   The food I am eating is salty.

2. 제가 가는 도시는 커요.
   The city I am on the way to is big.

3. 제가 운전하는 차는 빨라요.
   The car I am driving is fast.

4. 제가 쓰는 핸드폰은 아이폰이에요.
   The cell phone I am using is an iPhone.

5. 제가 읽는 책은 어려워요.
   The book I am reading is difficult.

● 16-4. Doing now VS habitual activities
The present tense direct modifier form (하는, 먹는 etc) has two possible meanings based on context. This can lead to some ambiguity.

The following sentence can have two completely different meanings.

제가 먹는 음식은 비싸요.
The food I am eating is expensive. (doing now)
The food I eat is expensive. (habitual)

This can be a problem when you are trying to say a specific thing. There are ways to FORCE the 하는, 먹는 verbs into the form you want.

Method 1: Word context

Force to DOING NOW
By adding words like 지금 (now) you can force the sentence into "doing now" form.

1. 제가 **지금** 먹는 음식은 비싸요.
   The food I am eating **now** is expensive.

Force to HABITUAL
Using words like 항상 (always) or 보통 (normally) you can force the sentence into "habitual" form.

2. 제가 **항상** 먹는 음식은 비싸요.
   The food I always eat is expensive.

3. 제가 **보통** 먹는 음식은 비싸요.
   The food I **normally** eat is expensive.

Method 2: Verb Tense

Force to DOING NOW
We can also change the tense of the verb to the ~고 있다 form to force it to always be "doing now" form without any ambiguity.

제가 **먹고 있는** 음식은 비싸요.
The food I **am eating** is expensive.

● **16-5. ~(으)ㄴ Directly modifying verbs (past tense)**
Past tense direct modifier form is made JUST like future tense except that instead of ㄹ you use ㄴ in its place.

Past tense direct modifier form

할 거예요   →   한
먹을 거예요 → 먹은

먹은 음식	the food I ate
간 도시	the city I went to
운전한 차	the car I drove
쓴 핸드폰	the cell phone I used
읽은 책	the book I read

Note: In English we like to use past tense with both the *direct modifier* and the following adjective / noun since it sounds more natural. The same is true for Korean. So to sound more natural we will use past tense in both cases.

Example sentences
1. 제가 먹은 음식은 짰어요.
   The food I ate was salty.

2. 제가 간 도시는 컸어요.
   The city I went to was big.

3. 제가 운전한 차는 빨랐어요.
   The car I drove was fast.

4. 제가 쓴 핸드폰은 낡았어요.
   The cell phone I used was old.

5. 제가 읽은 책은 무서웠어요.
   The book I read was scary.

Here are some more complicated examples.

Example conversation
1. A: 화요일에 백화점에서 산 물건은 어디에 있어요?
   B: 그날 산 것을 다 잃어버렸어요.
   A: 진짜요? 슬프네요.

   A: Where are the items you bought at the department store on Tuesday?
   B: I lost all of the things I bought that day.
   A: Oh really? That sure is sad.

2. A: 어떤 남자하고 결혼하고 싶어요?
   B: 오랫동안 한국어를 공부한 남자하고 결혼하고 싶어요.

   A: What type of man do you want to marry?
   B: I want to marry a man who has studied Korean for a long time.

● **16-6. Putting it all together for direct modifiers**
When there is a 받침 on the verb then you just add 을 (future), 는 (present), 은 (past) to the stem.

the apple I will eat

the apple I am eating

the apple I ate

When there isn't a 받침 on the verb then you just attach ㄹ (future), or ㄴ (past) to the stem. Notice that with present tense 는 is added regardless of if there is a 받침 or not.

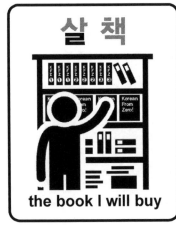

the book I will buy

the book I am buying

the book I bought

Example sentences
1. 제가 읽은 책의 제목은 모비딕이에요.
   The title of the book I read is Moby Dick.

2. 제가 읽을 책의 제목은 모비딕이에요.
   The title of the book I will read is Moby Dick.

3. 제가 읽는 책의 제목은 모비딕이에요.
   The title of the book I am reading is Moby Dick.

Special Information 특별 정보

Adjectives VS Nouns

Prior to learning how to *directly modify* with verbs, in book 1 we learned how to directly modify with adjectives. Adjectives do not directly modify in the "future" and "past" and ONLY use the present to describe the state of an object.

After learning how to directly modify with verbs, it's easy to mistake adjectives in direct modifier form as past tense since the (으)ㄴ pattern is used.

비싼 차	expensive car
작은 고양이	small cat
매운 음식	spicy food
나쁜 사람	bad person
예쁜 여자	beautiful girl

Also remember that adjectives with 있다 and 없다 in them, such as 재미있다, 맛있다, 재미없다, 맛없다 just add 는 to the verb stem.

재미있는 영화	interesting movie
맛없는 음식	tasteless food
재미없는 이야기	uninteresting story
맛있는 고기	delicious meat

● **16-7. 유명하다 (to be famous)**

TYPE	하다 adjectives	BASIC FORM	유명해

Example sentences

1. 싸이는 미국에서도 유명해요.
   PSY is famous in America also.

2. 브라질에는 유명한 축구 선수가 많아요.
   In Brazil there are many famous soccer players.

3. 제주도는 바다가 유명해서 사람들이 여름에 많이 가요.
   Jeju Island beaches are famous so in the summer many people go.

● 16-8. 팔다 (to sell)

TYPE	ㄹ irregular	BASIC FORM	팔아

The item being sold is marked with the 을/를 object marker.

Example sentences

1. 커피숍에서 케이크도 팔아요.
   Coffee shops also sell cakes too.

2. 그 CD 는 지금은 팔지 않아요.
   That CD isn't sold right now.

3. 쓰지 않는 물건은 팔거나 버리세요.
   Sell or throw away items you aren't using.

4. 저 식당에서는 맛있는 피자를 팔아요.
   They sell delicious pizza at that restaurant over there.

5. 어제 음식을 다 팔아서 지금은 못 팔아요.
   I sold all the food yesterday so now I can't sell anything.

● 16-9. Irregulars and direct modifier form

Irregular verbs are irregular because they don't follow the pattern of conjugation that the majority of other verbs follow. With direct modifier form the irregulars have a few irregularities.

HUGE IMPORTANT NOTE

The rules for irregulars are provided ONLY for reference. Please don't go crazy remembering all of the rules. Eventually the commonly used verbs will be learned through usage.

If you spend your energy on charts like the one that follows you will never move forward. Glance at it... use it for reference, then move on and keep learning.

The few mistakes you might make aren't as damaging as not moving forward. Think about all the people you know who speak English from foreign countries. You never focus on their many mistakes, and neither will Koreans focus on yours.

Use this chart as a reference for conjugating irregulars into direct modifier forms.

Irregular direct modifier pattern + sample verbs			
Irregular	**Future** the ~ that I will VERB	**Present** the ~ that is VERBing	**Past** the ~ that VERBed
ㄹ	no change	remove ㄹ add 는	ㄹ → ㄴ
팔다 (to sell)	팔 ~	파는 ~	판 ~
울다 (to cry)	울 ~	우는 ~	운 ~
놀다 (to play)	놀 ~	노는 ~	논 ~
ㄷ	ㄷ → ㄹ add 을	add 는	ㄷ → ㄹ add 은
듣다 (to listen)	들을 ~	듣는 ~	들은 ~
묻다 (to bury)	물을 ~	묻는 ~	물은 ~
싣다 (to load)	실을 ~	싣는 ~	실은 ~
ㅅ	remove ㅅ add 을	add 는	remove ㅅ add 은
짓다 (to build)	지을 ~	짓는 ~	지은 ~
낫다 (to heal)	나을 ~	낫는 ~	나은 ~
붓다 (to pour)	부을 ~	붓는 ~	부은 ~
ㅂ	remove ㅂ add 울	add 는	remove ㅂ add 운
줍다 (to pick up)	주울 ~	줍는 ~	주운 ~
돕다 (to help)	도울 ~	돕는 ~	도운 ~

Example sentences
1. 저는 매일 카페에서 커피를 파는 아르바이트를 하고 있어요.
   Everyday at the café I do a part-time job where I sell coffee.

2. 여동생이 사는 곳은 부산이에요.
   The place where my younger sister lives is Busan.

> 곳 is "place" in Korean. Don't confuse it with 것.

3. 오늘은 아는 노래만 부를 거예요.
   Today I am going to only sing songs that I know.

4. 엄마가 어제 만든 케이크를 먹고 싶어요?
   Do you want to eat the cake that mom made yesterday?

5. 내일 팔 김밥을 지금 만들고 있어요.
I am making the gimbap that I will sell tomorrow.

6. 제니퍼 씨가 지난 금요일에 논 클럽의 이름이 뭐였어요?
What was the name of the club that Jennifer hung out at last Friday?

● 16-10. 나오다 (to come out, to emerge, to appear (TV, movies))

TYPE	regular verb		BASIC FORM	나와

Example sentences
1. 오늘 집에서 아침 8 시에 나왔어요.
I came out of the house at 8 o'clock in the morning.

2. 다음 달에 아이폰 7 이 나올 거예요.
The iPhone 7 will come out next month.

3. 그 영화에 유명한 배우가 많이 나와요.
There are lots of famous actors in that movie.

4. 어제 집에서 나온 시간이 너무 늦어서 지하철을 못 탔어요.
The time that I left my house was too late, so I couldn't ride the subway.

5. 집에 물이 안 나와요.
We don't have any water in our house. (no water comes out)

● 16-11. 찾다 (to find, to search for), 찾아보다 (to search for)

찾다	TYPE	regular verb	BASIC FORM	찾아
찾아보다	TYPE	regular verb	BASIC FORM	찾아봐

The item being searched for or found is marked with 을/를.

The problem with 찾다
In English we have separate verbs for "find" and "search for" as they are two different activities. However, Korean has 찾다 for both activities. "To find" means the item you were looking for ***was found***, and "to search for" means the item you were looking for is ***still missing***.

The problem is, according to grammar logic, 찾았어요 can mean, "I found it." or "I looked for it." which are completely different meanings. However, in "Korean logic" 차잤어요 almost always translates to "I found it." However, if you say 찾고 있어요 now the meaning is always "I am searching for it." This will make you pull your hair out for sure!

There are two ways to avoid this confusion:

#1 - The context should help determine is 찾다 means "search" or "find".
For example, 못 찾았어요 can only mean "I couldn't find it".
And 30 분 동안 찾았어요 only makes sense as "I searched for 30 minutes".

#2 - Say 찾아보다 (to search for) instead of 찾다.
찾아보다 can ONLY mean "to search for" and never "to find".

Example sentences
1. 어제 지하철에서 잃어버린 휴대폰을 오늘 찾았어요.
   Today I found the cell phone that I lost yesterday on the subway.

2. 도서관에서 재미있는 책을 찾아봤지만 못 찾았어요.
   I looked for an interesting book at the library but I couldn't find one.

3. 어제 차 키를 잃어버렸지만 오늘 찾았어요.
   Yesterday I lost my car keys, but today I found them.

4. 지난 주에 잃어버린 강아지를 어제 공원에서 찾았어요.
   Yesterday I found the puppy that I lost last week at the park.

● 16-12. 입다 (to wear, to put on)

TYPE	regular verb	BASIC FORM	입어

입다 is the most commonly used generic way to say *wear*. However, other verbs will be introduced in book 3 for more specific ways of wearing. 입다 is used for the following clothing types:

dresses	shirts	pants
shorts	bras	sweaters
coats	pajamas	jackets
underwear	skirts	suits

Example sentences

1. 날씨가 너무 추워서 코트를 입었어요.
   The weather was very cold so I wore a coat.

2. 난 코트를 입었지만 아직 추워.
   I am wearing a coat but I am still cold.

3. 난 코트도 입고 스웨터도 입어서 춥지 않아.
   I'm wearing a coat and a sweater so I'm not cold.

4. 내일 입을 바지가 없어졌어요.
   The pants I am going to wear tomorrow have disappeared.

5. 다음 번에는 더 따뜻한 옷을 입을 거예요.
   Next time I will wear warmer clothes.

6. 오늘 밤에 입을 옷을 찾아볼게요.
   I'll look for clothes to wear tonight.

NOTE: 입는~ means "putting on at this very moment" and never just "wearing" in Korean. If you want to say "the girl wearing a dress" you must say the equivalent of "the girl who put on the dress" using 입은~.

7. 저기 드레스를 입은 여자가 제 여자 친구예요.
   The girl wearing the dress over there is my girlfriend.

● 16-13. 유행하다 (to be in fashion, to be trending)

TYPE	하다 verb	BASIC FORM	유행해

Koreans tend to be very in tune with fashion. 유행하다 is handy to know.

Example sentences

1. 백화점에 가서 유행하는 바지를 샀어요.
   I went to the department store and bought some fashionable pants.

2. 그 옷들은 요즘 너무 유행해서 난 입고 싶지 않아.
   Those clothes are too popular these days so I don't want to wear them.

3. 저 남자는 유행을 몰라. 항상 같은 옷만 입어.
   That guy doesn't know fashion. He always wears only the same clothes.

4. 지금 한국에선 짧은 치마가 유행하고 있어요.
   In Korea short skirts are popular now.

5. 이번 여름에는 짧은 머리가 유행할 거예요.
   This summer short hair will be popular.

> 머리 is short for 머리카락 which means "hair".

● **16-14 찍다 (to take a picture or film, to dip)**

TYPE	regular verb	BASIC FORM	찍어

찍다 is interesting since it can mean completely different things. The thing you are "dipping" or "taking a picture of" are marked with 을/를. The thing you are dipping into is marked with 에.

Example sentences
1. 공원에서 가족들하고 사진을 찍었어요.
   We took a picture with our family at the park.

2. 사진 좀 찍어 주세요.
   Please take a picture.

3. 저기에서 지금 영화를찍고 있어요.
   They are filming a movie over there right now.

4. 싱가폴에서 사진을 많이 찍었어요.
   I took many pictures in Singapore.
5. 작년에 찍은 사진을 다 잃어버렸어요.
   I lost all the pictures I took last year.

6. 나쵸를 치즈에 찍었어요.
   I dipped nachos into cheese.

7. 이번에 더 재미있는 사진을 찍으세요.
   This time take more interesting pictures.

● 16-15. 그런데, 근데 for background information

그런데 and its shorter version 근데 are commonly used in front of a statement to say "but" or "however", depending on the context. 하지만 might feel similar in meaning but 하지만 is much stronger and tends to show opposing information.

The information following 그런데 is normally just background information. It's sort of like saying "that's the case however…" or "yeah but…".

DO NOT get hung up on the English translation. In the following sentence the English is different, yet the meaning is still the same.

---

1. 영화 표를 두 장 받았어요. **그런데** 영화를싫어해요.
   I received 2 movie tickets. **However**, I don't like movies.
   I received 2 movie tickets. **But**, I don't like movies.
   I received 2 movie tickets. **Even though**, I don't like movies.

The goal is to give new information adding to the prior statement. It's our opinion that "however" is the most effective translation of 그런데. When the first sentence starts with 그런데 "But" sounds more natural.

Example sentences

1. 일본에 가고 싶어요. 그런데 일본어를 못 해요.
   I want to go to Japan. However, I can't speak Japanese.

2. 수업은 아직 안 끝났어요. 그런데 민수랑 약속이 두 시에 있어요.
   Class hasn't ended yet. However, I have an appointment with Minsu at 2 o'clock.

3. 빨리 달리고 싶어요. 그런데 다리가 아파요.
   I want to run fast. However, my legs hurt.

Special Information 특별 정보

Past Tense VS Present Tense (important!)
Korean usage of the *past tense* is often similar to how English uses the *present tense* form.

For example, in English we say, "I am married", or "I am divorced" and this shows the current state of the person. However, Koreans say, "I got married" or "I got divorced" to show that the person did the action.

These differences mean you might accidentally say, 결혼해요? (are you married?) when you should say 결혼했어요? (Did you get married?).

This past tense usage also pops up with the direct modifiers we learned in this lesson. If we follow the the rules taught in this lesson, the following translations should be correct:

1. 입은 옷 (the clothing that I wore)
2. 입는 옷 (the clothing that I am wearing)

With most verbs #2 works perfectly as taught, however with 입다 (to wear, to put on) if you say 입는 옷, it will never mean "the clothing that I am wearing", but instead, can only mean "the clothing that I wear" or "the clothing that I am putting on right now".

If you want to say "the clothing I am wearing" like we do in English you would have to say 입은 옷 which translates to "the clothing that I put on".

You could also say "the clothing I am wearing" using ~고 있다 form.

입고 있는 옷 (the clothing I am wearing)

16 Q&A 질문과 대답

1. 이 옷이 요즘 유행해요?
네. 유명한 선수가 입고 사진을 찍어서 유행해요.
네. 하지만 물건이 없어서 못 팔아요.

Are these clothes in fashion these days?
Yes. A famous athlete wore it and took a picture so it's in fashion.
Yes. However, I can't sell it too you since we don't have any stock (items).

2. 지난번 생일파티에 드레스를 입었어요?
아니오. 드레스를 찾지 못했어요.
네. 제가 입은 드레스는 아름다웠어요.

Did you wear a dress at your last birthday party?
No. I couldn't find a dress.
Yes. The dress I wore was beautiful.

3. 뭘 찾아요?
어제 산 물건이 없어져서 찾고 있어요.
책상 속에 티켓을 찾고 있었어요.

What are you looking for?
The items I bought yesterday are missing, so I am looking for them.
I am looking for tickets in the desk.

4. 지금 읽는 책은 유명해요?
제가 읽는 책은 지난달에 나와서 아직 안 유명해요.
당연하죠! 지금 서점에서 많이 팔고 있어요.
네. 제목은 모비딕이예요.

Is the book you are reading famous?
The book I am reading can't out last month, so it isn't famous yet.
Of course! It's selling a lot now at the book store.
Yes. The title is Moby Dick.

5. 같이 사진 찍고 싶어요?
싫어요. 지금 입은 옷이 별로 안 예뻐요.
좋아요. 근데 한번만 찍어요.

Do you want to take a picture together?
No. The clothing I am wearing (I put on) aren't that pretty.
Okay. However, just take one picture.

16 | Test Yourself Activities 연습 문제

● A16-1. Sentence Jumble
With the words provided, make Korean sentences that match the English. You can freely add particles, pronouns and conjugate verbs as needed.

1. 입다, 옷, 비싸다, 지금, 어제, 내일, 오늘

_____

The clothes that I am wearing today are expensive.

_____

The clothes that I wore yesterday were expensive.

_____

The clothes that I will wear tomorrow are not expensive.

2. 잊어버리다, 잃어버리다, 유행, 만들다, 지갑, 한국, 약속

_____

I lost my wallet.

_____

I forgot my appointment.

_____

Wallets made in Korea are fashionable.

3. 나오다, 영화, 어제, 언제, 재미있다

_____

Yesterday an interesting movie came out.

_____

When will the movie come out?

_____

The movie that came out yesterday is interesting.

● **A16-2. Fill in the blanks**
Fill in the missing word or particle based on the English sentence.

1. 지난달에 결혼_____ 친구가 지금 여행하고 있어요.
   My friend who got married last month is travelling now.

2. 어제 _____ 영화의 제목이 뭐였어요?
   What was the name of the movie you watched yesterday?

3. 제일 _____나라는 어디예요?
   Where is the country you want to go to the most?

4. 제가 항상 _____ 연필을 잃어버렸어요.
   I lost the pencil that I always use.

5. 내일 파티에서 _____ 옷을 이미 준비했어요.
   I already prepared the clothing that I will wear at the party tomorrow.

● **A16-3. Mark and Translate**
Mark the Korean sentence without mistakes then translate it.

1. ○ 저는 무겁을 가방을 싫어해요.
   ○ 저는 무겁는 가방을 싫어해요.
   ○ 저는 무거운 가방을 싫어해요.

   Translation:_____

2. ○ 작년에 돌아가신 아버지가 보고 싶어요.
   ○ 작년에 돌아가실 아버지가 보고 싶어요.
   ○ 작년에 돌아가시는 아버지가 보고 싶어요.

   Translation:_____

3. ○ 남동생이 항상 듣는 음악은 힙합이에요.
   ○ 남동생이 항상 들는 음악은 힙합이에요.
   ○ 남동생이 항상 들어는 음악은 힙합이에요.

   Translation:_____

16 | Self Test Answers 연습 문제 정답

● **A16-1. Sentence Jumble**
1. 제가 오늘 입은 옷은 비싸요.
   제가 어제 입은 옷은 비쌌어요.
   제가 내일 입을 옷은 비싸지 않아요.

2. 지갑을 잃어버렸어요.
   약속을 잊어버렸어요.
   한국에서 만든 지갑이 유행해요.

3. 어제 재미있는 영화가나왔어요.
   영화가언제 (나올 거예요 / 나와요)?
   어제 나온 영화는 재미있어요.

● **A16-2. Fill in the blanks**
1. 지난달에 결혼한 친구가 지금 여행하고 있어요.
2. 어제 본 영화의 제목이 뭐였어요?
3. 제일 가고 싶은 나라는 어디예요?
4. 제가 항상 쓰는 연필을 잃어버렸어요.
5. 내일 파티에서 입을 옷을 이미 준비했어요.

● **A16-3. Best Sentence Search**

1. ○ 저는 무겁을 가방을 싫어해요.
   ○ 저는 무겁는 가방을 싫어해요.
   ✓ 저는 무거운 가방을 싫어해요.
   Translation: I don't like heavy bags.

2. ✓ 작년에 돌아가신 아버지가 보고 싶어요.
   ○ 작년에 돌아가실 아버지가 보고 싶어요.
   ○ 작년에 돌아가시는 아버지가 보고 싶어요.
   Translation: I miss my father who passed away last year.

3. ✓ 남동생이 항상 듣는 음악은 힙합이에요.
   ○ 남동생이 항상 들는 음악은 힙합이에요.
   ○ 남동생이 항상 들어는 음악은 힙합이에요.
   Translation: The music that my younger brother normally listens
                 to is hip hop.

16 | Vocabulary Builder 단어 구축

Learning new words is not a game. But you can make it a game by installing "ANKI" or any other popular SRS (spaced repetition system) app on your smart phone.

■ Group M: Toys and Games 장난감과 게임

윷놀이	yut (traditional Korean board game)
가위 바위 보	paper scissors rock
화투	flower cards (card game)
숨바꼭질	hide-n-seek
까꿍	peek-a-boo
줄넘기	jump rope
장난감	toy
게임	game

■ Vocabulary Sentences

The following sentences might contain words and concepts not yet taught. Focus on the new vocabulary more than the grammar.

1. 설날에는 윷놀이를 해요.
   During Korean New Years, we play "yut".

2. 아이들은 가위 바위 보를 자주 해요.
   Kids play rock paper scissors often.

3. 한국 가족들은 만나면 화투를 쳐요.
   Often when Korean families meet, they play "hwatu".

4. 숨바꼭질을 할 때 사람이 많으면 더 재미있어요.
   If there are many people when you play hide-n-seek it's more interesting.

5. 아기에게 까꿍을 해 주면 좋아해요.
   Babies like it when you play peek-a-boo.

6. 학생들은 줄넘기를 하면서 운동해요.
   Student exercise by doing jump ropes.

17 Lesson 17: Before and After

17 | New Vocabulary 새로운 단어

New Nouns etc.

불	lights (in house etc)
에어컨	air conditioning
히터	heater
성격	personality
멋	style
맛	flavor, taste
새 차	new car

New Adjectives

멋있다	to be stylish, cool
밝다	to be bright
어둡다	to be dark

New Verbs

연락하다	to contact
사귀다	to date; go out with; make friends with
헤어지다	to break up, to split
버리다	to throw away
끄다	to turn off
켜다	to turn on

17 | Grammar and Usage 문법과 사용법

● 17-1. 있는, 없는 as direct modifiers

있다 and 없다 were not included in the examples concerning direct modifiers in the last lesson, however they are very commonly used in everyday Korean.

있는 is used to say things like 서울에 있는 가게 (a store in Seoul). Because 있다 also means "to have" you can also say things such as, 돈이 있는 사람 (people that have money). 없는 is simply the opposite of 있는.

Example sentences

1. 식탁 위에 있는 지갑은 누구의 것입니까?
   Who's is the wallet on the dining table?

2. 친구가 없는 사람들은 슬퍼요.
   People that have no friends are sad.

3. 우리 학교에는 돈이 있는 사람도 있고 없는 사람도 있어요.
   There are people with and people without money at our school.

● 17-2. The difference between ~하고 있는 and ~하는

The ongoing present tense form ~고 있다 taught in book 1 is commonly used as a direct modifier and generally has the same meaning as ~는.

Example sentences

1. 중국어를 배우고 있는 학생들
   This means, "students learning Chinese".

2. 중국어를 배우는 학생들
   This can mean both, "students who learn Chinese" and "students learning Chinese".

If you want to talk about people who learn Chinese, and not people actually learning at this very moment, then 배우는 is more grammatically correct.

But realistically both of these mean the same thing and most Koreans wouldn't be able to tell you why they are different.

● 17-3. ~전 (before) ~후 (after) nouns and times

By using ~전 and ~후 after nouns and time spans you can say things like 수업 전 (before class) and 수업 후 (after class). When using 전 and 후 you normally attach the time marker 에.

Example sentences

1. 일 년 전에 결혼했어요.
   I got married 1 year ago.

2. 한 달 후에 한국에 돌아올 거예요.
   I will return back to Korea after one month.

3. 삼 일 후에 대학생이 될 거예요.
   I will become a college student in three days.

Example conversation

1. A: 두 달 전에 한국에 왔지만, 아직 한국어를 잘 못해요.
   B: 괜찮아요! 시간이 걸릴 거예요.

   A: 2 months ago I came to Korea, but I still can't speak Korean well.
   B: It's okay! It will take time.

> Don't be confused. The first 전 in B: is short for 저는.

2. A: 수업 전에 뭐 해요?
   B: 전 보통 스타벅스에서 커피를 마셔요.
   A: 저도 같이 마시고 싶지만 아침에 일찍 일어나지 못해요.

   A: What do you do before class?
   B: I normally drink coffee at Starbucks.
   A: I also want to drink together but I can't wake up in the morning.

3. A: 2분 후에 지하철이 올 거예요. 빨리 오세요!
   B: 알았어요. 거의 도착했어요.

   A: 2 minutes from now the subway will come. Hurry up and come!
   B: I know. I have almost arrived.

4. A: 저녁을 먹은 후에 영화를보자.
   B: 그래.

   A: After eating dinner, Let's watch a movie
   B: Okay.

● **17-4. ~기 전 Before (verbs)**
To use "before" with a verb use the STEM + 기 전 pattern. It doesn't matter
if the stem has a 받침 you still just add 기 전.

Examples
1. 하기 전   before doing
2. 보기 전   before seeing
3. 가기 전   before going
4. 먹기 전   before eating
5. 끝나기 전   before it ends

Example sentences
1. 전화번호를 잊어버리기 전에 쓰세요.
   Before you forget the phone number write it down.

2. 처음에 한국에 가기 전에 한국어를 거의 매일 공부했어요.
   Before I went to Korea for the first time I studied Korean almost
   everyday.

3. 티비를 보기 전에 숙제를 해!
   Do your homework before you watch TV.

Example conversation
1. A: 오늘 몇 시에 집에 돌아와요?
   B: 아마 7 시쯤에 돌아갈 거예요.
   A: 왜 더 일찍 돌아오지 못해요?
   B: 집으로 돌아가기 전에 도서관에서 책을 빌리고 싶어요.

> The person at the house uses 돌아오다 (come home) and the one not   home uses 돌아가다 (go home).

   A: What time will you come home today?
   B: I will go home maybe around 7 o'clock.
   A: Why can't you come home earlier?
   B: Before I go home I want to borrow a book from the library.

2. A: 이 가방은 유행하기 전에 런던의 유명한 가게에서 샀어요.
   B: 얼마였어요?
   A: 20 만 원이었어요.
   B: 와! 싸네요!

   A: I bought this bag at a famous store in London before it was trendy.
   B: How much was it?
   A: It was 200,000 won.
   B: Wow! That's cheap!

● 17-5. ~(으)ㄴ 후(에) After (verbs)

To use "after" with a verb we will use the past tense direct modifier form taught in the last lesson. To say "after I did" you would say 한 후(에).

Example sentences

1. 영화가**끝난 후에** 친구랑 놀았어요.
   After the movie ended I hung out with friends.

2. 남자 친구를 **만난 후에** 식당에 갔어요.
   After meeting my boyfriend we went to a restaurant.

3. 술을 많이 **마신 후에** 머리가 아팠어요.
   After I drank a lot of alcohol my head hurt.

4. **공부한 후에** 저에게 다시 전화해 주세요.
   After studying call me again.

5. 낡은 차를 **판 후에** 새 차를 샀어요.
   After selling my old car I bought a new car.

● 17-6. 멋있다 (cool, stylish)

TYPE	regular adjective	BASIC FORM	멋있어

멋있다 literally means "to have style".

Example sentences

1. 우리 삼촌은 축구를 잘해서 정말 멋있어요.
   Because our uncle is good at soccer he is really cool.

2. 내 남자 친구가 학교에서 제일 친절하고 멋있어!
   My boyfriend is the kindest and most stylish boy in school!

3. 박민수 씨는 키가 크고 멋있는 옷을 많이 입어요.
   Minsu Park is tall and wears a lot of cool clothes.

4. 예성 씨는 노래를 부를 때 진짜 멋있어요.
   When Yesung sings he is really cool.

5. 조지는 갑자기 멋있어졌어요.
   George suddenly got cool.

> 예성 is a Korean singer and actor.
> He is a member of "Super Junior".

┌─── **Special Information 특별 정보** ───┐

멋지다 is a similar word to 멋있다. 멋지다 means "wonderful", "awesome" and other similar words. The meaning really isn't much different from 멋있다 as they both contain 멋 except that 멋지다 is a stronger meaning.

● **17-7. 밝다 (to be bright), 어둡다 (to be dark)**

밝다	TYPE	regular verb	BASIC FORM	밝아

어둡다	TYPE	ㅂ irregular adjective	BASIC FORM	어두워

Example sentences

1. 동생이 입고 있는 치마는 밝은 노란색이에요.
The skirt that my sibling is wearing is bright yellow.

2. 시험이 끝난 후에 학생들의 얼굴이 밝아졌어요.
After the test ends the student's faces got bright.

3. 일몰 후 서울이 점점 어두워졌어요.
After the sunset, Seoul gradually got dark.

4. 제 책상 옆에 있는 램프는 밝지 않아요.
The lamp next to my desk isn't bright.

5. 오늘은 꼭 어두워지기 전에 집에 돌아와!
Definitely come home before it gets dark today!

┌─── **Special Information 특별 정보** ───┐

밝다 (to be bright) and 어둡다 (to be dark) can be used to talk about a person or animal's personality. Typically you are talking about a change in the personality so you would say 밝아지다 (to become bright, brighten) and 어두워지다 (to become dark, darken).

1. 대니가 결혼한 후에 성격이 밝아졌네요.
After Danny got married his personally sure did brighten.

2. 대니는 아버지가 돌아가신 후에 성격이 어두워졌네요.
After Danny's father passed away his personally sure did darken.

● **17-8. 연락하다 (to contact, to keep in touch)**

TYPE	regular verb	BASIC FORM	그만둬

Remember that 연락 must be pronounced as 열락. The person you are contacting is marked with 에게 / 한테.

> **Example sentences**
> 1. 한국에 가기 전에 연락해 주세요.
>   Contact me before you go to Korea.
>
> 2. 선생님에게 연락했지만 아직 대답이 안 왔어요.
>   I contacted the teacher but he/she hasn't answered yet.
>
> 3. 주말에 너무 바빠서 연락을 못 했어요.
>   Since I was too busy on the weekend, I couldn't contact you.
>
> 4. 일이 끝난 후에 연락할게요.
>   I'll contact you after work ends.

● **17-9. 사귀다 (to date), 헤어지다 (to break up with)**

밝다	TYPE	regular verb	BASIC FORM	밝아
어둡다	TYPE	ㅂ irregular adjective	BASIC FORM	어두워

The person you break up with or date is marked with 와/과, 랑/이랑, or 하고.

> **Example sentences**
> 1. 일 년 정도 그녀와 사귀었어요.
>   I dated her for about one year.
>
> 2. 대학교에 입학한 후에 새로운 친구를 사귀었어요.
>   After entering college, I made new friends.
>
>   > 친구를 사귀다 means "to make friends".
>
> 3. 지난주에 남자 친구와 헤어져서 너무 외로워요.
>   I broke up with my boyfriend last week so I am really sad.
>
> 4. 둘이 사귀어요?
>   Are you two dating?
>
>   > 둘이 is commonly used to say "you two" and 우리둘이 means "us two"
>
> 5. 한달 전에 여자 친구랑 헤어진 후 매일 그녀가 꿈에 나와요.
>   After breaking up with my girlfriend 1 month ago, she appears in my dreams everyday.

● 17-10. 버리다 (to throw away)

TYPE	regular verb	BASIC FORM	버려

Example sentences

1. 여기에 쓰레기를 버리지 마세요.
   Don't throw away trash here.

2. 작년에 버린 책을 다시 읽고 싶어졌어요.
   I want to read the book again that I threw away last year.

> ~졌어요 here shows a change in the desire to read the book.

3. 싱크대 위의 칫솔이 너무 오래되어서(돼서) 버렸어요.
   The toothbrush on top of the sink was old so I threw it away.

4. 생각 없이 어제 산 만화책을 버렸어요.
   Without thinking I threw away the comic book that I bought yesterday.

● 17-11. 켜다 (to turn on), 끄다 (to turn off)

켜다	TYPE	regular verb	BASIC FORM	켜

끄다	TYPE	regular verb	BASIC FORM	꺼

Example sentences

1. 컴퓨터를 끄고 텔레비전을 켜세요.
   Turn off the computer and turn on the TV.

> ~졌어요 here shows the state of the lamp changing to "on".

2. 침대 옆의 램프가 이유 없이 켜졌어요.
   For no reason the lamp next to the bed turned on.

3. 영화관에서는 핸드폰을 항상 끄세요.
   Always turn off your phone in the movie theatre.

4. 여름에는 너무 더워서 항상 에어컨을 켜요.
   Since it's really hot in summer we always turn on the air conditioner.

5. 공부하기 전에 음악을 끄세요.
   Turn off the music before you study.

6. 자기 전에 텔레비전도 끄고 불도 끄세요.
   Before you sleep turn off the TV and also turn off the light.

17 | Q&A 질문과 대답

1. **언제 결혼했어요?**
   세 달 전에 결혼했어요.
   아직 결혼 안 했어요. 혼자 살아서 외로워요.

   When did you get married?
   I got married 3 months ago.
   I am not married yet. I am lonely because I live alone.

2. **남자친구 있어요?**
   연락하는 남자가 있어요.
   사귀는 남자가 있어요.
   오늘 헤어졌어요.

   Do you have a boyfriend?
   There is a boy I keep in touch with.
   There is a boy I am dating.
   I broke up today.

3. **왜 아직 안 자요?**
   불이 너무 밝아서 못 자요.
   밥을 먹은 후에 잘 거예요.

   Why won't you go to sleep yet?
   I can't sleep because the lights are too bright.
   I will sleep after I eat dinner.

4. **아버지가 새 차를 사 줬어요?**
   아니요. 어머니가 사 주었어요.
   네. 정말 멋있는 차를 사 줬지만 히터가 안 나와요.

   Did your father by a new car for you?
   No. My mother bought it for me.
   Yes. He bought a really cool car for me, but the heater isn't working.

5. **식탁 위에 있는 음식은 맛있어요?**
   별로 맛이 없어요.
   정말 맛있어서 다 먹고 싶어요..

   Is the food on the table tasty?
   It doesn't have that much taste.
   I want to eat it all because it is so tasty.

> Literally we are saying "the heater doesn't come out".

17 | Test Yourself Activities 연습 문제

● A17-1. Sentence Jumble

With the words provided, make Korean sentences that match the English.
You can freely add particles, pronouns and conjugate verbs as needed.

1. 히터, 어둡다, 밝다, 불, 에어컨, 끄다, 켜다, 춥다, 돕다

   _____

   It's dark. Please turn on the light.

   _____

   It's bright. Please turn off the light.

   _____

   It's hot. Please turn on the air conditioning.

2. 지난해, 나쁘다, 사람, 멋있다, 새 차, 성격, 사귀다, 좋다, 옷, 비싸다

   _____

   Stylish clothing is expensive.

   _____

   I want to date a cool person.

   _____

   The person I dated last year was cool, but his personality was bad.

3. 성격, 남동생, 춥다, 돕다, 밤, 아침, 어둡다, 밝다, 방

   _____

   My room is cold at night and hot in the morning.

   _____

   My room is dark at night and bright in the morning.

   _____

   My younger brother's personality is bright.

● A17-2. Fill in the blanks
Fill in the missing word or particle based on the English sentence.

1. 지난주에 남자 친구와 _____서 너무 외로워요.
   I broke up with my boyfriend last week so I am really sad.

2. 생각 없이 어제 산 만화책을 _____요.
   Without thinking I threw away the comic book that I bought yesterday.

3. 처음에 한국에 _____에 한국어를 거의 매일 공부했어요.
   Before I went to Korea for the first time I studied Korean almost everyday.

4. 영화가_____에 친구랑 놀았어요.
   After the movie ended I hung out with friends.

5. 식탁에 _____ 음식은 누구의 음식이에요?
   Whose food is the food on the table?

● A17-3. Mark and Translate
Mark the Korean sentence without mistakes then translate it.

1. ○ 사무실에 돌아가기 전에 화장실에 가고 싶어요.
   ○ 사무실에 돌아가기 후에 화장실에 가고 싶어요.
   ○ 사무실에 돌아갈 거예지만 화장실에 가기전 싶어요.

   Translation:_____

2. ○ 남자 친구랑 결혼하고 싶었지만 어젯밤에 헤어졌어요.
   ○ 남차 찐구랑 결혼하고 싶었지만 어젯밤에 헤어졌어요.
   ○ 남친 자구랑 결혼하고 십었지만 어젯밤에 헤어졌어요.

   Translation:_____

3. ○ 어두워기 전에 숙제를 다 했어요
   ○ 어둡기 후에 숙제를 다 할 거예요.
   ○ 어두워지기 전에 숙제를 다 했어요

   Translation:_____

17 | Self Test Answers 연습 문제 정답

● A17-1. Sentence Jumble

1. 어두워요. 불을 켜 주세요.
   밝아요. 불을 꺼 주세요.
   더워요. 에어컨을 켜 주세요.

2. 멋있는 옷은 비싸요.
   멋있는 사람(이랑 / 과 / 하고) 사귀고 싶어요.
   지난해에 사귄 사람은 멋있었지만 성격이 나빴어요.

3. 제 방은 밤에(는) 춥고 아침에(는) 더워요.
   제 방은 밤에(는) 어둡고 아침에(는) 밝아요.
   제 남동생의 성격이 밝아요.

● A17-2. Fill in the blanks

1. 지난주에 남자 친구와 <u>헤어져서</u> 너무 외로워요.

2. 생각 없이 어제 산 만화책을 <u>버렸어요</u>.

3. 처음에 한국에 <u>가기 전</u>에 한국어를 거의 매일 공부했어요.

4. 영화가<u>끝난 후</u>에 친구랑 놀았어요.

5. 식탁에 <u>있는</u> 음식은 누구의 음식이에요?

● A17-3. Best Sentence Search

1. ✓ 사무실에 돌아가기 전에 화장실에 가고 싶어요.
   ○ 사무실에 돌아가기 후에 화장실에 가고 싶어요.
   ○ 사무실에 돌아갈 거예지만 화장실에 가기전 싶어요.
   Translation: Before I return to the office I want to go to the bathroom.

2. ✓ 남자친구랑 결혼하고 싶었지만 어젯밤에 헤어졌어요.
   ○ 남차찐구랑 결혼하고 싶었지만 어젯밤에 헤어졌어요.
   ○ 남친자구랑 결혼하고 십었지만 어젯밤에 헤어졌어요.
   Translation: I wanted to marry with my boyfriend, but we broke up last night.

3. ○ 어두워기 전에 숙제를 다 했어요
   ○ 어둡기 후에 숙제를 다 할 거예요.
   ✓ 어두워지기 전에 숙제를 다 했어요
   Translation: Before it got dark I did all of my homework.

17 | Vocabulary Builder 단어 구축

You are probably sick of the cheesy things in this spot. It's a tough job making these puns. But someone has to do it.

■ Group N: Jobs 직업

의사	doctor
공무원	government worker
회사원	an office worker
소방관	firefighter
과학자	scientist
정치가	politician
간호사	nurse
작가	writer
가수	singer
요리사	chef

공무원

■ Vocabulary Sentences

The following sentences might contain words and concepts not yet taught. Focus on the new vocabulary more than the grammar.

1. 저는 의사가 되고 싶어요.
   I want to become a doctor.

2. 많은 한국사람들은 공무원이 되고 싶어해요.
   Many Koreans want to become government workers.

3. 회사원의 월급은 공무원보다 많아요.
   Office workers monthly salary is more than government workers.

4. 소방관은 목숨을 걸고 다른 사람을 구해 줘요.
   Firefighters risk their lives to save other people.

5. 과학자가 되고 싶으면 공부를 많이 해야 돼요.
   If you want to become a scientist, you need to study a lot.

6. 정직한 정치가가 없는 것 같아요.
   I think there aren't any honest politicians.

7. 제 누나는 남자 간호사와 사귀어요.
   My sister is dating a male nurse.

8. 작가가 되기 위해서는 책을 많이 읽어야 돼요.
   In order to become a writer, you need to read a lot of books.

9. 요즘 한국 가수들은 춤과 노래를 많이 연습해요.
   Recently Korean singers practice a lot of singing and dancing.

10. 많은 요리사는 통통해요.
    Many chefs are chubby.

SR! Super Review and Quiz #4: Lessons 16-17

SR | Question and Answer 질문과 대답

Hide the English and try to translate the Korean. Take notes on words or grammar patterns that confuse you then review them if necessary.

1. **Q: 이것은 뭐예요?**
   A: 제가 만든 음식이에요.
   A: 제가 지금 만드는 음식이에요.
   A: 맛없어서 버릴 음식이에요.

   Q: What's this food here?
   A: It's the food that I made yesterday.
   A: It's the food that I am making right now.
   A: It's food that I will throw away because it doesn't taste good.

2. **Q: 지금 뭘 하고 있어요?**
   A: 아르바이트를 하기 전에 밥을 먹고 있어요.
   A: 내일 같이 일할 사람이랑 밥을 먹고 있어요.
   A: 지금은 일하고 있지만, 일이 끝난 후 클럽으로 갈 거예요.

   Q: What are you doing right now?
   A: I am eating food before I do my part time job.
   A: I'm eating food with the people that I will work with tomorrow.
   A: I'm working right now, but after work ends I'll go to a night club.

3. **Q: 오늘 같이 운동할까요?**
   A: 오늘은 벌써 운동했지만 내일은 같이 할 수 있어요.
   A: 미안해요. 한 시간쯤 전에 했어요.
   A: 네, 같이 운동합시다.

   Q: Shall we exercise together today?
   A: Today, I've already exercised, but tomorrow we can do it together.
   A: Sorry. I exercised about an hour ago.
   A: Yes, let's exercise together.

4. **Q:** 지난 여름에 한국에 갔을 때 뭘 했어요?
   A: 재미있는 게임도 하고 무서운 영화도 봤어요.
   A: 거의 일만 해서 진짜 화가나요.
   A: 이번 가을에 가르칠 수업을 준비했어요.

Q: What did you do last summer?
A: I played a fun game and saw a scary movie.
A: I only mostly worked, so I'm really mad.
A: I prepared for a class that I will teach this fall.

SR | Conversation 대화 K-E

1. **Conversation between newly made friends.**
   A: 이 노래를 부른 가수를 알아요?
   B: 네, 노래도 잘 부르고 춤도 잘 추는 가수예요.
   A: 이름이 뭐예요?
   B: 보아예요. 일본에서도 아주 유명한 가수예요.

   A: Do you know the singer who sang this song?
   B: Yes, she's a singer that dances well and also sings well.
   A: What's her name?
   B: It's BOA. She's also a very famous singer in Japan.

2. **Polite conversation between neighbors.**
   미나: 조지 씨, 지금 뭐 해요?
   조지: 내일 파티에서 먹을 케이크를 만들고 있어요.
   미나: 빨리 먹고 싶어요.
   　　　조지 씨가 지난번에 만든 케이크가 정말 맛있었어요.
   조지: 그래요? 그럼 더 만들어 줄게요.

   Mina: George, what are you doing right now?
   George: I'm making the cake we'll eat tomorrow at the party.
   Mina: I want to eat right away.
   　　　The cake you made last time was really delicious.
   George: Really? Well then, I'll make more for you.

3. **Mixed conversation between student and a mean teacher.**

요코: 선생님, 이건 뭐예요?

선생님: 다음 주 매일 아침마다 할 숙제야.

요코: 와! 하지만 숙제는 싫어요.

선생님: 싫어해? 그럼 저녁마다 할 숙제도 줄게.

Yoko: Teacher, what is this?

Teacher: It's homework that you will do next week each morning every day.

Yoko: Wow! But, I don't like homework.

Teacher: You don't like it? Then I will also give you homework to do each evening.

4. **Casual conversation between two friends**

준호: 이 사진은 어디에서 찍었어?

요코: 작년 크리스마스에 교회에서 찍은 사진이야.

준호: 요코 씨 옆에 있는 이 남자는 누구야?

요코: 몰라. 그날 교회에서 처음 만난 남자야.

Junho: Where did you take this picture?

Yoko: It's a picture I took on Christmas day at the church.

Junho: Who is this man next to you in the picture?

Yoko: I don't know. It's a man I met that day for the first time at church.

SR | **Quiz Yourself 퀴즈**

● 1. Particle and conjugation check

Properly conjugate all verbs and adjectives and add any required particles.
Then on the following line translate the completed sentence into English.
MAINTAIN THE SAME ORDER and only add particles when required.

Sample
Ex. 이것 / 미국 / 오다 (past) / 과일
Combined:　이것은 미국에서 온 과일입니다.
Translation:　<u>This is a fruit that came from America.</u>

---

1. 이 사진 / 어제 / 찍다 / 사진 / 이다

   Combined: _____

   Translation:_____

2. 지금 / 팔다 / 책 / 무슨 / 책 / 이다

   Combined: _____

   Translation:_____

3. 지난 / 여름 / 가다 / 도시 / 런던 / 이다

   Combined: _____

   Translation:_____

4. 어제 / 마시다 / 음료수 / 맛있다 (past)

   Combined: _____

   Translation:_____

5. 내일 / 타다 / 비행기 / 어디 / 가다

   Combined: _____

   Translation:_____

● **2. Translation**
If the following sentence is in English, translate it into Korean.
If the following sentence is in Korean, translate it into English.

> Sample
> Ex. 가구를 사기 전에 한번 앉으세요.
> Translation: <u>Before buying furniture, sit on it once.</u>
>
> Ex. After I eat, I'll go.
> Translation: <u>밥을 먹은 후에 갈 거예요.</u>

1. Before exercising, I want to take a nap for 10 minutes.

    Translation:_____

2. The car that I'm driving tomorrow is a Hyundai.

    Translation:_____

3. I ate the sandwich that my wife made me in the morning.

    Translation:_____

4. 어제 읽은 책은 어디에 있어요?

    Translation:_____

5. 이것은 운동하기 전에 마실 물이에요.

    Translation:_____

6. 이 약은 밥을 먹은 후에 먹을 약이에요.

    Translation:_____

● **3. Fill in the Blank**

Read the conversation, then from the provided list choose the Korean that makes sense for the blank portion. Translations are in the answer key.

1. **Co-workers are discussing plans.**
   A: 이번 겨울에 여행 하고 싶은 나라가 있어요?
   B: 네, 이번 겨울에는 유럽에 있는 나라를 여행할 거에요.
   A: 유럽에 있는 어떤 나라에 가고 싶어요?
   B: _____ 나라에 가고 싶어요.

   ○ 예쁜 산 보고 싶어
   ○ 음식이 맛있는
   ○ 구경을 많이 할 수 있는
   ○ 영어를 잘 못해서

2. **Co-workers are discussing plans.**
   A: 넌 내일 이 식당에서 뭘 먹을 거야?
   B: 이 식당은 내가 먹을 수 있는 음식이 없어.
   A: 그런데 여기에는 _____이 많아.
   B: 나는 지금 다이어트해서 못 먹어.

   ○ 네가 항상 먹는 음식
   ○ 네가 절대 안 먹는 음식
   ○ 귀여운 동물
   ○ 네가 빨리 먹어 싶은 음식

3. **Co-workers talking prior to lunch.**
   A: 아이고! 지갑을 잃어버렸어요.
   B: 어디서?
   A: 지하철에서 내릴 때 잃어버렸어요. 아마도...
   B: 그래요? 그럼 제가 돈을 빌려 줄_____.
   A: 고맙습니다!

   ○ 겠어요.
   ○ 게요.
   ○ 개요.
   ○ 께요.

4. A newlywed is talking to his friend who has been married for years.

A: 결혼을 _____ 무엇이 달라요?

B: 항상 집에서 나를 기다리는 사람이 있어요.

A: 와! 좋네요!

B: 아니요, 우리 집에 있는 사람은 제 월급만 기다려요.

○ 할 전과 하기 후는
○ 하기 전과 한 후는
○ 하기 전과 할 후는
○ 할 전과 한 후은

SR | Answer Key 대답 키

● 1. Particle and conjugation check

1. 이 사진은 어제 찍은 사진(입니다 / 이에요).
   This is a picture that I took yesterday.

2. 지금 파는 책은 무슨 책(입니까 / 이에요)?
   What's the book you are selling right now?

3. 지난 여름에 간 도시는 런던(입니다 / 이에요).
   The city that I went to last summer is London.

4. 어제 마신 음료수는 맛있었어요.
   The beverage that I drank yesterday was delicious.

5. 내일 탈 비행기는 어디로 가요?
   Where does the plane you are taking tomorrow go?

● 2. Translation

1. 운동하기 전 10 분 동안 자고 싶어요.

2. (제가) 내일 운전할 차는 현대예요.

3. 아내가 아침에 만들어준 샌드위치를 먹었어요.

4. Where's the book that you read yesterday?

5. This is the water that I will drink before exercising.

6. This medicine is a medicine that you take after eating food / a meal.

● **3. Fill in the Blank**

1. A: Is there a country you want to travel to this winter?
   B: Yes. I will visit countries in Europe this winter.
   A: What country in Europe do you want to visit?
   B: I want to go to a country that <u>I can do a lot of sightseeing.</u>

   ○ 예쁜 산 보고 싶어
   ○ 음식이 맛있는
   ✓ 구경을 많이 할 수 있는
   ○ 영어를 잘 못해서

2. A: What are you going to eat in this restaurant tomorrow?
   B: This restaurant doesn't have any food I can eat.
   A: Why can't you eat? There is a lot of <u>food that you always eat</u> here.
   B: I'm currently on a diet. That's why I cannot eat.

   ✓ 네가 항상 먹는 음식
   ○ 네가 절대 안 먹는 음식
   ○ 귀여운 동물
   ○ 네가 빨리 먹어 싶은 음식

3. A: Oh man! I lost my wallet!
   B: Where at?
   A: When I got off of the subway I lost it. Maybe…
   B: Is that so? Well then, I <u>will</u> loan money to you.
   A: Thank you!

   ○ 겠어요.
   ✓ 게요.
   ○ 개요.
   ○ 께요.

4. A: What's different <u>before and after</u> marriage?
   B: There is always someone waiting for me at home.
   A: Wow! That sure is nice!
   B: No, the person at my house is waiting just for my monthly salary.

   ○ 할 전과 하기 후는
   ✓ 하기 전과 한 후는
   ○ 하기 전과 할 후는
   ○ 할 전과 한 후은

Verb and Adjective Reference Guide

This is an alphabetical list of all the verbs introduced in this book.

English Meaning	Korean Verb	Lesson
to answer	대답하다	5
to apologize	사과하다	11
to appear, to be seen	보이다	12
to arrive	도착하다	5
to be bashful, shy, embarrassed	부끄럽다	10
to be beaten, old, worn	낡다	12
to be beautiful	아름답다	14
to be born	태어나다	14
to be bright	밝다	17
to be clean	깨끗하다	5
to be comfortable, convenient	편하다	14
to be continue on, continued	계속되다	12
to be continued, continue on	계속되다	12
to be convenient, comfortable	편하다	14
to be cool. stylish,	멋있다	17
to be dark	어둡다	17
to be depressed	우울하다	11
to be dirty	더럽다	5

to be embarrassed, shy, bashful	부끄럽다	10
to be exhausted, rough	힘들다	6
to be famous	유명하다	16
to be fulfilled, to be happy	행복하다	11
to be happy, to be fulfilled	행복하다	11
to be heavy	무겁다	13
to be in fashion, trending	유행하다	16
to be inconvenient, uncomfortable	불편하다	14
to be kind	친절하다	13
to be late	늦다	13
to be light	가볍다	13
to be mad	화가나다	11
to be new	새롭다	12
to be not kind	불친절하다	13
to be old, worn, beaten	낡다	12
to be prepared	준비되다	12
to be reserved	예약되다	12
to be roomy, spacious, wide	넓다	5
to be rough, exhausted	힘들다	6
to be sad, lonely	외롭다	11
to be scared	무섭다	11
to be seen, to appear	보이다	12
to be short	키가 작다	15

to be shy, embarrassed, bashful	부끄럽다	10
to be sleepy	졸리다	6
to be slow	느리다	14
to be spacious, roomy, wide	넓다	5
to be stylish, cool	멋있다	17
to be tall	키가 크다	15
to be tired, to be tiring	피곤하다	6
to be trending, in fashion	유행하다	16
to be uncomfortable, inconvenient	불편하다	14
to be warm	따뜻하다	5
to be wide, spacious, roomy	넓다	5
to be worn, old, beaten	낡다	12
to become	되다	7
to become broken / shattered	깨지다	6
to break up, to split	헤어지다	17
to break, to shatter	깨다	6
to build	짓다	16
to bury	묻다	16
to buy	사다	6
to buy for someone	사 주다	6
to cancel	취소하다	10
to carry, to hold, to lift, to raise	들다	14
to come out	나오다	16

to contact	연락하다	17
to continue	계속하다	10
to continue	계속하다	12
to cry	울다	15
to cry	울다	16
to dance	춤을 추다	14
to date, go out with, make friends with	사귀다	17
to depart	출발하다	5
to die	죽다	14
to disappear, to run out	없어지다	15
to do	하다	6
to do a part-time job	아르바이트하다	15
to do for someone	해 주다	6
to do homework	숙제하다	5
to drive	운전하다	7
to end	끝나다	5
to exercise	운동하다	5
to express anger	화를 내다	11
to fight	싸우다	11
to find	찾다	16
to forget	잊어버리다	13
to go out with, date, make friends with	사귀다	17
to go sightseeing, to watch	구경하다	15

to grab	잡다	12
to have a meeting	미팅하다	5
to have, to hold	가지다	14
to heal	낫다	16
to help	돕다	16
to hold, to carry, to lift, to raise	들다	14
to hug	안다	12
to keep, to protect	지키다	10
to laugh	웃다	15
to lift, to carry, to hold, to raise	들다	14
to listen	듣다	16
to live	살다	8
to load	싣다	16
to loan, to borrow, to rent	빌리다	8
to look for, to search	찾아보다	16
to love	사랑하다	5
to make	만들다	6
to make a promise	약속하다	10
to make friends with, date, go out with	사귀다	17
to make up	화해하다	11
to oversleep	늦잠을 자다	15
to pass away	돌아가시다	14
to pay, to put out	내다	10

to phone / call	전화하다	5
to pick up	줍다	16
to play	놀다	16
to pour	붓다	16
to practice	연습하다	5
to prepare	준비하다	12
to question	질문하다	5
to raise, to carry, to hold, to lift	들다	14
to reserve	예약하다	12
to rest, to take a break	쉬다	8
to return, to come back	돌아오다	5
to return, to go back	돌아가다	5
to run	달리다	7
to run out, to disappear	없어지다	15
to sell	팔다	16
to sell	팔다	16
to shatter, break	깨다	6
to shower	샤워하다	5
to sing	노래하다	5
to sing a song	노래를 부르다	14
to sleep	잠을 자다	15
to study	공부하다	5
to swim	수영하다	5

to take a nap	낮잠을 자다	15
to take a picture or film, to dip	찍다	16
to take time	걸리다	8
to talk, to chat	이야기하다	10
to teach	가르치다	13
to throw away	버리다	17
to travel	여행하다	5
to turn off	끄다	17
to turn on	켜다	17
to wait	기다리다	5
to wear, to put on	입다	16
to work	일하다	5
to write	쓰다	6
to write for someone	써 주다	6

Popular Korean Boy Names

Popular Korean Boy Names Top 10		
Rank	1968	1975
#1	성호 achieve goodness	정훈 teaching righteous
#2	영수 paving road	성호 achieve goodness
#3	영호 good road	성훈 achieve meritorious deed

#4	영철 bright road	성진 true achievement
#5	정호 understand brightness	정호 understand brightness
#6	영진 truest road	상훈 achieve greatness
#7	병철 combine brightness	성민 achieve strength
#8	진호 true happiness	영진 truest road
#9	성수 achieve purity	상현 even more intelligent
#10	재호 happy again	준호 name of example
Rank	1978	1988
#1	정훈 teaching righteous	지훈 teach intelligence
#2	성훈 achieve meritorious deed	성민 achieve strength
#3	상훈 achieve greatness	현우 kind and righteous help
#4	성진 true achievement	정훈 teaching righteous
#5	지훈 teach intelligence	동현 one goodness
#6	성호 achieve goodness	준영 following the light
#7	진호 true happiness	민수 collect cleverness
#8	준호 name of example	준호 name of example
#9	성민 achieve strength	상현 even more intelligent
#10	민수 collect cleverness	진우 truly sufficient

Popular Korean Boy Names Top 10

Rank	1998	2005
#1	동현 one goodness	민준 strong example
#2	지훈 teach intelligence	현우 kind and righteous help
#3	성민 achieve strength	동현 one goodness
#4	현우 kind and righteous help	준혁 following the light
#5	준호 name of example	민재 clever talent
#6	민석 protect the gentle	도현 righteous path
#7	민수 collect cleverness	지훈 teach intelligence
#8	준혁 following the light	준영 following the light
#9	준영 following the light	현준 comparable kindness
#10	승현 continue sunlight	승민 continue strength
Rank	2008	2013
#1	민준 strong example	민준 strong example
#2	지훈 teach intelligence	서준 comparable wisdom
#3	현우 kind and righteous help	주원 best life
#4	준서 deepen wisdom	하준 astonishing intelligence
#5	우진 true friend	예준 excellent talent
#6	건우 stand above friends	준우 collect blessings
#7	예준 excellent talent	도윤 guiding light
#8	현준 comparable kindness	지후 knowing warmth
#9	도현 righteous path	준서 deepen wisdom
#10	동현 one goodness	지호 knowing goodness

Popular Korean Girl Names

Popular Korean Girl Names Top 10		
Rank	**1968**	**1975**
#1	미경 beautiful sight	미영 beautiful fame and fortune
#2	미숙 beautiful achievement	은정 lasting purity
#3	경희 sight of happiness	은주 lasting beauty
#4	경숙 achieving joy	은영 lasting fame and fortune
#5	영숙 Jade road	현주 true beauty
#6	미영 beautiful fame and fortune	은경 lasting brightness
#7	영미 lasting beauty	지영 intelligent wealth and fame
#8	정희 fathoms happiness	미경 beautiful sight
#9	정숙 fast understanding	현정 true compassion
#10	현숙 true cleanliness	미정 beautiful will
Rank	**1978**	**1988**
#1	지영 intelligent wealth and fame	지혜 wisdom
#2	은정 lasting purity	지은 blessing of wisdom
#3	미영 beautiful fame and fortune	수진 calm water
#4	현정 true compassion	혜진 true blessing
#5	은주 lasting beauty	은지 knowing blessing
#6	은영 lasting fame and fortune	지영 intelligent wealth and fame
#7	현주 true beauty	아름 beauty
#8	선영 shining fame	지현 true wisdom
#9	지연 flowering intelligence	지연 flowering intelligence
#10	민수 collect cleverness	진우 truly sufficient

Popular Korean Girl Names Top 10		
Rank	1998	2005
#1	유진 true softness	서연 indwelling beauty
#2	민지 clever wisdom	민서 indwelling cleverness
#3	수빈 exceptional shine	서현 sparkling dew at dawn
#4	지원 best intelligence	수빈 exceptional shine
#5	지현 true wisdom	유진 true softness
#6	지은 blessing of wisdom	민지 clever wisdom
#7	현지 kind intelligence	서영 indwelling fame and fortune
#8	은지 knowing blessing	지원 best intelligence
#9	예진 true talent	수민 receiving warmth
#10	예지 true intelligence	예원 best cleverness
Rank	2008	2013
#1	서연 indwelling beauty	서윤 indwelling light
#2	민서 indwelling cleverness	서연 indwelling beauty
#3	지민 clever will	민서 indwelling cleverness
#4	서현 sparkling dew at dawn	서현 sparkling dew at dawn
#5	서윤 indwelling light	지민 clever will
#6	예은 widom and blessing	하은 providing comfort
#7	하은 providing comfort	하윤 providing beauty
#8	지우 bountiful wisdom	지유 possessing intelligence
#9	수빈 exceptional shine	지우 bountiful wisdom
#10	윤서 providing wisdom	지아 knowing purity

Glossary
E-K

1

1 day - 일 일
1 day - 하루
1 hour - 한 시간
1 minute - 일 분
1 month - 한 달
1 time - 한 번
1 week - 일 주
10 days - 십 일
10 hours - 열 시간
10 minutes - 십 분
10 months - 열 달
10 times - 열 번
10 weeks - 십 주
11 days - 십일 일
11 hours - 열한 시간
11 minutes - 십일 분
11 months - 열한 달
11 times - 열한 번
11 weeks - 십일 주
12 days - 십이 일
12 hours - 열두 시간
12 minutes - 십이 분
12 months - 열두 달
12 times - 열두 번
12 weeks - 십이 주

2

2 days - 이 일
2 days - 이틀
2 hours - 두 시간
2 minutes - 이 분
2 months - 두 달
2 times - 두 번
2 weeks - 이 주

3

3 days - 삼 일
3 days - 사흘
3 hours - 세 시간
3 minutes - 삼 분
3 months - 세 달
3 times - 세 번
3 weeks - 삼 주

4

4 days - 사 일
4 hours - 네 시간
4 minutes - 사 분
4 months - 네 달
4 times - 네 번
4 weeks - 사 주

5

5 days - 오 일
5 hours - 다섯 시간
5 minutes - 오 분
5 months - 다섯 달
5 times - 다섯 번
5 weeks - 오 주

6

6 days - 육 일
6 hours - 여섯 시간
6 minutes - 육 분
6 months - 여섯 달
6 times - 여섯 번
6 weeks - 육 주

7

7 days - 칠 일
7 hours - 일곱 시간

7 minutes - 칠 분

7 months - 일곱 달

7 times - 일곱 번

7 weeks - 칠 주

8

8 days - 팔 일

8 hours - 여덟 시간

8 minutes - 팔 분

8 months - 여덟 달

8 times - 여덟 번

8 weeks - 팔 주

9

9 days - 구 일

9 hours - 아홉 시간

9 minutes - 구 분

9 months - 아홉 달

9 times - 아홉 번

9 weeks - 구 주

A

a doll - 인형

a little - 조금, 좀

a lot, many - 많이

about~ - ~정도

academy, private education academy - 학원

after a short while, later - 이따가

after school academy - 학원

air conditioning - 에어컨

airfare - 항공료

alcohol, liquor - 술

all - 다

almost~ - 거의

alone, myself - 혼자

already - 이미

always - 항상

always - 항상

an office worker - 회사원

answer - 대답

antibiotic - 항생제

around~ - ~쯤

arrival - 도착

art - 예술

aspirin - 아스피린

autumn - 가을

autumn, fall - 가을

B

back side, behind, backward direction - 뒤쪽

backward direction, behind, back side - 뒤쪽

baggage, luggage - 짐

bakery - 빵집

barbecue restaurant - 고깃집

battlefield - 전쟁터

beach - 해변

behind, back side, backward direction - 뒤쪽

below, underneath, down direction, lower side - 아래쪽

bias (toward), prejudice (against) - 편견

big city, metropolis - 대도시

birth control - 피임약

blanket - 담요

bookcase - 책장

boss, president (of company) - 사장님

bowl - 그릇

bread - 빵

bus fare - 버스비

business meeting - 회의

but, however - 그런데

but, however, even though - 근데

but, however, even though - 그런데

butterfly - 나비

C

café - 카페

California - 캘리포니아

camping - 캠핑

car keys - 차 키

card (credit card) - 카드(신용카드)

cash - 현금

chef - 요리사

chopsticks - 젓가락

circle - 원

city - 도시

clouds - 구름

club, night club - 클럽

comics - 만화책

company worker, employee - 회사원

completely - 완전히

connection - 연결

continent - 대륙

cost, fee - 비용

cough medicine - 기침약

cousin - 사촌

cow - 소

crane - 학

cream, ointment - 연고

crime - 범죄

criminal - 범죄자

cup - 컵

customer, guest - 손님

D

Danny - 대니

day - 날

day off - 휴가

day, one day - 하루

days - ~일

definitely - 꼭

departure - 출발

desert - 사막

dessert - 디저트

dinner table - 식탁

dish, plate - 접시

doctor - 의사

dolphin - 돌고래

down direction, underneath, lower side - 아래쪽

driver's license - 운전면허증

E

earrings - 귀걸이

east; east side; east direction - 동쪽

education - 교육

Emily - 에밀리

employee, company worker - 회사원

error, mistake - 잘못

Europe - 유럽

even though, however, but - 근데

even though, however, but - 그런데

ever, never, not at all, totally - 전혀

exercise - 운동

exercise, physical activity - 운동

eye drops - 안약

F

fall, autumn - 가을

fan (of singer, tv show etc) - 팬

fee based (to have a charge) - 유료

fee, cost - 비용

feelings, mood - 기분

firefighter - 소방관

fishing - 낚시

flavor, taste - 맛

flower cards (card game) - 화투

for a long time - 오랫동안

for no reason, without reason - 이유 없이

forest - 숲

fork - 포크

forward direction, in front, front side - 앞쪽

fox - 여우

free (no charge) - 무료

freezer - 냉동고

front side, in front, forward direction - 앞쪽

G

garbage can - 쓰레기통

George - 조지

ghost, spirit - 귀신

giraffe - 기린

golf - 골프

goodness!, oh my!, ouch! (sigh...) - 아이고

government worker - 공무원

grade - 점수

gradually - 점점

grasslands - 초원

guest, customer - 손님

guitar - 기타

H

heater - 히터

here; this way, side, direction - 이쪽

hexagon - 육각형

hide-n-seek - 숨바꼭질

hiking - 등산

hill - 언덕

hobby - 취미

homework - 숙제

Hongdae (place in Seoul) - 홍대

horror movie - 공포영화

hours - ~시간

How many days? - 며칠? (not 몇 일)

How many hours? - 몇 시간?

How many minutes? - 몇 분?

How many months? - 몇 달?

How many times? - 몇 번?

How many weeks? - 몇 주?

how many, how much - 얼마나

how much, how many - 얼마나

however, but, even though - 근데

however, but, even though - 그런데

I

I (casual) - 난 short for 나는

I (polite) - 전 short for 저는

ice - 얼음

immediately, right away - 곧

in front, front side, forward direction - 앞쪽

in, on, at (shortened form) - 서 short for 에서

in, on, at (stressed) - 에선 short for 에서는

injection, shot - 주사

interest - 관심

international - 국제

internet - 인터넷

iPhone - 아이폰

island - 섬

item; product - 물건

J

jacket - 자켓

Jennifer - 제니퍼

Jessie - 제시

joke - 농담

jump rope - 줄넘기

K

knee(s) - 무릎

knife - 칼

Korean language (similar to 한국어) - 한국말

L

lake - 호수

lamp - 램프

language - 언어

last time - 지난번

last~ - 지난

later - 나중에

later, after a short while - 이따가

leave of absence from school - 휴학

letters, text (message) - 문자

lightning - 번개

lights (in house etc) - 불

lion - 사자

liquor, alcohol - 술

lodging expenses - 숙박비

long time ago; the old days - 옛날

love - 사랑

lower side, underneath, down direction - 아래쪽

luggage, baggage - 짐

M

machine - 기계

major - 전공

many, a lot - 많이

married life - 결혼생활

meeting - 미팅

method - 방법

metropolis, big city - 대도시

microwave - 전자레인지

minor - 부전공

minutes - ~분

mistake, error - 잘못

monthly pay - 월급

months (Chinese) - ~개월

months (Korean) - ~달

mood, feelings - 기분

more~, ~er - 더~

most~, ~est - 제일~

mountain - 산

muscles - 근육

myself, alone - 혼자

N

name, title - 제목

nap - 낮잠

necklace - 목걸이

never ever - 절대로

never, not at all, totally, ever - 전혀

new car - 새 차

next time - 다음 번

next, the side - 옆쪽

next~ - 다음

night club, club - 클럽

No. ~ exit (train stations etc) - ~번 출구

normally - 보통

North Korea - 북한

north; north side; north direction - 북쪽

not at all, never, totally, ever - 전혀

not much - 별로

not yet - 아직

nurse - 간호사

O

often - 자주

often - 자주

oh my!, goodness!, ouch! (sigh...) - 아이고

ointment, cream - 연고

on top, upper side, up direction - 위쪽

one day, day - 하루

ouch! (sigh...), goodness!, oh my! - 아이고

over there; that way, side, direction - 저쪽

owl - 올빼미

P

paper scissors rock - 가위 바위 보

parrot - 앵무새

part time job - 아르바이트

peek-a-boo - 까꿍

pentagon - 오각형

perfume, scent - 향기

period of time - ~동안

personality - 성격

phone - 전화

physical activity, execsise - 운동

pill - 알약

pillow - 베개

plate - 접시

plate, dish - 접시

play (theater) - 연극

player - 선수

police - 경찰

politician - 정치가

politics - 정치

power outlet - 콘센트

practice - 연습

prejudice (against), bias (toward) - 편견

preparations - 준비

prescription - 처방전

president (of company), boss - 사장님

prison - 감옥

private education academy, academy - 학원

professor - 교수님

promise - 약속

Q

question - 질문

quickly, right away - 빨리

quietly - 조용히

R

razor - 면도기

recently, these days - 요즘

rectangle - 직사각형

Reed - 리드

refrigerator - 냉장고

report - 보고서

Republic of Korea - 대한민국

reservations - 예약

right away, immediately - 곧

right away, quickly - 빨리

river - 강

rock, stone - 바위

rule - 규칙

S

safety belt (seat belt) - 안전벨트

scent, perfume - 향기

school expenses - 학비

scientist - 과학자

score - 점수

screen (LCD) - 액정

scuba diving - 스쿠버 다이빙

secretary - 비서

semester - 학기

shampoo - 샴푸

shape - 모양

shot, injection - 주사

shower - 샤워

side dish - 반찬

silkworm - 번데기

Singapore - 싱가폴

singer - 가수

sink - 싱크대

slightly - 약간

slowly - 천천히

snack - 간식

soap - 비누

sofa - 소파

sometimes - 가끔

song - 노래

south; south side; south direction - 남쪽

spicy rice cake (stir fried) - 떡볶이

spirit, ghost - 귀신

spoon - 숟가락

spring - 봄

square - 사각(형)

stairs - 계단

stone, rock - 바위

storm - 폭풍

stream - 개울(가)

studies - 공부

studying abroad - 유학

style - 멋

stylish, cool - 멋있다

suddenly - 갑자기

summer - 여름

sunrise - 일출

sunset - 일몰

swimming - 수영

T

taste, flavor - 맛

taxes - 세금

taxi fare - 택시비

text (message), letters - 문자

that - 그건 short for 그것은

that - 그게 short for 그것이

that day - 그날

that direction, way, side; over there - 저쪽

that direction, way, side; there - 그쪽

that side, way, direction; over there - 저쪽

that side, way, direction; there - 그쪽

that way, side, direction; over there - 저쪽

that way, side, direction; there - 그쪽

the side, next - 옆쪽

there; that way, side, direction - 그쪽

these days, recently - 요즘

thing - 걸 short for 것을

thing - 게 short for 것이

this - 이건 short for 이것은

this - 이게 short for 이것이

this direction, way, side; here - 이쪽

this side, way, direction; here - 이쪽

this time - 이번

this way, side, direction; here - 이쪽

this~ - 이번

thunder - 천둥

ticket - 표

tickets (concerts, movies) - 티켓

times - ~번

title, name - 제목

to (stressed) - 엔 short for 에는

to answer - 대답하다

to apologize - 사과하다

to appear, to be seen - 보이다

to arrive - 도착하다

to be rough, exhausted - 힘들다

to be bashful, shy, embarrassed - 부끄럽다

to be beaten, old, worn, - 낡다

to be beautiful - 아름답다

to be born - 태어나다

to be bright - 밝다

to be clean - 깨끗하다

to be comfortable, convenient - 편하다

to be continued, continue on - 계속되다

to be convenient, comfortable - 편하다

to be cool, stylish   - 멋있다

to be dark - 어둡다

to be depressed - 우울하다

to be dirty - 더럽다

to be embarrassed, shy, bashful - 부끄럽다

to be exhausted, rough - 힘들다

to be famous - 유명하다

to be fulfilled, to be happy - 행복하다

to be happy, to be fulfilled - 행복하다

to be heavy - 무겁다

to be in fashion, trending - 유행하다

to be inconvenient, uncomfortable - 불편하다

to be kind - 친절하다

to be late - 늦다

to be light - 가볍다

to be lonely, sad - 외롭다

to be mad - 화가나다

to be new - 새롭다

to be not kind - 불친절하다

to be old, worn, beaten - 낡다

to be prepared - 준비되다

to be reserved - 예약되다

to be roomy, wide, spacious - 넓다

to be sad, lonely - 외롭다

to be scared - 무섭다

to be seen, to appear - 보이다

to be short - 키가 작다

to be shy, embarrassed, bashful - 부끄럽다

to be sleepy - 졸리다

to be slow - 느리다

to be spacious, roomy, wide - 넓다

to be stylish, cool - 멋있다

to be tall - 키가 크다

to be tired, to be tiring - 피곤하다

to be tiring, to be tired - 피곤하다

to be trending, in fashion - 유행하다

to be uncomfortable, inconvenient - 불편하다

to be warm - 따뜻하다

to be wide, spacious, roomy - 넓다

to be worn, old, beaten - 낡다

to become - 되다

to become broken / shattered - 깨지다

to borrow, to loan, to rent - 빌리다

to break up, to split - 헤어지다

to break, to shatter - 깨다

to build - 짓다

to bury - 묻다

to buy - 사다

to buy for someone - 사 주다

to cancel - 취소하다

to carry, to hold, to lift, to raise - 들다

to chat, to talk - 이야기하다

to come back, to return - 돌아오다

to come out - 나오다

to contact - 연락하다

to continue - 계속하다

to continue on, to be continued - 계속되다

to cry - 울다

to cry - 울다

to dance - 춤을 추다

to date; go out with; make friends with - 사귀다

to depart - 출발하다

to die - 죽다

to dip, to take a picture or film - 찍다

to disappear, to run out - 없어지다

to do - 하다

to do a part-time job - 아르바이트하다

to do for someone - 해 주다

to do homework - 숙제하다

to drive - 운전하다

to end - 끝나다

to exercise - 운동하다

to express anger - 화를내다

to fight - 싸우다

to find - 찾다

to forget - 잊어버리다

to go back, to return - 돌아가다

to go sightseeing, to watch - 구경하다

to grab - 잡다

to have a meeting - 미팅하다

to have, to hold - 가지다

to heal - 낫다

to help - 돕다

to hold, to carry, to lift, to raise - 들다

to hold, to have - 가지다

to hug - 안다

to keep, to protect - 지키다

to laugh - 웃다

to lift, to carry, to hold, to raise - 들다

to listen - 듣다

to live - 살다

to load - 싣다

to loan, to borrow, to rent - 빌리다

to look for, to search - 찾아보다

to love - 사랑하다

to make - 만들다

to make a promise - 약속하다

to make up - 화해하다

to oversleep - 늦잠을 자다

to pass away - 돌아가시다

to pay, to put out - 내다

to phone / call - 전화하다

to pick up - 줍다

to play - 놀다

to pour - 붓다

to practice - 연습하다

to prepare - 준비하다

to protect, to keep - 지키다

to put on, to wear - 입다

to put out, to pay - 내다

to question - 질문하다

to raise, to carry, to hold, to lift - 들다

to rent, to loan, to borrow - 빌리다

to reserve - 예약하다

to rest, to take a break - 쉬다

to return, to come back - 돌아오다

to return, to go back - 돌아가다

to run – 달리다

to run out, to disappear - 없어지다

to search, to look for - 찾아보다

to sell - 팔다

to shatter, to break - 깨다

to shower - 샤워하다

to sing - 노래하다

to sing a song - 노래를 부르다

to sleep - 잠을 자다

to split, to break up - 헤어지다

to study - 공부하다

to swim - 수영하다

to take a break, to rest - 쉬다

to take a nap - 낮잠을 자다

to take a picture or film, to dip - 찍다

to take time - 걸리다

to talk, to chat - 이야기하다

to teach - 가르치다

to the left; left side; left direction - 왼쪽

to the right; right side; right direction - 오른쪽

to throw away - 버리다

to travel - 여행하다

to turn off - 끄다

to turn on - 켜다

to wait - 기다리다

to watch, to go sightseeing - 구경하다

to wear, to put on - 입다

to work - 일하다

to write - 쓰다

to write for someone - 써 주다

TOEIC (a test of English proficiency) - 토익

toilet - 변기(통)

toilet paper - 화장지

toothbrush - 칫솔

toothpaste - 치약

totally, never, not at all, ever - 전혀

towel - 수건

travel - 여행

triangle - 삼각(형)

tuition - 수업료

U

underneath, down direction, lower side - 아래쪽

up direction, on top, upper side - 위쪽

upper side, on top, up direction - 위쪽

us - 우린 short for 우리는

V

vaccine - 백신

valley - 계곡

W

wall - 벽

war - 전쟁

wedding hall - 결혼식장

weeks - ~주

west; west side; west direction - 서쪽

whale - 고래

what - 뭘 short for 무엇을

what - 뭘 short for 뭐를

which direction?, which side? - 어느 쪽

which side?, which direction? - 어느 쪽

why? - 왜

winter - 겨울

winter - 겨울

without reason, for no reason - 이유 없이

without thinking, without thought - 생각 없이

wolf - 늑대

work - 일

wow! - 와!

writer - 작가

Y

years - ~년

Yoko - 요코

you (casual) - 넌 short for 너는

yut (traditional Korean board game) - 윷놀이

Z

zoo - 동물원

Glossary
K-E

ㄱ

가끔 - sometimes
가르치다 - to teach
가볍다 - to be light
가수 - singer
가수 - singer
가위 바위 보 - paper scissors rock
가을 - fall, autumn
가지다 - to have, to hold
간식 - snack
간호사 - nurse
감옥 - prison
갑자기 - suddenly
강 - river
개울(가) - stream
개월 - months (Chinese)
거의 - almost~
걸 short for 것을 - thing
걸리다 - to take time
게 short for 것이 - thing
겨울 - winter
결혼생활 - married life
결혼식장 - wedding hall
경찰 - police
계곡 - valley
계단 - stairs
계속되다 - to be continued, continue on
계속하다 - to continue
고깃집 - barbecue restaurant
고래 - whale
곧 - right away, immediately
골프 - golf
공무원 - government worker
공부 - studies
공부하다 - to study
공포영화 - horror movie
과학자 - scientist
관심 - interest
교수님 - professor
교육 - education

구 분 - 9 minutes
구 일 - 9 days
구 주 - 9 weeks
구경하다 - to go sightseeing, to watch
구름 - clouds
국제 - international
귀걸이 - earrings
귀신 - ghost, spirit
규칙 - rule
그건 short for 그것은 - that
그게 short for 그것이 - that
그날 - that day
그런데 - but, however
그릇 - bowl
그쪽 - that way, side, direction; there
근데 -   (short for 그런데)
근육 - muscles
기계 - machine
기다리다 - to wait
기린 - giraffe
기분 - feelings, mood
기침약 - cough medicine
기타 - guitar
까꿍 - peek-a-boo
깨끗하다 - to be clean
깨다 - to break, to shatter
깨지다 - to become broken / shattered
꼭 - definitely
끄다 - to turn off
끝나다 - to end

ㄴ

나비 - butterfly
나오다 - to come out
나중에 - later
낚시 - fishing
난 short for 나는 - I (casual)
날 - day
낡다 - to be old, worn, beaten
남쪽 - south; south side; south direction
낫다 - to heal

낮잠 - nap
낮잠을 자다 - to take a nap
내다 - to pay, to put out
냉동고 - freezer
냉장고 - refrigerator
넌 short for 너는 - you (casual)
넓다 - to be spacious, roomy, wide
네 달 - 4 months
네 번 - 4 times
네 시간 - 4 hours
년 - years
노래 - song
노래를 부르다 - to sing a song
노래하다 - to sing
놀다 - to play
농담 - joke
느리다 - to be slow
늑대 - wolf
늦다 - to be late
늦잠을 자다 - to oversleep

ㄷ

다 - all
다섯 달 - 5 months
다섯 번 - 5 times
다섯 시간 - 5 hours
다음 - next~
다음 번 - next time
달 - months (Korean)
달리다 - to run
담요 - blanket
대니 - Danny
대답 - answer
대답하다 - to answer
대도시 - big city, metropolis
대륙 - continent
대한민국 - Republic of Korea
더~ - more~, ~er
더럽다 - to be dirty
도시 - city
도착 - arrival

도착하다 - to arrive
돌고래 - dolphin
돌아가다 - to return, to go back
돌아가시다 - to pass away
돌아오다 - to return, to come back
돕다 - to help
동물원 - zoo
동안 - period of time
동쪽 - east; east side; east direction
되다 - to become
두 달 - 2 months
두 번 - 2 times
두 시간 - 2 hours
뒤쪽 - behind, back side, backward direction
듣다 - to listen
들다 - to carry, to hold, to lift, to raise
등산 - hiking
디저트 - dessert
따뜻하다 - to be warm
떡볶이 - spicy rice cake (stir fried)

ㄹ

램프 - lamp
리드 - Reed

ㅁ

만들다 - to make
만화책 - comics
많이 - a lot, many
맛 - flavor, taste
멋 - style
멋있다 - to be stylish, cool
며칠? (not 몇 일) - How many days?
면도기 - razor
몇 달? - How many months?
몇 번? - How many times?
몇 분? - How many minutes?
몇 시간? - How many hours?
몇 주? - How many weeks?
모양 - shape

목걸이 - necklace
무겁다 - to be heavy
무료 - free (no charge)
무릎 - knee(s)
무섭다 - to be scared
문자 - letters, text (message)
묻다 - to bury
물건 - item; product
뭘 short for 무엇을 - what
뭘 short for 뭐를 - what
미팅 - meeting
미팅하다 - to have a meeting

ㅂ

바위 - rock, stone
반찬 - side dish
밝다 - to be bright
방법 - method
백신 - vaccine
버리다 - to throw away
버스비 - buse fare
번 - times
번 출구 - No. ~ exit (train stations etc)
번개 - lightning
번데기 - silkworm
범죄 - crime
범죄자 - criminal
베개 - pillow
벽 - wall
변기(통) - toilet
별로 - not much
보고서 - report
보이다 - to be seen, to appear
보통 - normally
봄 - spring
부끄럽다 - to be shy, embarrassed, bashful
부전공 - minor
북쪽 - north; north side; north direction
북한 - North Korea
분 - minutes
불 - lights (in house etc)

불친절하다 - to be not kind
불편하다 - to be uncomfortable, inconvenient
붓다 - to pour
비누 - soap
비서 - secretary
비용 - fee, cost
빌리다 - to loan, to borrow, to rent
빨리 - quickly, right away
빵 - bread
빵집 - bakery

ㅅ

사 분 - 4 minutes
사 일 - 4 days
사 주 - 4 weeks
사 주다 - to buy for someone
사각(형) - square
사과하다 - to apologize
사귀다 - to date; go out with; make friends with
사다 - to buy
사랑 - love
사랑하다 - to love
사막 - desert
사자 - lion
사장님 - boss, president
사촌 - cousin
사흘 - 3 days
산 - mountain
살다 - to live
삼 분 - 3 minutes
삼 일 - 3 days
삼 주 - 3 weeks
삼각(형) - triangle
새 차 - new car
새롭다 - to be new
생각 없이 - without thinking, without thought
샤워 - shower
샤워하다 - to shower
샴푸 - shampoo
서 short for 에서 - in, on, at (shortened form)
서쪽 - west; west side; west direction

선수 - player
섬 - island
성격 - personality
세 달 - 3 months
세 번 - 3 times
세 시간 - 3 hours
세금 - taxes
소 - cow
소방관 - firefighter
소파 - sofa
손님 - customer, guest
수건 - towel
수업료 - tuition
수영 - swimming
수영하다 - to swim
숙박비 - lodging expenses
숙제 - homework
숙제하다 - to do homework
숟가락 - spoon
술 - alcohol, liquor
숨바꼭질 - hide-n-seek
숲 - forest
쉬다 - to rest, to take a break
스쿠버 다이빙 - scuba diving
시간 - hours
식탁 - dinner table
싣다 - to load
십 분 - 10 minutes
십 일 - 10 days
십 주 - 10 weeks
십이 분 - 12 minutes
십이 일 - 12 days
십이 주 - 12 weeks
십일 분 - 11 minutes
십일 일 - 11 days
십일 주 - 11 weeks
싱가폴 - Singapore
싱크대 - sink
싸우다 - to fight
써 주다 - to write for someone
쓰다 - to write
쓰레기통 - garbage can

ㅇ

아래쪽 - below, down direction, lower side
아르바이트 - part time job
아르바이트하다 - to do a part-time job
아름답다 - to be beautiful
아스피린 - aspirin
아이고 - oh my!, goodness!, ouch! (sigh...)
아이폰 - iPhone
아직 - not yet
아홉 달 - 9 months
아홉 번 - 9 times
아홉 시간 - 9 hours
안다 - to hug
안약 - eye drops
안전벨트 - safety belt (seat belt)
알약 - pill
앞쪽 - in front, front side, forward direction
액정 - screen (LCD)
앵무새 - parrot
약간 - slightly
약속 - promise
약속하다 - to make a promise
어느 쪽 - which side?, which direction?
어둡다 - to be dark
언덕 - hill
언어 - language
얼마나 - how many, how much
얼음 - ice
없어지다 - to disappear, to run out
에밀리 - Emily
에선 short for 에서는 - in, on, at (stressed)
에어컨 - air conditioning
엔 short for 에는 - to (stressed)
여덟 달 - 8 months
여덟 번 - 8 times
여덟 시간 - 8 hours
여름 - summer
여섯 달 - 6 months
여섯 번 - 6 times
여섯 시간 - 6 hours

여우 - fox
여행 - travel
여행하다 - to travel
연결 - connection
연고 - cream, ointment
연극 - play (theater)
연락하다 - to contact
연습 - practice
연습하다 - to practice
열 달 - 10 months
열 번 - 10 times
열 시간 - 10 hours
열두 달 - 12 months
열두 번 - 12 times
열두 시간 - 12 hours
열한 달 - 11 months
열한 번 - 11 times
열한 시간 - 11 hours
옆쪽 - the side, next
예술 - art
예약 - reservations
예약되다 - to be reserved
예약하다 - to reserve
옛날 - long time ago; the old days
오 분 - 5 minutes
오 일 - 5 days
오 주 - 5 weeks
오각형 - pentagon
오랫동안 - for a long time
오른쪽 - to the right; right side; right direction
올빼미 - owl
와! - wow!
완전히 - completely
왜 - why?
외롭다 - to be sad, lonely
왼쪽 - to the left; left side; left direction
요리사 - chef
요즘 - these days, recently
요코 - Yoko
우린 short for 우리는 - us
우울하다 - to be depressed
운동 - exercise

운동 - physical activity, exercise
운동하다 - to exercise
운전면허증 - driver's license
운전하다 - to drive
울다 - to cry
웃다 - to laugh
원 - circle
월급
위쪽 - on top, upper side, up direction
유럽 - Europe
유료 - fee based (to have a charge)
유명하다 - to be famous
유학 - studying abroad
유행하다 - to be in fashion, trending
육 분 - 6 minutes
육 일 - 6 days
육 주 - 6 weeks
육각형 - hexagon
윷놀이 - yut (traditional Korean board game)
의사 - doctor
이 분 - 2 minutes
이 일 - 2 days
이 주 - 2 weeks
이건 short for 이것은 - this
이게 short for 이것이 - this
이따가 - later, after a short while
이미 - already
이번 - this time
이번 - this~
이야기하다 - to talk, to chat
이유 없이 - without reason, for no reason
이쪽 - this way, side, direction; here
이틀 - 2 days
인터넷 - internet
인형 - a doll
일 - days
일 - work
일 분 - 1 minute
일 일 - 1 day
일 주 - 1 week
일곱 달 - 7 months
일곱 번 - 7 times

일곱 시간 - 7 hours
일몰 - sunset
일출 - sunrise
일하다 - to work
입다 - to wear, to put on
잊어버리다 - to forget

ㅈ

자주 - often
자켓 - jacket
작가 - writer
잘못 - mistake, error
잠을 자다 - to sleep
잡다 - to grab
저쪽 - that way, side, direction; over there
전 short for 저는 - I (polite)
전공 - major
전자레인지 - microwave
전쟁 - war
전쟁터 - battlefield
전혀 - never, not at all, totally, ever
전화 - phone
전화하다 - to phone / call
절대로 - never ever
점수 - grade
점수 - score
점점 - gradually
접시 - plate
접시 - plate, dish
젓가락 - chopsticks
정도 - about~
정치 - politics
정치가 - politician
제니퍼 - Jennifer
제목 - title, name
제시 - Jessie
제일~ - most~, ~est
조금, 좀 - a little
조용히 - quietly
조지 - George
졸리다 - to be sleepy

좀, 조금 - a little
주 - weeks
주사 - injection, shot
죽다 - to die
준비 - preparations
준비되다 - to be prepared
준비하다 - to prepare
줄넘기 - jump rope
줍다 - to pick up
지난 - last~
지난번 - last time
지키다 - to keep, to protect
직사각형 - rectangle
질문 - question
질문하다 - to question
짐 - luggage, baggage
짓다 - to build
쯤 - around~
찍다 - to take a picture or film, to dip

ㅊ

차 키 - car keys
찾다 - to find
찾아보다 - to look for, to search
책장 - bookcase
처방전 - prescription
천둥 - thunder
천천히 - slowly
초원 - grasslands
출발 - departure
출발하다 - to depart
춤을 추다 - to dance
취미 - hobby
취소하다 - to cancel
치약 - toothpaste
친절하다 - to be kind
칠 분 - 7 minutes
칠 일 - 7 days
칠 주 - 7 weeks
칫솔 - toothbrush

ㅋ

카드(신용카드) - card (credit card)
카페 - café
칼 - knife
캘리포니아 - California
캠핑 - camping
컵 - cup
켜다 - to turn on
콘센트 - power outlet
클럽 - night club, club
키가 작다 - to be short
키가 크다 - to be tall

ㅌ

태어나다 - to be born
택시비 - taxi fare
토익 - TOEIC (a test of English proficiency)
티켓 - tickets (concerts, movies)

ㅍ

팔 분 - 8 minutes
팔 일 - 8 days
팔 주 - 8 weeks
팔다 - to sell
팔다 - to sell
팬 - fan (of singer, tv show etc)
편견 - prejudice (against), bias (toward)
편하다 - to be comfortable, convenient
포크 - fork
폭풍 - storm
표 - ticket
피곤하다 - to be tired, to be tiring
피임약 - birth control

ㅎ

하다 - to do
하루 - 1 day

하루 - one day, day
학 - crane
학기 - semester
학비 - school expenses
학원 - after school academy
학원 - private education academy, academy
한 달 - 1 month
한 번 - 1 time
한 시간 - 1 hour
한국말 - Korean language (similar to 한국어)
항공료 - airfare
항상 - always
항생제 - antibiotic
해 주다 - to do for someone
해변 - beach
행복하다 - to be fulfilled, to be happy
향기 - scent, perfume
헤어지다 - to break up, to split
현금 - cash
호수 - lake
혼자 - alone, myself
홍대 - Hongdae (place in Seoul)
화가나다 - to be mad
화를내다 - to express anger
화장지 - toilet paper
화투 - flower cards (card game)
화해하다 - to make up
회사원 - an office worker
회사원 - employee, company worker
회의 - business meeting
휴가 - day off
휴학 - leave of absence from school
히터 - heater
힘들다 - to be exhausted, rough

SOUTH KOREA 대한민국
Provinces & Major Cities Map

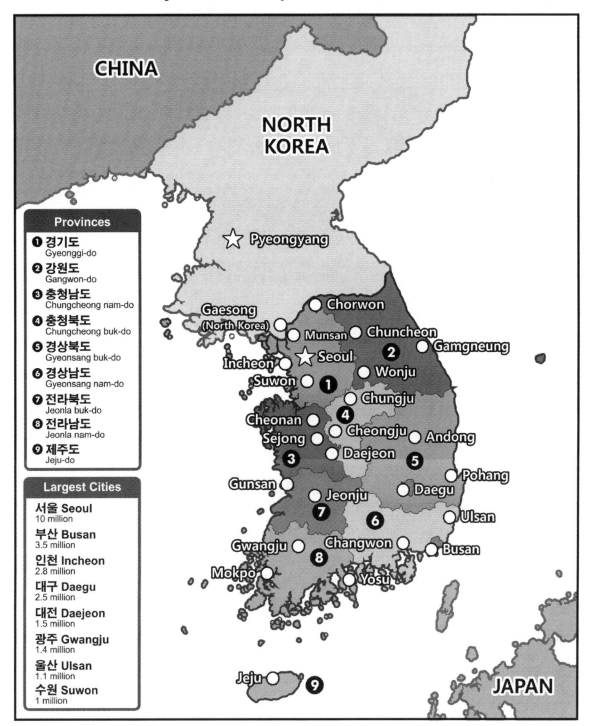

Provinces

❶ 경기도
Gyeonggi-do

❷ 강원도
Gangwon-do

❸ 충청남도
Chungcheong nam-do

❹ 충청북도
Chungcheong buk-do

❺ 경상북도
Gyeonsang buk-do

❻ 경상남도
Gyeonsang nam-do

❼ 전라북도
Jeonla buk-do

❽ 전라남도
Jeonla nam-do

❾ 제주도
Jeju-do

Largest Cities

서울 Seoul
10 million

부산 Busan
3.5 million

인천 Incheon
2.8 million

대구 Daegu
2.5 million

대전 Daejeon
1.5 million

광주 Gwangju
1.4 million

울산 Ulsan
1.1 million

수원 Suwon
1 million

CHINA

NORTH KOREA

Pyeongyang

Gaesong (North Korea)

Chorwon

Munsan

Chuncheon

Gamgneung

Incheon

Seoul

❷

Wonju

Suwon

❶

Chungju

Cheonan

❹

Cheongju

Andong

Sejong

Daejeon

❺

❸

Pohang

Gunsan

Daegu

Jeonju

❼

❻

Ulsan

Gwangju

Changwon

Busan

❽

Mokpo

Yosu

Jeju

❾

JAPAN

HANGUL CHARACTER NAME CHART

Romanization	g/k	n	d/t	r/l	m	b/p	s
hangul consonants	ㄱ	ㄴ	ㄷ	ㄹ	ㅁ	ㅂ	ㅅ
name	기역	니은	디귿	리을	미음	비읍	시옷

Romanization	null/ng	j	ch	k	t	p	h
hangul consonants	ㅇ	ㅈ	ㅊ	ㅋ	ㅌ	ㅍ	ㅎ
name	이응	지읒	치읓	키읔	티읕	피읖	히읗

Romanization	pp	jj	dd	kk	ss
hangul consonants	ㅃ	ㅉ	ㄸ	ㄲ	ㅆ
name	쌍비읍	쌍지읒	쌍디귿	쌍기역	쌍시옷

Romanization	a	ya	eo	yeo	o	yo	u
hangul vowels	ㅏ	ㅑ	ㅓ	ㅕ	ㅗ	ㅛ	ㅜ
name	아	야	어	여	오	요	우

Romanization	yu	eu	i	ae	e	yae	ye
hangul vowels	ㅠ	ㅡ	ㅣ	ㅐ	ㅔ	ㅒ	ㅖ
name	유	으	이	아이	어이	야이	여이

Romanization	wa	wae	oe	wo	we	wi	ui
hangul vowels	ㅘ	ㅙ	ㅚ	ㅝ	ㅞ	ㅟ	ㅢ
name	와	왜	외	워	웨	위	의

Cut out for reference.

Korean Keyboard Layout

© 2014 KoreanFromZero.com

Grammar Reference Guide

Grammar Point	Section
(으) form	7-9
(으)ㄴ After (verbs)	17-5
(으)ㄴ Directly modifying verbs (past tense)	16-5
(으)ㄹ Directly modifying verbs (future tense)	16-2
(으)ㄹ 게요 I'll do it!	15-9
(으)세요 future, present tense	7-11
(으)세요 Polite command form	7-10
(이)나 Using "or" with nouns	9-7
20 powerful and useful adverbs	7-2
BASIC + 주다 Doing something for someone	6-3
BASIC + 하다 Other people's emotions and intentions	11-1
Changing the "frequency" verb	5-1
Common Korean contractions	15-1
Directions	13-5
Directly modifying with adjectives	3-4
Doing now VS habitual activities	16-4
Formal VS Polite VS Casual Korean	2-2
Irregulars and direct modifier form	16-9
NOUN + 서 (because noun~)	6-2
Overview of directly modifying with verbs	16-1

Other From Zero! Books

**Chinese From Zero!
Coming in 2016!**

Made in the USA
Middletown, DE
19 September 2019